W9-ALU-439

# Measurement and Control Basics

# Measurement and Control Basics

## Thomas A. Hughes

**Resources for Measurement and Control Series**

**Instrument Society of America**

Copyright ©Instrument Society of America 1988

All rights reserved

Printed in the United States of America

No part of this publication may be reproduced, stored in a
retrieval system, or transmitted, in any form or by any means,
electronic, mechanical, photocopying, recording or otherwise,
without the prior written permission of the publisher.

INSTRUMENT SOCIETY OF AMERICA
67 Alexander Drive
P.O. Box 12277
Research Triangle Park
North Carolina 27709


Library of Congress Cataloging-in-Publication Data
Hughes, T.A.
  Measurement and control basics.

  Includes index.
  Bibliography: p.
  1. Process control.  2. Mensuration.  I. Title.
TS156.8.H84  1988       670.42      88-8303
ISBN 1-55617-097-1


Second Printing, 1991
ISBN: 1-55617-097-1

*To my wife Ellen and my daughter Audrey*
*for their love, patience, and understanding.*

# Contents

# Preface

This book provides a thorough and comprehensive coverage of the fundamental principles of process control and instrumentation. It is written for engineers, technicians, and marketing, sales, and management personnel who are new to process control and measurement and need to understand the basic principles of the field. It is also intended as an easy-to-read reference manual for experienced personnel who need a quick reference source on the subject.

The book discusses the basic principles of process control in Chapters 1 and 2 from a practical point of view, and the use of mathematics is kept to a minimum. The third and fourth chapters provide a review of electronics and digital logic fundamentals; those chapters may be skipped by the reader with a background in these subjects. The middle chapters (5 through 8) cover the fundamentals of pressure, level, flow, and analytical measurement. Chapter 9 discusses final control elements, such as control valves, motors, and pumps. The last two chapters discuss the design and application to process control of industrial computers. The book approaches the subject from a design and applications point of view and contains numerous practical design examples.

I would like to express my appreciation to my daughter Audrey for typing the original manuscript, and to my wife Ellen for the long hours spent reviewing the book. I would also like to thank Mr. Ralph L. Moore and Mr. John R. Lavigne for making many constructive comments that improved the overall presentation.

Tom Hughes
Arvada, CO
Aug. 1988

# About the Author

Thomas A. Hughes, a Senior Member of the Instrument Society of America, has twenty years experience in the design and application of instrumentation and control systems, including ten years in the management of instrumentation projects.

He is the author of two books: *Measurement and Control Basics*, 1988, and *Programmable Controllers*, 1989, published by ISA.

He received his B.S. in engineering physics from the University of Colorado and his M.S. in engineering from Colorado State University.

Mr. Hughes holds professional engineering licenses in the states of Colorado and Alaska, and has held engineering positions with Dow Chemical, B. K. Sweeney Manufacturing, Stearns-Roger Engineering, and Rockwell International. He has taught numerous courses in electronics, mathematics, and instrumentation and control systems at the college level and in industry. He is currently Manager of Instrumentation and Control Engineering at EG&G in Golden, Colorado.

# 1

# Introduction to Process Control

**Introduction**   To study the basic concept of industrial process control effectively, it is necessary to have an overall, general understanding of process control principles, which this chapter provides along with definitions used in industrial control and an introduction to the "intuitive" approach to process control.

**Definition of Process Control**   The operations associated with process control have always existed in nature. We can define "natural" process control as an operation that regulates some internal physical characteristic important to a living organism. Examples of natural regulation include body temperature, blood pressure, and heart rate.

Early man found it necessary to regulate some of his external environmental parameters to maintain life. This regulation can be defined as "artificial" process control. This type of process control was accomplished by observation of the parameter, comparison with some desired value, and action to bring the parameter as close as possible to the desired value. One of the first examples of such control was the use of fire by early man.

The term "process control" was widely used when people learned to adapt automatic regulatory procedures to the more efficient manufacture of products or the processing of material. Such procedures are automatic because no human (manual) intervention is required for regulation of a process.

The following example can be used to define the essential features of process control. In Figure 1-1, a level detector, a level controller, and a control valve are used to control liquid level in a tank.

The purpose of this control system is to maintain the fluid level at some prescribed height (H) from the bottom of the tank. We assume that the rate of flow into the tank is random. The level detector and transducer is a device that senses and *measures* the fluid level in the tank. The level controller *evaluates* the measurement, compares it to a desired set point (H) and produces a series of corrective

1

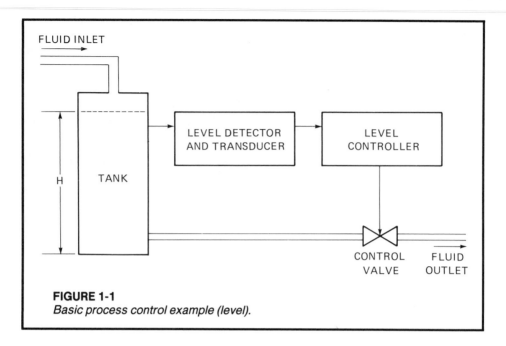

**FIGURE 1-1**
*Basic process control example (level).*

outputs. The valve *controls* the flow of fluid in the outlet pipe. Therefore, the three essential elements of a control loop are *measurement*, *evaluation*, and *control*.

## Elements of a Process Control System
A process control system consists of four elements: *process*, *measurement*, *evaluation*, and *control*. A model can be made using blocks to represent each element of a control loop, as shown in Figure 1-2.

**Definition of a Process**
In general, a process consists of an assembly of equipment and material that relates to some manufacturing sequence. In the example presented in Figure 1-1, the process to be placed under control with respect to the fluid level includes such variables as the liquid, the flow of liquid in and out of the tank, and the size of the tank itself. Many dynamic variables can be involved in a

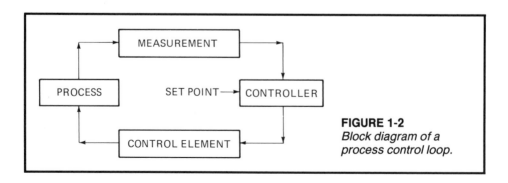

**FIGURE 1-2**
*Block diagram of a process control loop.*

given process, and it may be desirable to control all these variables. There are single-variable processes in which only one variable is controlled, as well as multi-variable processes in which many variables, some interrelated, may require regulation.

**Measurement**  In order to control a dynamic variable in a process, there must be information on the variable itself. This information is obtained from a measurement of the variable. In general, a measurement refers to the conversion of the variable into an analog signal of the variable, such as pneumatic pressure, an electrical voltage, or current. A device that performs the initial measurement and energy conversion of a dynamic variable into an electrical or pneumatic signal is a converter or transducer.

Transducers can be classed as level, temperature, pressure, flow, and analytical types. These instruments will be discussed in greater detail in later chapters. The result of any measurement is the conversion of a dynamic variable into some proportional information required by the other elements in the process control loop.

**Evaluation**  In the process control sequence, the evaluation step examines the measurement and determines the corrective action to be taken. This part of the loop is called either the controller or the evaluation performed by a controller. The evaluation may be performed manually by an operator, or automatically by electronic signal processing, pneumatic signal processing, a computer, or a combination of all these.

The controller requires both a measurement of the dynamic variable and a representation of the desired value of the variable in order to function. This desired value of the dynamic variable is called the set point (SP). Therefore, the evaluation consists of a comparison of the measurement and the set point and then a determination of the action required to bring the controlled variable to the set point value. This is the essential feature of a process control loop.

**Final Control Element**  The final element in a process control loop is the device that exerts a direct influence on the process. This element accepts an input from the controller and transforms it into some proportional operation performed on the process. In most cases in the process industry, this final control element will be a control valve that adjusts the flow of fluid in the process. Electrical motors and pumps are also used as final control elements. A detailed discussion of final control elements can be found in Chapter 9.

## Process and Instrument Drawings

In the process industry, a standard set of symbols is used to prepare drawings of processes. The instrument symbols used in these drawings are generally based on Instrument Society of America (ISA) Standard S5.1. These drawings are called Process and Instrument Diagrams (P&ID's) and they show the interconnection of process equipment and the instrumentation used to control the process. A typical example of a P&ID is shown in Figure 1-3.

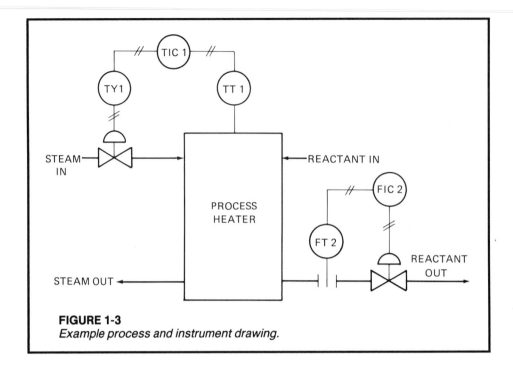

**FIGURE 1-3**
*Example process and instrument drawing.*

In standard P&IDs, the process flow lines, such as reactant flow and steam in Figure 1-3, are shown as heavy solid lines. The instrumentation signal lines are shown in a way that indicates whether they are pneumatic or electric. A cross-hatched line is used for pneumatic lines, for example, a 3-15 psi signal. The electric current line, usually 4-20 mA, is represented by a dashed line.

A balloon symbol with an enclosed two- or three-letter code is used to represent the instrumentation associated with the process control loops. For example, the balloon in Figure 1-3 with TT enclosed is a temperature transducer, and that with TIC enclosed is a temperature-indicating controller. Generally, a number is assigned to each control loop, and combining the letter code and number into an instrument tag number labels the specific device in the loop as illustrated in Figure 1-3.

Special items such as control valves and in-line instruments (for instance, orifice plates) have special symbols as shown in Figure 1-3. Refer to the Appendix for a more detailed discussion of instrument symbols.


## General Requirements of a Control System
The primary requirement of a control system is that it must be reasonably stable. In other words, the speed of response must be fairly fast and this response must show reasonable damping. A control system must also be able to reduce the system error to zero or to a value near zero.

**System Error**   The system error is a measure of the difference between the controlled variable set point value and the value of the process variable maintained by the system or expressed in equation form:

$$e(t) = PV(t) - SP(t) \qquad (1\text{-}1)$$

where:   $e(t)$  = system error as a function of time $(t)$
$PV(t)$ = process variable as a function of time
$SP(t)$ = set point as a function of time

**System Response**   The main purpose of a control loop is to maintain some dynamic process variable (flow, temperature, level, etc.) at a prescribed operating point or set point. System response is the ability of a control loop to recover from a disturbance that causes a change in the controlled process variable. There are two general types of response: underdamped (cyclic response) and damped. Figure 1-4 shows an underdamped or cyclic response of a system where the process variable oscillates around the set point after a process disturbance. Figure 1-5 shows a damped response where the control system is able to bring the process variable back to the operating point with no oscillations.

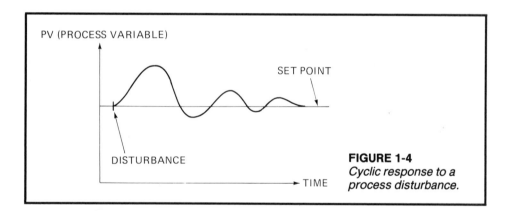

**FIGURE 1-4**
*Cyclic response to a process disturbance.*

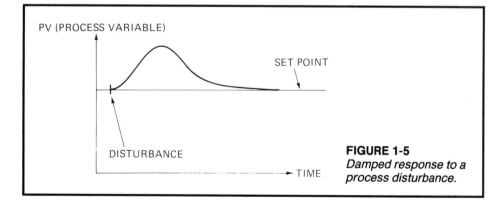

**FIGURE 1-5**
*Damped response to a process disturbance.*

A process control system can also be adjusted to produce either a cyclic or a damped response following a change in set point. In the cyclic response shown in Figure 1-6, the actual value of the process variable overshoots the new set point and then oscillates about this point before stabilizing. In the damped response shown in Figure 1-7, the process variable never overshoots the set point or oscillates, but approaches the new set point slowly.

**Control Loop Design Criteria**    Numerous criteria are employed in the evaluation of a process control loop response to an input change. The most common criteria used are settling time, maximum error, offset error and error area. These criteria are illustrated in Figure 1-8.

In the event of a process disturbance or a change in set point, the settling time is defined as the time required by the process control loop to bring the process variable back to within an allowable error. The maximum error is simply the maximum allowable deviation of the dynamic variable (set point). The error area ($A_e$) is de-

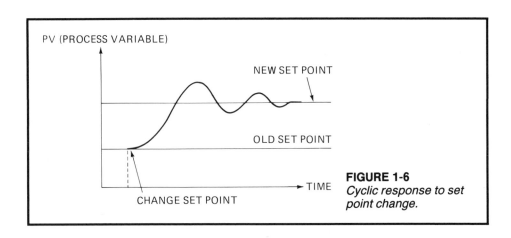

FIGURE 1-6
*Cyclic response to set
point change.*

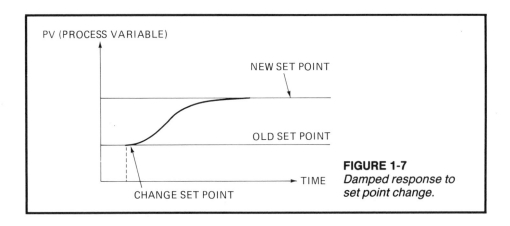

FIGURE 1-7
*Damped response to
set point change.*

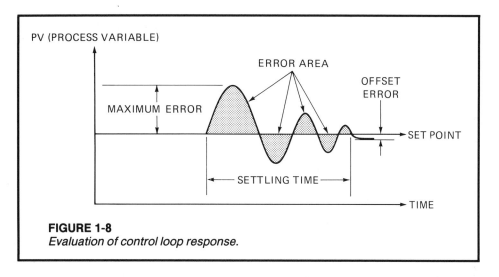

**FIGURE 1-8**
*Evaluation of control loop response.*

fined as the integral of the absolute magnitude of the error over the span of the disturbance. The error area is

$$A_e = \int |e(t)| \, dt \qquad (1\text{-}2)$$

Most control loops have certain inherent nonlinear qualities that prevent the system from returning the process variable to the set point following a system change. This condition is generally called "offset error."

The evaluation criteria discussed above are overall measures of control loop behavior used to determine the adequacy of the loop to perform some desired function. But we still do not have a clear understanding of process control. Perhaps the best way to obtain a good feel for process control is to take an intuitive approach.

## Intuitive Approach to Process Control Concepts

The practice of process control came long before the theory or analytical methods. Processes and controllers were designed using empirical methods based on intuition (feel) and extensive process experience. Most of the reasoning involved was nonmathematical. This approach was unscientific trial and error, but it was a successful control method.

Consider, for example, an operator looking into an early metal processing furnace to determine if the product was finished. Flame color, amount of smoke, and process time were used to make this judgment. From this early method evolved most of the control concepts and hardware installed today. Theories and mathematical techniques came later to explain how and why the systems responded as they did.

In this section, we will approach the study of control fundamentals in much the same way that control knowledge developed, that is, through a step-by-step procedure from manual control to ever-increasing automatic control. Suppose we have a process as shown in Figure 1-9.

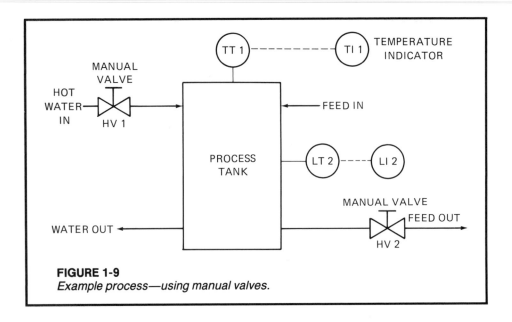

**FIGURE 1-9**
*Example process—using manual valves.*

A source of feed liquid flows into a tank at a varying flow rate from somewhere else in a process plant. There is a need to heat this feed so that it emerges at a desired temperature, $T_d$, as a hot liquid. To do this, hot water, which is available from another part of the plant, flows through heat exchanger coils in the tanks to

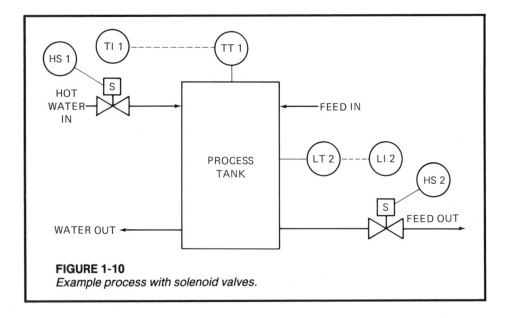

**FIGURE 1-10**
*Example process with solenoid valves.*

heat the liquid. By controlling the flow of hot water we can obtain the desired temperature, $T_d$.

A further process requirement is that the level of the tanks must neither overflow nor get too low.

The temperature is measured in the tank, and a temperature transmitter (TT1) converts the signal to a 4-20 mA direct current (dc) signal to drive a temperature indicator (TI1), which is mounted near the hot water inlet valve. Similarly, a level indicator is mounted in the operator's view of the hot feed outlet valve (HV2).

Suppose a process operator has the task of holding the temperature, T, near the desired temperature, $T_d$, while making sure the tank doesn't overflow. The question is how the operator would cope with his task over a period of time. He would mainly adjust the hot water inlet valve (HV1) to maintain the temperature and occasionally adjust the outlet valve (HV2) to maintain the correct level in the tank.

The operator would have several problems: first, both indicators would have to be within operator view; and, second, the manual valves would have to be near and easy to adjust.

**ON–OFF Control**    To make the operator's work easier, suppose we installed electrically operated solenoid valves in place of the manual valves as shown in Figure 1-10. We can also install two hand switches (HS1 and HS2) so that the solenoid valves can be operated from a common location. The valves can assume two states, either fully open (on) or fully closed (off). This type of control is called two-position or ON-OFF control.

Assume for the moment that the level is holding steady and that the main concern is control of temperature. The operator has been told to keep the temperature at a set point of 100°F. He compares the reading of the temperature indicator with this mental target and adopts a control strategy that might be called the "mode of control". The most obvious control mode would be to close the hot water inlet valve when the temperature gets above 100°F and to open it when it gets below 100°F. The problem with this method is that the operator would be opening and closing the valve almost continually and the temperature would be oscillatory. Also, because it takes time for energy to flow into and out of the tank, the temperature swings through a range of values above and below 100°F. The amplitude of oscillation depends primarily on the lags of the process and the attentiveness of the operator in determining the error (e) between the set point (SP) and the actual process variable (PV), the tank liquid temperature. The operator will maintain a neutral zone around the set point. Part of it is intentional, to keep the valve from wearing due to opening and closing too often, and part is due to human variability (see Figure 1-11).

This mode of control can be expressed mathematically as follows:
Let e = SP – PV

where:    e    = error
          SP   = set point
          PV   = process variable

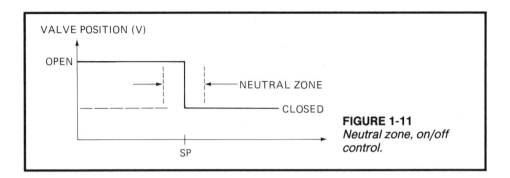

**FIGURE 1-11**
*Neutral zone, on/off control.*

Then, valve position (V) is:

  (a)  open when e is +

  (b)  closed when e is –

so that valve position (V) is a function (f) of the sign of the error (e), or expressed mathematically, V = f(sign e).

**Proportional Control**   Viewing the process as a balance between energy-in and energy-out, it is clear that smoother control would result if we maintained a steady flow of water, rather than the sudden changes between ON and OFF. The problem is to find the correct value of steady flow required for proper control. Obviously, for each rate of feed flow in and out of the tank, there is some ideal amount of inlet water flow that will hold the outlet temperature, T, at 100°F. This suggests two modifications to our *control mode* or strategy. The first is to establish some steady flow value for the hot water that, at average operating conditions, tends to hold the process variable (temperature) at the desired value or set point (100°F). Then, once that average flow valve has been established for the hot water, let increases or decreases of error = (SP – PV) cause corresponding increases and decreases in water flow from this normal value.

  This establishes the concept of *proportional control* (i.e., corrective valve action that is in some proportion to the change in error or deviation of the process variable from set point).

  Before this can be implemented on our process, the solenoid valves must be changed to proportioning valves. This means that they can be positioned to any degree of opening from fully closed to fully opened. This capability is achieved through the choice of a valve actuator mechanism, which is generally either an electric or pneumatic diaphragm actuator. The process now looks like Figure 1-12, using pneumatic actuators on control valves.

  With control valves in the system, the operator can now make gradual adjustments to the valves as he observes the temperature deviating from the desired set point. Therefore, we would expect less-frequent adjustments of the control valves, since they can now maintain a steady flow of process liquid, which should be in closer balance to the average need of the process.

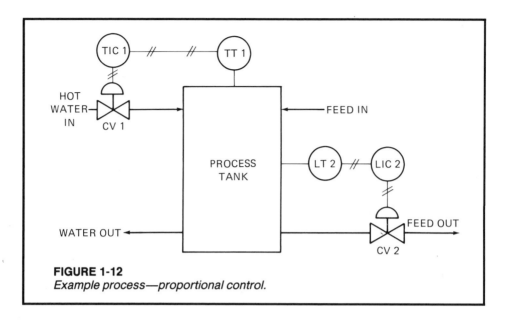

**FIGURE 1-12**
*Example process—proportional control.*

Proportional control can be described mathematically as follows:

$$V = K_c e + m \qquad\qquad (1\text{-}3)$$

where:  V = valve position
K_c = proportional gain in a process controller
m = constant, which is the position of the valve when the error is zero
e  = error

The $K_c$ factor is a measure of the sensitivity of the valve change to a given error.
Proportional control can be illustrated using the three graphs of Figure 1-13 and setting the proportional constant to three different values (i.e., $K_c = 1$, $K_c > 1$ and $K_c < 1$). As shown in these graphs, the amount of valve change ($\Delta V$) for a given error can be quite variable. We can have a one-to-one relationship as shown in Figure 1-13a. In that case, the valve would move 1% of its full travel for a corresponding 1% change in error or in a 1 to 1 ratio. In Figure 13b, where a low gain (K < 1) is selected, a large change in error is required before the valve would be fully opened or closed. Finally, Figure 1-13c shows the case of high gain (K > 1), where a very small error would cause a large change in the valve position.
The term "proportional gain" or, simply, "gain" has been brought in by the use of analytical methods in process control. Historically, this proportionality between error and valve action was called proportional band, abbreviated PB. Proportional band is the expression stating the percent of change in error required to move the valve full scale. Again, this had intuitive plausibility because it gave an operator a feel for how small an error caused full corrective action. Thus, a 10% proportional band meant that a 10% error between SP and PV would cause the

output to go full scale. This definition can be related to proportional gain $K_c$ by noting that:

$$K_c = \frac{100\%}{PB\%} \tag{1-4}$$

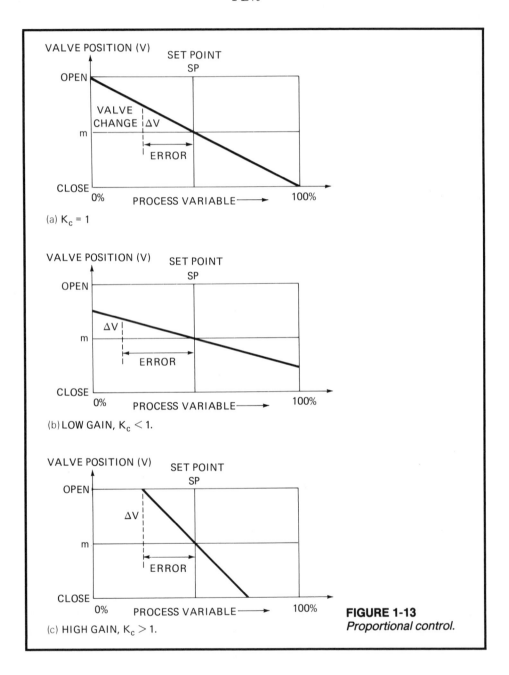

**FIGURE 1-13**
*Proportional control.*

The modern way of considering this mode is to think in terms of *gain* ($K_c$). The m term, as can be seen from Equation 1-3, has to be that valve position which supplies just the right amount of hot water to make the temperature 100°F, that is, PV = SP. The position, indicated in Figures 13a, b, and c, is often called the *manual (m)* reset.

When a controller is designed to provide this mode of control, it must contain at least these two adjustments, one for the $K_c$ term, and one for the m term. Control has become more complicated, for it is now necessary to know where to set $K_c$ and m for best control.

It would not take too long before the operator of this process would discover a serious problem with proportional control. Namely, proportional control rarely ever keeps the process variable at the set point if there are frequent disturbances to the process. For example, suppose the flow to the tank suddenly increases. If the temperature of the tank is to be maintained at 100°F at this new rate of feed flow, more hot water must be supplied. This calls for a change in valve position. If Equation 1-3 is examined, the only way that the valve position (V) can be changed is for the error (e) to change. Remember that m is a constant. Thus, an error will occur and the temperature will drop below 100°F until an equilibrium is reached between hot water flow and new feed flow. How much this drop will be depends on the value of $K_c$ set in the controller. The larger $K_c$ is, the less this *offset* will be. However, it can be shown that you cannot increase $K_c$ indefinitely because the control loop will become unstable. So, some error is inevitable if the feed rate changes. A plot of the process characteristics for hot feed temperature vs. hot water flow rate (valve position) for both low feed flow and high feed flow is illustrated in Figure 1-14.

For the valve in position 1 and the feed coming in at a low flow rate, the process would heat the fluid and produce hot feed at temperature $T_1$. If suddenly the feed went to the high flow rate and the valve were not changed, the temperature would drop to $T_2$. At this new high flow rate, the valve must be moved to position (2) if the original temperature $T_1$ is to be restored. Figure 1-15 shows the extent to which proportional control is able to achieve this restoration.

One way to deal with this problem is through the manual adjustment of m. When we adjust the m term (usually a knob on the controller), we are moving the valve to a new position that allows the PV to equal SP under the new conditions of load. In this case, with an increase in the feed flow, Equation 1-3 (i.e., V = $K_c$e + m ) clearly shows that the only way to get a new valve for V if e is to be zero is by changing the m term. So, if process changes are frequent or large, it may become necessary to make m adjustments frequently. It is apparent that some different type of control mode is needed.

**Proportional-Plus-Reset (Integral) Control**    Suppose that the m adjustment of the proportional controller described in the previous section is performed automatically by the controller instead of the operator. This would eliminate the offset error due to process changes. The question is, on what basis should the manual reset be automated? One innovative concept would be to move the valve at some rate as long as the error is not zero. Eventually, the correct control valve position would be found, but there are many rates at which to move the valve.

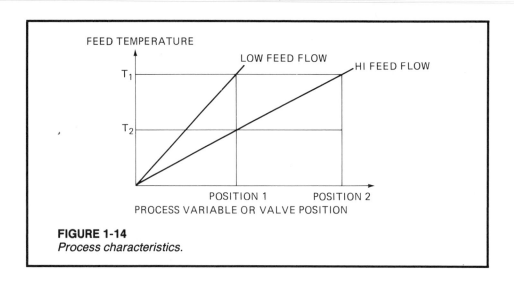

**FIGURE 1-14**
*Process characteristics.*

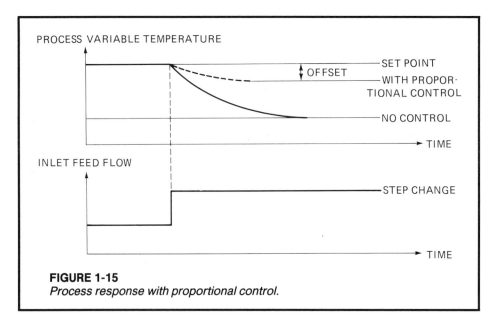

**FIGURE 1-15**
*Process response with proportional control.*

The most common practice used in the instrumentation field is to design controllers that move the valve at a speed proportional to the error. This has some logical sense to it, in that it would seem plausible to move the valve faster as the error got larger. This added control mode is called *automatic reset*. It is usually used in conjunction with proportional control because it eliminates the offset.

The proportional-plus-reset functions are shown in Figure 1-16. Assume a step change in set point at a point in time as shown. First, there is a sudden change in valve position equal to $K_c e$ due to the *proportional* function. At the same time,

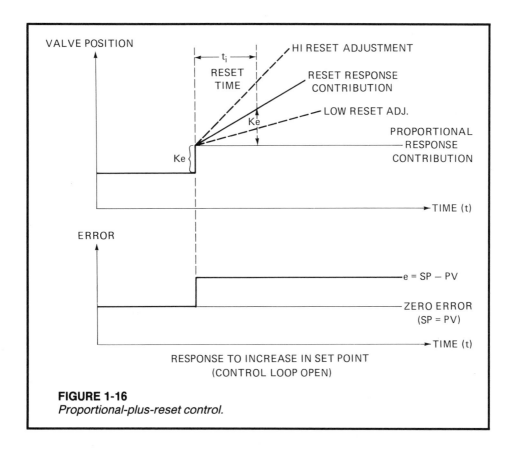

**FIGURE 1-16**
*Proportional-plus-reset control.*

the *reset* function, sensing there is an error, begins to move the valve at a rate proportional to that error. Since the illustration shows a constant error, the valve rate will be constant. This figure also illustrates relationships that explain some of the historical terminology of control. It will be seen that after an interval of time, $t_i$, an increase in valve position equal to the original proportional change will have taken place. This is called the *reset time*. It is an adjustment that is made to a reset controller that determines the slope of the reset response portion of the graph. The dotted lines show adjustments for low reset and high reset.

This relationship leads to alternate means of expressing the reset adjustment in a controller. When time is used to express reset action, it is called the *reset time*. Quite commonly, its reciprocal is used, in which case it is called reset in "repeats per minute," abbreviated RPM. This term refers to the number of times per minute that the reset action is repeating the valve change produced by proportional control alone. Process control systems personnel call $t_i$ the integral time.

The improvement in control after adding the reset function is illustrated in Figure 1-17. The same process change that was previously assumed under proportional-only control is used. Note how, after the initial upset, the reset action returns the error to zero and there is no offset.

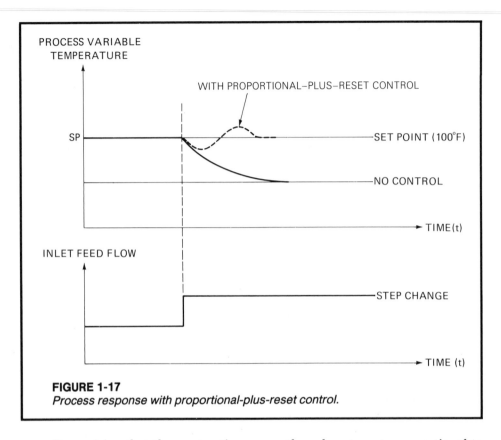

**FIGURE 1-17**
*Process response with proportional-plus-reset control.*

Recognizing that the reset action moves the valve at a rate proportional to error, this control mode can be described mathematically as follows:

$$dV/dt = K_i e$$

where dV/dt is the derivative of the valve position with respect to time (t) and $K_i = K_c/t_i$.

We can find the position of the valve at any time by integrating the derivative equation above, as follows:

$$V = K_i \int_0^t e\, dt$$

This equation shows that the valve position is proportional to the integral of the error. This way leads to the label "integral control". The quantity that was previously called "reset time" can also be referred to as the "integral time".

Finally, combining proportional and reset control gives the total expression of a two-mode controller:

$$V = K_c e + \frac{K_c}{t_i} \int_0^t e\, dt + m \tag{1-5}$$

There is one problem with PI control that needs to be mentioned. If a control loop is using PI control, there is a possibility with the integral (reset) mode that the controller will continue to integrate and change the output even outside the operating range of the controller. This condition is called "reset windup". For example, the heat exchanger shown in Figure 1-18 can be designed and built to heat 50 gpm of process fluid from 70°F to 140°F. If the process flow should suddenly increase to 100 gpm, there may be no way to supply sufficient steam to maintain the process fluid temperature at 140°F even when the control valve is wide open (100%) as shown in Figure 1-19. In this case, the reset mode, having opened the valve all the way (the controller output is perhaps 15 psig), would continue to integrate the error signal and increase the controller output all the way to the supply pressure of the pneumatic system. Once past 15 psig, the valve will open no further and the continued integration serves no purpose. The controller has "wound up" to a maximum output value.

Furthermore, if the process flow should then drop to 50 gpm (back to the operable range of the process), there would be some period of time during which the controlled temperature is above the set point while the valve remains wide open. A period of time is required for the integral mode to integrate (reset) downward from this wound-up condition to 15 psig before the valve begins to close and control the process.

It is possible to prevent this problem of controller reset windup with a controller operational feature that limits the integration and the controller output. This feature is normally called *anti-reset windup*. For those processes subject to periodic operation outside the capacity of the process, the anti-reset windup feature is recommended.

**Proportional-Plus-Rate (Derivative) Control**   We can now add another control action based on the rate of change of error. This establishes a function under which there is a valve movement proportional to the rate of change of error.

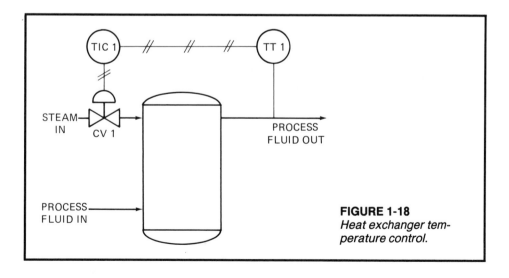

**FIGURE 1-18**
*Heat exchanger temperature control.*

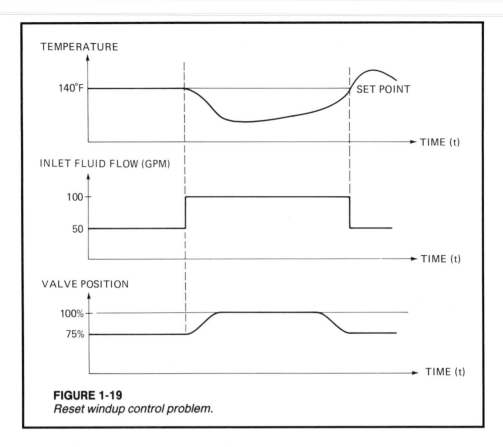

**FIGURE 1-19**
*Reset windup control problem.*

Note that this additional correction exists only while the error is changing; it disappears when the error stops changing, even though there may still be a large error.

This control function can be expressed mathematically as follows:

$$V = K_d \ \frac{de}{dt}$$

where $K_d$ is the derivative constant.

We can relate the derivative constant $K_d$ to the proportional constant as follows:

$$K_d = K_c t_d$$

where $t_d$ is the derivative time.

Combining this derivative control function with proportional control, we obtain proportional-plus-derivative (PD) control as follows:

$$V = K_c e + K_c t_d \frac{de}{dt} + m \qquad (1\text{-}6)$$

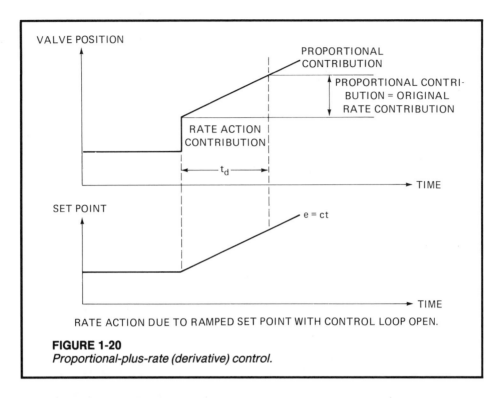

RATE ACTION DUE TO RAMPED SET POINT WITH CONTROL LOOP OPEN.

**FIGURE 1-20**
*Proportional-plus-rate (derivative) control.*

To illustrate PD control, let's assume that the error is changing at a constant rate. This could be done by changing the set point at a constant rate (i.e., SP = ct) as shown in Figure 1-20.

Derivative or rate action contributes an immediate valve change proportional to the rate of change of the error. In Figure 1-20 it is equal to the slope of the set point line. As the error increases, the proportional action contributes additional control valve movement. Later, the contribution of the proportional action will have equaled the initial contribution of the rate action. The time it takes this to happen is called the rate or derivative time, $t_d$.

The ramped set point can be expressed mathematically as

$$e = Ct$$

where:  e  = error
C  = constant (slope of set point change)
t  = time

The control valve change in position from Equation 1-6 becomes:

$$V - m = K_c C(t + t_d)$$

This indicates that the valve position is ahead by time $t_d$, the position that straight proportional control would have established for the same error. The control action leads to improved control in many applications, particularly in temperature control loops where the rate of change of the error is very important. In temperature loops, there are generally large time delays between the application of corrective action and the process response; therefore, derivative action is required to control steep temperature changes.

**Proportional-Integral-Derivative Control**  Finally, the three control functions proportional, integral, and derivative (PID) can be combined as shown in Equation 1-6 to obtain full three-mode or PID control.

$$V = K_c e + \frac{K_c}{t_i} \int_0^t e \, dt + K_c t_d \frac{de}{dt} + m \qquad (1\text{-}7)$$

## EXERCISES

1.1  List several examples of open and closed control systems found in a home and describe the operation of each system.

1.2  Draw a block diagram of a home heating system and explain the input disturbances that might exist in the system. Also, identify the device that serves as the controller for the system.

1.3  Draw a P&ID, using standard instrument symbols, for the level control loop shown in Figure 1-1.

1.4  For a proportional controller: (a) what gain corresponds to a proportional band of 150%? and (b) what proportional band corresponds to a gain of 0.4?

1.5  Explain why proportional-only controllers exhibit offset at steady state.

1.6  Explain what effects a large change in liquid level will have on the temperature control example of Figure 1-13.

## BIBLIOGRAPHY

1. Murrill, P.W., *Fundamentals of Process Control Theory*, Instrument Society of America, 1981.

2. The Staff of Chemical Engineering (ed.), *Practical Process Instrumentation and Control*, Chemical Engineering McGraw-Hill Publications Co., 1980.

3. Kirk, F.W., and Rimboi, N.R.; *Instrumentation*, Third Edition, American Technical Publishers, Inc., 1975.

4. Johnson, C.D., *Process Control Instrumentation Technology*, Second Edition, John Wiley & Sons, Second Edition, 1982.

5. Ogata, K., *Modern Control Engineering*, Prentice-Hall, Inc., 1970.

6. Weyrick, R.C., *Fundamentals of Automatic Control*, McGraw-Hill Book Company, 1975.

7. Honeywell International, Process Management Systems Division, *An Evolutionary Look at Process Control*, 1981.

# 2
# Process
# Control
# Loops

**Introduction**    The general concept of process control was discussed in Chapter 1. In this chapter, we will discuss process control loops. Since feedback control is the most common type of control loop encountered in automatic process control, it will be discussed in detail. We will then discuss other types of control loops, such as *cascade*, *ratio*, and *feedforward*. And finally, we will examine tuning of control loops.

## Single Feedback Control Loop    In a feedback control loop, a measurement is made of the variable to be controlled and this measurement value is compared with a reference point (set point). If a difference or error exists between the actual value and the desired value of the process, the automatic controller will take the necessary corrective action. A typical single feedback loop is shown in Figure 2-1.

The output variable is sensed or measured through the appropriate instrumentation, such as temperature, flow, or level detectors, and this sensed value is then compared to the set point. The comparison is used by the controller to calculate a signal to adjust the manipulated variable. Since the manipulated variable in the process industry is most often a flow, the output of the controller usually is a signal to a control valve, as shown in Figure 2-1. During a continuous operation, disturbances may enter the process and tend to drive the output in one direction or another. The single manipulated variable is used to compensate for all such changes produced by the disturbances. Furthermore, if there are changes in the set point, the manipulated variable is altered to produce the needed change in the output.

**Block Diagrams**    Block diagrams are used to provide a simple pictorial representation of a control system. Block diagrams have two basic symbols, the circle and the function block.

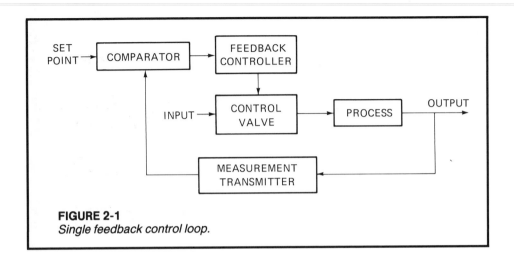

**FIGURE 2-1**
*Single feedback control loop.*

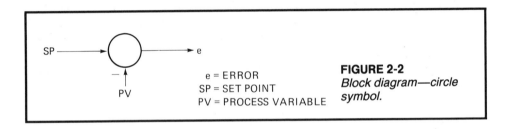

**FIGURE 2-2**
*Block diagram—circle symbol.*

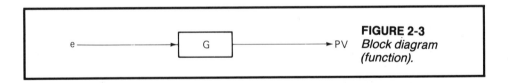

**FIGURE 2-3**
*Block diagram (function).*

   The arrows entering and leaving the circle represent the flow of information and the head of each arrow has an algebraic sign associated with it, either plus or minus. The small circle is a simple way to represent addition or subtraction. The symbol shown in Figure 2-2 represents the algebraic equation $e = SP - PV$.

   The other symbol used in block diagrams is a simple block with one arrow entering and one arrow leaving as shown in Figure 2-3.

   Figure 2-3 represents a multiplication; the output is equal to the block (G) times the input (e), or $PV = Ge$.

   These symbols can be combined into networks to show simple or complex control loops and will be used throughout this text. A block diagram of a very simple negative feedback control loop is shown in Figure 2-4.

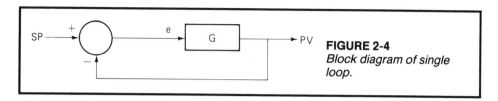

**FIGURE 2-4**
*Block diagram of single loop.*

**Functional Block Diagram of a Feedback Loop**  A functional block dia-gram of the single feedback control loop is shown in Figure 2-5. Functionally, the loop can be separated into two broad parts: one part is inside the controller case and the other is the balance of the process loop.

There must be a provision for either the operator or some hardware to provide a set point to the control loop. The set point must have the same dimensions as the controlled variable; i.e., if the controlled variable is pounds per hour, then the set point also must be pounds per hour. The input element converts the set point signal into the operating units of the controller: millivolts, milliamps, air pressure, etc.

The controlled variable is detected by a sensor and the value is transmitted back to the controller case along with the correct operating units. Inside the con-troller, a comparator takes the algebraic difference between the set point and the controlled variable and produces an error signal. The error signal becomes the input to the feedback controller. Based on the error, the controller calculates and sends a signal to the final control element, and this in turn controls the manipu-lated variable input to the process.

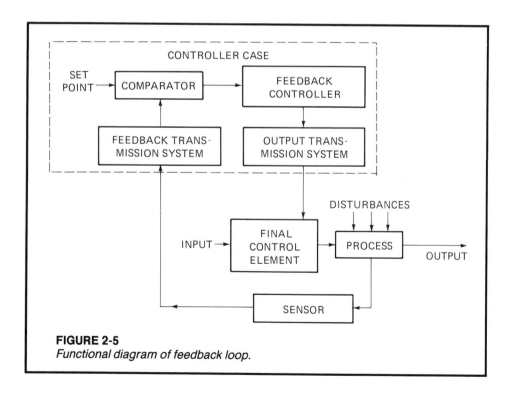

**FIGURE 2-5**
*Functional diagram of feedback loop.*

## Time Elements of a Feedback Loop   The various blocks of the

feedback control loop shown in Figure 2-5 require time to sense an input change
and to transform this new condition to an output change. The time of response of
the control loop is the combination of the responses of the sensor, the feedback
transmitter, the controller, the output transmitter, the final control element, and
the process.

An important objective in control system design is to correctly match the
time response of the control system to that of the process. To reach this objective,
it is necessary to understand the following types of time elements: first-order lag,
time constants, higher-order lag, and dead time.

The first-order lag is the most common type of time element encountered in
process control. To study this, it may be useful to look at the response curves when
the system is subjected to a step input as shown in Figure 2-6.

The advantage of using a step input as a forcing function is that the input is at
steady state before the change, and then is instantaneously switched to a new
steady-state value. When the output curve is studied, the transition of the system
can be observed as it passes from one steady state to a new one. For a first-order
linear system, the response to a step input is shown in Figure 2-7.

The time of response shown in Figure 2-7 is called a "first-order lag" because
the output lags behind the input, and the differential equation for the system is a
linear first-order differential equation.

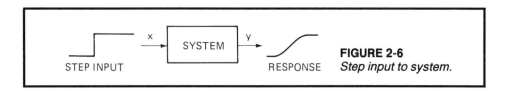

**FIGURE 2-6**
*Step input to system.*

The system equation is:

$$\tau \ \frac{dy}{dt} + y = Kx$$

where:   y  = output
         x  = input
         K = gain
         τ  = time constant

In block diagram form, we have:

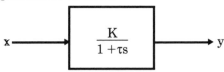

where s is the operator d/dt.

These systems are characterized by the capacity to store matter or energy, and the dynamic shape of their response curves is described by a time constant. This time constant ($\tau$) is meaningful both in a physical sense and in a mathematical sense. Mathematically, it predicts, at any instant, the future time period required to obtain 63.2% of the change remaining.

The response curve in Figure 2-7 shows that response of the system is always decreasing; i.e., the rate of response is maximum in the beginning and is continuously decreasing from that time onward. The time constant also gives an insight into the physical response of a system. Figure 2-8 shows four different response curves, all for first-order systems, but each has a different time constant.

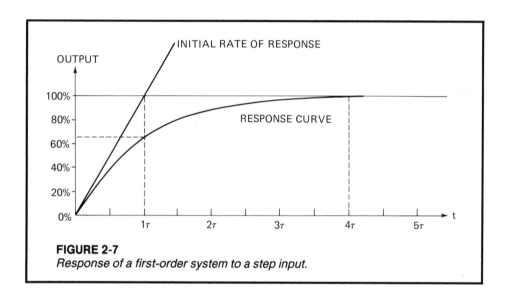

**FIGURE 2-7**
*Response of a first-order system to a step input.*

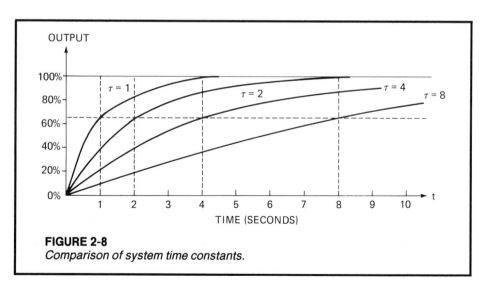

**FIGURE 2-8**
*Comparison of system time constants.*

It can be seen from the four curves that as the time constant gets larger, the response of the system becomes slower.

## Comparison of Basic Physical Systems
To gain some understanding about process time constants, we can look at some common physical systems. The three systems to be examined are electrical, liquid, and thermal. All three physical systems can be said to have resistance and capacitance. It will be shown that resistance times capacitance of a system produces the process time constant.

### Electrical Systems
The characteristics of an electric circuit having pure resistance and pure capacitance in series are quite similar to the characteristics of fluid and thermal systems. Resistance in an electric circuit is defined by Ohm's Law, which states that the potential (voltage) required to send an electric current through a resistor is equal to the current times the resistance, $V = IR$, where $V =$ electric potential (volts) and $I =$ current (amperes = coulombs/sec), so that electric resistance is:

$$R = \frac{V}{I} = \frac{\text{potential}}{\text{flow}} \tag{2-1}$$

The relationship for capacitance states that the charge on a capacitor is equal to the capacitance times the potential across the capacitor, $q = CV$, where $q =$ charge (coulombs), $C =$ capacitance (farads), and $V =$ potential (volts). Thus, capacitance is given by :

$$C = \frac{q}{V} = \frac{\text{charge quantity}}{\text{potential}} \tag{2-2}$$

A series electrical RC network is shown in Figure 2-9. To understand the concept of time constants, the system equation for the circuit needs to be derived.

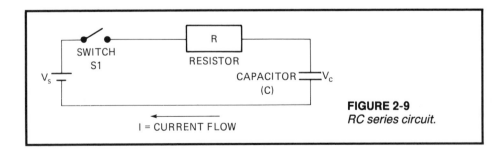

FIGURE 2-9
RC series circuit.

The sum of the voltages in the circuit equals the applied voltage $V_s$ as follows:

$$V_s = V_R + V_c = IR + V_c$$

Differentiating Equation 2-2 with respect to time (t) gives

$$dq/dt = C \, dV/dt$$

By definition,

$$I = dq/dt = C \, \frac{dV_c}{dt}$$

so,

$$V_s = RC\frac{dV_c}{dt} + V_c$$

or

$$V_s = \tau\frac{dV_c}{dt} + V_c$$

where $\tau = RC$ is the time constant for the system.

It can be shown in the following that R times C has the units of time:

$$RC = \left[ \frac{V}{I} \right] \cdot \left[ C = \frac{q}{V} \right] = \left[ \frac{volts}{coulombs/sec} \right] \cdot \left[ \frac{coulombs}{volts} \right] = \left[ seconds \right]$$

This RC time constant is the time required to charge the capacitor to 63.2% of its maximum value in the series RC circuit shown in Figure 2-9 after the switch S1 is closed.

**Liquid Systems**   To illustrate the concept of time constants in a physical system, the analogy between an RC electric circuit and a liquid flow system will be examined. Liquid flow in a pipe is shown in Figure 2-10 with a restricting device (valve) providing a hydraulic resistance (R) to the flow.

Two different types of flow can take place in liquid systems: *laminar flow* and *turbulent flow*. Laminar flow occurs where the fluid velocity is relatively low and the liquid flows in layers, so that the flow is directly proportional to pressure differential or head. Unfortunately, laminar flow is seldom encountered in actual practice and usually occurs only with very viscous fluids at low velocity.

Turbulent flow occurs when the fluid velocity is relatively high and the velocity of the liquid at any point varies irregularly. When turbulent flow occurs from a tank discharging under its own head, the flow is found using Bernoulli's Law:

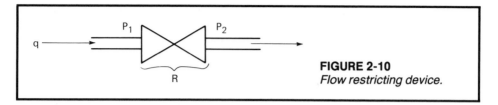

**FIGURE 2-10**
*Flow restricting device.*

$$q = KA\sqrt{2gh} \tag{2-3}$$

where:   $q$ = flow rate, ft$^3$/sec
         $K$ = a flow coefficient
         $A$ = area of restriction, ft$^2$
         $g$ = acceleration due to gravity, ft/sec$^2$
         $h$ = $P_0 - P_1$ = head of liquid, ft

We can define hydraulic resistance to flow as

$$R \cong \frac{\text{potential}}{\text{flow}} = \frac{h}{q}$$

or

$$R = \frac{dh}{dq} \tag{2-4}$$

Rearranging Equation 2-3,

$$(h)^{1/2} = q/KA(2g)^{1/2} \tag{2-5}$$

and differentiating Equation 2-5 with respect to q gives

$$\frac{dh}{dq} = \frac{2(h)^{1/2}}{KA(2g)^{1/2}} \tag{2-6}$$

If we substitute Equation 2-5 into Equation 2-6 to eliminate the constant term $KA\,(2g)^{1/2}$, we obtain:

$$\frac{dh}{dq} = \frac{2h}{q} \tag{2-7}$$

From Equations 2-4 and 2-7,

$$R = \frac{dh}{dq} = \frac{2h}{q} \tag{2-7a}$$

This compares with Ohm's Law for resistance, but the difference lies in the fact that turbulent flow involves the square root of potential. Also, hydraulic resistance is not constant as is electrical resistance, since it depends on the flow (q) and the pressure differential at any given time (refer to Figure 2-11.).

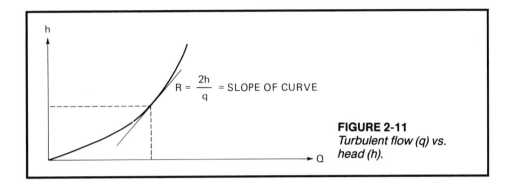

$$R = \frac{2h}{q} = \text{SLOPE OF CURVE}$$

**FIGURE 2-11**
*Turbulent flow (q) vs.
head (h).*

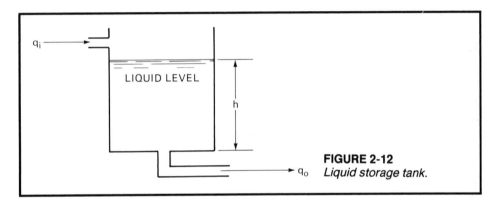

**FIGURE 2-12**
*Liquid storage tank.*

However, liquid capacitance is directly analogous to electrical capacitance. Figure 2-12 shows a tank being filled with a liquid and the equation for the liquid volume is given by:

$$V = Ah \qquad (2\text{-}8)$$

where:    $V$ = volume, $ft^3$
          $h$ = head or height, ft
          $A$ = area, $ft^2$

Equation 2-8 states that the volume (quantity) of liquid in the tank is equal to the cross-sectional area (A) times the head of the liquid (h) or:

$$A = \frac{V}{h} = \frac{\text{quantity}}{\text{potential}} \qquad (2\text{-}9)$$

Comparing Equation 2-9 to Equation 2-2, $C = q/V$ shows that liquid capacitance is simply the surface area of the liquid or $C = A$.

Furthermore, if we differentiate Equation 2-9 with respect to time, we have by definition:

$$\frac{dV}{dt} = A \frac{dh}{dt} \quad q_i - q_o \tag{2-10}$$

Assuming turbulent flow from the tank, $q = 2h/R$, Equation 2-10 becomes:

$$q_i = \frac{2h}{R} + A \frac{dh}{dt} \tag{2-11}$$

Equation 2-11 is a first-order linear differential equation that expresses liquid level as a function of time with the fluid flow in ($q_i$) as the forcing function.

Again, we can draw an analogy between two different physical systems. Comparing the variables in the liquid system with electrical quantities, we see that differential pressure (head), flow, and hydraulic resistance are analogous to voltage, current, and electrical resistance.

**EXAMPLE 2-1**

**Problem:** The tank shown in Figure 2-12 has a operating head (h) of 5 ft and a normal output flow of 0.2 ft³/s. The cross-sectional area of the tank is 10 ft². Determine the differential equation for the output flow ($q_o$) as a function of time, assuming turbulent flow.

**Solution:** Using Equation 2-7, the resistance to flow over the operating range is

$$R = \frac{2h}{q} = 50 \text{ sec/ft}^2$$

Since $dh = Rdq$, $dh/dt = R(dq/dt)$. From Equation 2-10

$$q_i = q_o + AR \frac{dq_o}{dt}$$

In this example $AR = 10 \text{ ft}^2 \times 50 \text{ sec/ft}^2 = 500 \text{ sec}$,

so that $q_i = q_o + 500 \frac{dq_o}{dt}$.

It is important to note that in the differential flow equation of Example 2-1 (i.e., $q_i = q_o + AR \frac{dq_o}{dt}$), the term AR has units of time and this term is the system time constant ($\tau$). Remember that for a liquid system capacitance (C) was equal to the liquid surface area (A), so the system time constant $\tau$ is given by $\tau = RC$.

**Thermal Systems**   The last physical process we need to examine is thermal systems. The basic thermal processes encountered in the process industries are the mixing of hot and cold fluids, the exchange of heat through adjoining bodies, and the generation of heat by combustion or chemical reaction.

Two laws of thermodynamics are used in the study of thermal systems. The first controls the way in which heat energy is produced and determines the amount generated. The second governs the flow of heat.

Temperature change in a body is a result of the first law of thermodynamics. For a given body, heat input raises the internal energy, and the rate of change of body temperature will be proportional to the heat flow to the body. The constant relating temperature change and heat flow is called the *thermal capacity* of the body.

$$C \ \frac{dT}{dt} = q \qquad\qquad (2\text{-}12)$$

where:  $C$ = thermal capacitance in Btu/°F
  $\dfrac{dT}{dt}$ = rate of change of temperature in °F/second
  $q$ = heat flow in Btu/second

The thermal capacitance of a body is found by multiplying the specific heat of the material by the weight of the body.

$$C = WS \qquad\qquad (2\text{-}13)$$

where:  $W$ = weight of the body in pounds (lbs)
  $S$ = specific heat of material in (Btu/lb/°F

Thermal capacitance is analogous to electric capacitance. For example, in Figure 2-13, heat flowing into a body with thermal capacitance C causes the temperature (T) to rise above the ambient value $T_o$.

It can be seen that heat flow and charge flow as well as temperature and voltage are analogous quantities.

Heat transmission takes place by *conduction, convection,* and *radiation.* Conduction involves transmission through adjoining bodies, convection involves transmission and mixing, and radiation uses electromagnetic waves to transfer heat.

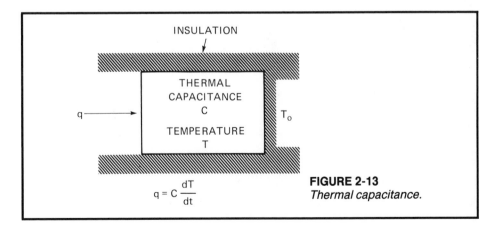

**FIGURE 2-13**
*Thermal capacitance.*

The rate of heat flow through a body is determined by its *thermal resistance.* This is defined as the change in temperature resulting from a unit change in heat flow rate. Thermal resistance is normally a linear function, in which case,

$$R = \frac{T_1 - T_2}{q} \tag{2-14}$$

where:   $R$ = thermal resistance in °F/(Btu/sec)
$T_1 - T_2$ = temperature change in °F
$q$ = heat flow in Btu/sec

Thermal resistance is analogous to the electric resistance of a resistor in an electric circuit.

If the temperature of a body is considered to be uniform throughout, its thermal behavior can be described by a linear differential equation. This assumption is generally true for small bodies or for gases or liquids where perfect mixing takes place. For such a system, thermal equilibrium requires that at any instant the heat added ($q_i$) to the system equals the heat stored($q_s$) plus the heat removed. Thus

$$q_i = q_s + q_o \tag{2-15}$$

### EXAMPLE 2-2

**Problem:** Derive the differential equation for the water temperature, $T_w$, for the insulated tank of water heated by an electric heater as shown in Figure 2-14. Assume that the rate of heat flow from the heating element is $q_i$, that the water is at a uniform temperature, and that there is no heat storage in the insulation.

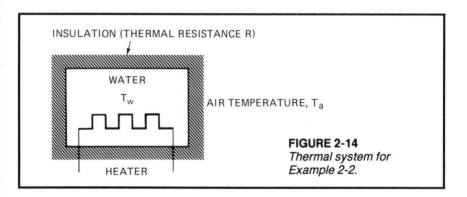

INSULATION (THERMAL RESISTANCE R)

WATER

$T_w$

AIR TEMPERATURE, $T_a$

HEATER

**FIGURE 2-14**
*Thermal system for Example 2-2.*

**Solution:** Using Equation 2-12, the heat stored in the water is

$$q_w = C \, \frac{dT}{dt}$$

where C is the thermal capacitance of the water. From Equation 2-14, the heat loss through the insulation is

$$q_o = \frac{T_w - T_a}{R}$$

where $T_a$ is the temperature of the air outside the tank. Applying Equation 2-15, we have

$$q_i = q_s + q_o$$

or:

$$q_i = C \frac{dT_w}{dt} + \frac{T_w - T_a}{R}$$

If we multiply this equation by R and let the system time constant equal $\tau$, we obtain

$$Rq_i = RC \frac{dT_w}{dt} + T_w - T_a$$

or:

$$Rq_i + T_a = \tau \frac{dT_w}{dt} + T_w$$

which is a first-order differential equation for water temperature $T_w$.

Table 2-1 gives a broader comparison of the variables in different physical systems.

**TABLE 2-1**
**Comparison of Physical Units**

| Variable | Electrical | Liquid Level | Thermal |
|----------|-----------|--------------|---------|
| Quantity | coulomb (C) | cubic foot ($ft^3$) | Btu |
| Potential | volt (V) | foot (ft) | degree |
| Flow | ampere (A) | $ft^3$/sec | Btu/sec |
| Resistance | ohms ($\Omega$) | ft/$ft^3$/sec | °F/Btu/sec |
| Capacitance | farads (F) | ft/$ft^3$ | Btu/°F |
| Time | seconds (sec) | seconds | seconds |

It was important to have a general idea of the physical meaning of process variables so that a process can be observed with some feel for its capacity to store material or energy. In this way, insight may be gained into the process dynamics of a system. Such an understanding is very important in process control design.

## Higher-Order Process Time Lags

In general, not all process systems will be neatly characterized by first-order lags. In some cases, a process will produce a response curve as shown in Figure 2-15.

We can note that the maximum rate of change for the output does not occur at time zero ($t_0$) but at some later time ($t_1$). This implies that some higher-order system is involved. For example, in the liquid level systems shown in Figures 2-16 and 2-17, we obtain two different responses. In Figure 2-16, the height of the liquid in the second tank does not influence the flow of liquid out of the first tank.

However, in Figure 2-17, it is clear that the height of the liquid in the second tank will influence the rate at which liquid flows out of the first tank.

When stages are interacting with one another, the process response will always be more sluggish than a simple first-order system connected as independent stages. This becomes an important factor in thermal systems since a thermal process response is usually slow.

Pure dead time is the period of time ($\theta$) that elapses between the moment a change is introduced into a process and the moment the output begins to change, as shown in Figure 2-18.

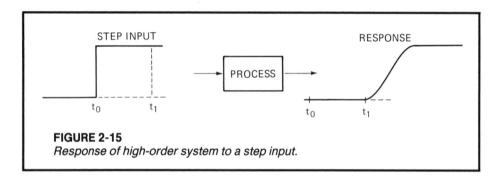

**FIGURE 2-15**
*Response of high-order system to a step input.*

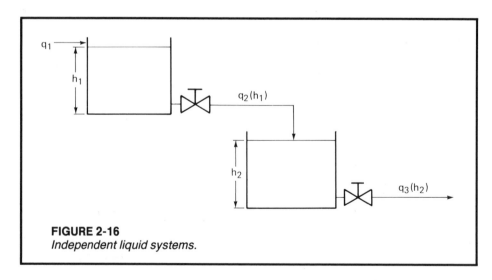

**FIGURE 2-16**
*Independent liquid systems.*

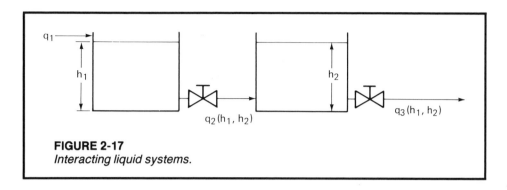

**FIGURE 2-17**
*Interacting liquid systems.*

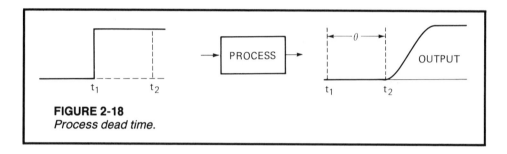

**FIGURE 2-18**
*Process dead time.*

Dead time is the most difficult situation to control, because during dead time there is no process response and therefore no information available to initiate corrective action.

To illustrate the concept of dead time, the temperature feedback control system shown in Figure 2-19 will be discussed. In this control loop, steam is injected into a water tank to produce hot water. There is a temperature bulb in the outlet stream to measure the temperature of the hot water produced. The control system increases or decreases the steam flow to hold the outlet water at a fixed temperature.

In the design of this control loop, the location of the temperature-sensing bulb is critical. It is tempting to say that the bulb should be installed farther down the outlet pipe and close to the water usage point. This sounds correct because the temperature of the water in the tank or at the tank exit is of little importance. This type of reasoning can be disastrous because, as the bulb is moved farther and farther down the line, a dead time is introduced into the feedback loop. In this example, the dead time ($\theta$) is equal to the distance (d) between the process hot water tank and the sensor, divided by the velocity (V) of the water flowing through the pipe (i.e., $\theta = d/V$). As a result of the additional dead time introduced into the temperature loop, the overall loop control deteriorates, and it may reach a point where it is impossible to achieve stable control.

Dead times may occur in many types of control applications and are the most difficult dynamic elements to control. Dead times can be determined from the

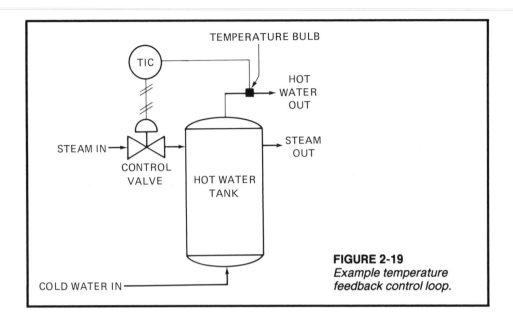

**FIGURE 2-19**
*Example temperature feedback control loop.*

process response curves by measuring the amount of time that elapses before any output response occurs after an input is applied to a system. We will discuss process reaction curves in a later section.

## Review of Control Modes
In Chapter 1 we discussed an intuitive approach to control modes; in this section, we will review this material and give further insight into the various types of standard control modes. We will also discuss some practical examples of process control.

**On-Off Control**   All types of control action may be considered as either continuous or discontinuous control. "On-off" control is discontinuous control. Two-position control action, or on-off control, is undoubtedly the easiest type of control to implement. A typical example of this type of control would be the liquid level in a tank. Typically, a level switch is used to turn on a fill or drain valve on the tank to maintain the tank level at a set point.

Figure 2-20 shows an example of two-position control, where the flow into a liquid storage tank is random and we are controlling the level in the tank by turning the outlet valve on or off using a level switch.

The instruments used for on-off control are cheap, rugged, and virtually foolproof. On-off control is basically oscillatory in character, but for many systems the amplitude of such oscillation of the controlled variable can be quite small.

An example of two-position control with differential gap is controlling tank level between two level switches, a level switch high (LSH) and a level switch low (LSL). In this example, a pump is turned on and off to maintain the liquid level between the two switches. The process shown in Figure 2-21 uses steam at a regulated

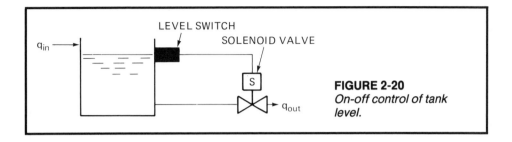

**FIGURE 2-20**
*On-off control of tank level.*

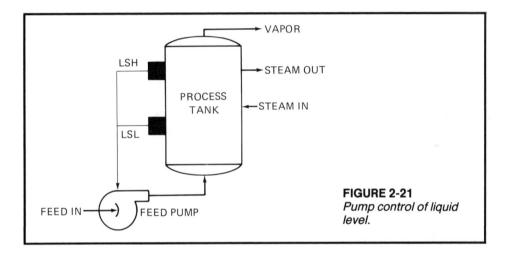

**FIGURE 2-21**
*Pump control of liquid level.*

rate to boil down liquid to produce a more concentrated solution that is drained off periodically.

The electrical circuit used to control the feed pump and hence the liquid level in the process tank is shown in Figure 2-22. These circuits are called ladder diagrams because they look like ladders with rungs. Each rung of the ladder is numbered in order that we can cross reference between sections in the diagram. For example, the contacts from the control relay CR1 are used in rungs 2 and 3, so we list these rung numbers (2, 3) on the right-hand side of the ladder next to the control relay (i.e., CR1) to reference where the relay contacts are used in the control circuit.

To explain the operation of the control circuit shown in the ladder diagram of Figure 2-22, we will assume the tank is empty, the low level switch is energized, and the high level switch is de-energized. When a level switch is energized, the normally open contacts (-|⊢) are closed and the normally closed contacts (-|/⊢) are opened. To start the system, the operator depresses the start push button (PB1) and this energizes relay CR1, which seals in the start push button with the first set of contacts [CR1(1)]. At the same time, control relay 2 (CR2) is energized in rung 3 through contacts of LSH, CR1(2) and LSL. This turns on the pump motor starter relay K1 using the second set of relay contacts [CR2(2)]. The first set of contacts on CR2 are used to seal in the low level switch (LSL), so that when the level in the tank rises above the position of the low level switch the pump will remain "ON".

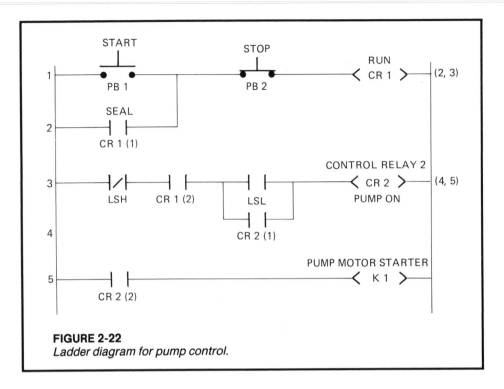

**FIGURE 2-22**
*Ladder diagram for pump control.*

The pump will remain "ON" until the level in the tank reaches the high level switch. After the LHS is energized, the system will cycle ON and OFF between the two level switches, hence the name ON/OFF control.

**Proportional Control**    The basic continuous control mode is proportional control in which the controller output is algebraically proportional to the error input signal to the controller. A simple block diagram model of the controller shown below illustrates this:

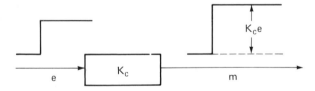

In this case, the controller output m is calculated as:

$$m = K_c e$$

This equation is called the control *algorithm.*

Proportional control action is the simplest and most commonly encountered of all the continuous control modes. In effect, there is a continuous linear relationship between the controller input and output.

The proportional gain of the controller is the term $K_c$, also referred to as the proportional sensitivity of the controller. $K_c$ indicates the change in the manipulated variable per unit change in the error signal. In a true sense, the proportional sensitivity or gain is a multiplication term and represents a parameter on a piece of actual hardware that must be adjusted by a technician or engineer; i.e., the gain is a knob to adjust.

This gain-adjusting mechanism on many industrial controllers is not expressed in terms of proportional sensitivity or gain but in terms of proportional band (PB). Proportional band is defined as the span of values of the input that corresponds to a full or complete change in the output. This is usually expressed as a percentage. It is related to proportional gain by

$$PB = \frac{1}{K_c} \times 100$$

Since most controllers have a scale indicating the value of the final controlled variable, the proportional band can be conveniently expressed as the range of values of the controlled variable corresponding to the full operating range of the final control valve.

As a matter of practice, *wide bands* (high percentages of PB) correspond to less sensitive response, and *narrow bands* (low percentages) correspond to more sensitive response.

Proportional control is quite simple and the easiest of the continuous controllers to tune since there is only one parameter to adjust. It also provides very rapid response and is relatively stable.

Proportional control has one major disadvantage, however. At steady state, it exhibits offset; i.e., there is a difference at steady state between the desired value or set point and the actual value of the controlled variable.

**Reset (Integral) Control**   *Reset action* is really an integration of the input error signal e. In effect, this means that in reset action (often called *integral action*), the value of the manipulated variable m is changed at a rate proportional to the error e. Thus, if the deviation is doubled over a previous value, the final control element is moved twice as fast. When the controlled variable is at the set point, the final control element remains stationary. In effect, this means that at steady state, when reset action is present, there can be no offset; therefore, the steady-state error must be zero.

Reset or integral control action is usually combined with proportional control action. The combination is termed *proportional-reset* or *proportional-integral action*; this is referred to as PI control. The combination is favorable in that some of the advantages of both types of control action are available. The basic control action for proportional-plus-integral action is as follows:

$$e \longrightarrow \boxed{K_c\left(1 + \frac{1}{t_i s}\right)} \longrightarrow m$$

where $K_c$ is the proportional gain, $t_i$ is the *integral time*, e is the error signal, m is controller output, and s implies the action of taking the derivative with respect to time, d/dy; therefore, 1/s implies integration with respect to time, $\int$ .. dt.

The advantage of including the integral mode with the proportional mode is that the integral action eliminates offset. Typically, there is some decreased stability due to the presence of the integral mode, i.e., the addition of the integral action makes the total loop slightly less stable. One significant exception to this is in liquid flow control. Liquid flow control loops are extremely fast and quite often tend to be very noisy. As a result, integral control is often added to the feedback controller in liquid flow control loops to provide a dampening or filtering action for the loop. Of course, the advantage of eliminating any offset is still present, but this is not the principal motivating factor in such cases.

Tuning a PI controller is more difficult than tuning a simpler proportional controller; now there are two separate tuning adjustments that must be made, and each depends on the other. As a matter of fact, the difficulty of tuning a controller increases dramatically with the number of adjustments that must be made.

**Proportional-plus-Derivative (PD) Control**    It is conceivable to have a control action that is based solely on the rate of change of the error signal e. While this is theoretically possible, it is not practical because, while the error might be large, if it were unchanging, the controller output would be zero. Thus, *rate control* or *derivative control* is usually found in combination with proportional control. The typical descriptive block diagram for a proportional-rate controller or PD controller is shown below:

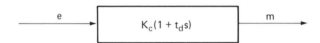

All of the terms are as defined earlier; in addition, $t_d$ is the derivative time and, as before, s implies the operation of taking the derivative with respect to time.

By adding derivative action to the controller, lead time is added in the controller to compensate for lag around the loop. Almost any process has a time delay or lag around the loop; therefore, the theoretical advantages of lead in the controller are appealing. However, it is quite a difficult control action to implement and adjust, and its usage is limited to cases in which there is an extensive amount of lag in the process. This often occurs with large temperature control systems.

The addition of rate control to the controller makes the loop more stable if it is correctly tuned. Since the loop is more stable, the proportional gain may be higher, and thus it can decrease offset above proportional action alone (but, of course, it does not eliminate offset).

**PID Control**    A typical block diagram for a three-mode controller or PID (proportional-plus-integral-plus-derivative) controller is shown on page 41.

The three-mode control gives rapid response and exhibits no offset, but it is very difficult to tune, because now there are three terms to adjust. As a result, it is

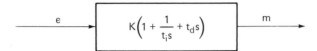

$$K\left(1 + \frac{1}{t_i s} + t_d s\right)$$

used only in a very small number of applications, and it often requires extensive and continuing adjustment to keep it properly tuned. It does, however, offer excellent control when proper tuning is used.

## Other Types of Control Loops
Up to this point we have discussed only single-loop feedback control. This section will now expand the discussion to include *cascade, ratio,* and *feedforward* control to cover most of the control strategies used in process control.

**Cascade Control Loops**   The general concept of cascade control is to place one feedback loop inside another feedback loop. In effect, one takes the process being controlled and finds some intermediate variable within the process to use as the set point for the main loop.

Cascade control exhibits its real value when a very slow process is being controlled. When this occurs, errors can exist for very long periods of time, and, when disturbances enter the process, there may be a significant wait before any corrective action is initiated. Also, when corrective action is taken, one may have to wait a long time for results. Cascade control affords one the opportunity to find intermediate controlled variables and to take corrective action on disturbances more promptly.

In general, cascade control has significant advantages to the user and is one of the least utilized feedback control techniques. Most plants could increase the usage of cascade control to significant advantage.

An important question in implementing cascade control is how to find the most advantageous secondary controlled variable. In the selection of this intermediate point, quite often a large number of choices are available to the designer. The overall strategy or goal should be to get as much of the process lag into the outer loop as possible while, at the same time, having as many of the disturbances as possible enter the inner loop.

Figure 2-23 shows a general layout of a furnace that is used to increase the temperature of a fluid passing through it, with the feedback control of this arrangement shown. Also shown in Figures 2-24a and b are two different cascade control arrangements. In both cases the primary controlled variable is the same, but in each case a different intermediate controlled variable has been selected. The question then is which type of cascade control is best.

In order to determine the best cascade control arrangement, it is necessary to make a specific determination of the most likely disturbances to the system. It is helpful to make a list of these in order of increasing importance. Once this has been done, the designer may review the various cascade control options available and determine which best meets the overall strategy outlined earlier, i.e., to have the inner loop as fast as possible while at the same time receiving the bulk of the important disturbances.

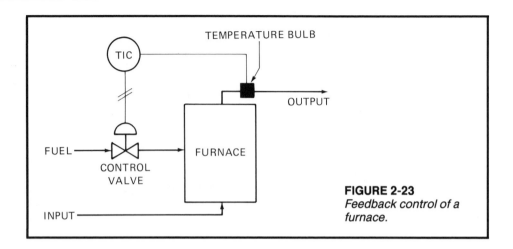

**FIGURE 2-23**
*Feedback control of a furnace.*

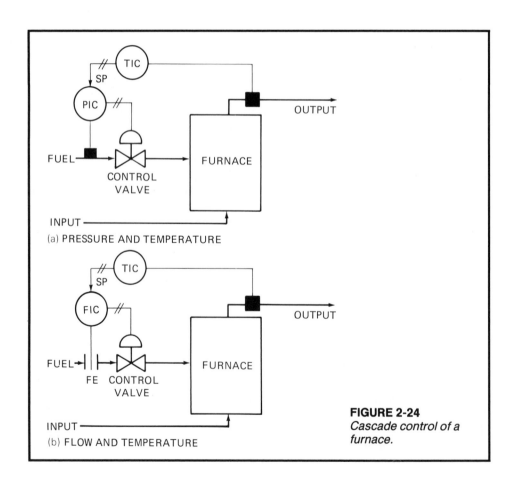

(a) PRESSURE AND TEMPERATURE

(b) FLOW AND TEMPERATURE

**FIGURE 2-24**
*Cascade control of a furnace.*

If both controllers of a cascade control system are three-mode controllers, there are a total of six tuning adjustments. It is doubtful if such a system could ever be tuned in an effective manner. Therefore, the modes to be included in both the primary and secondary controllers of a cascade arrangement should be selected with care.

For the secondary (or inner or slave) controller, it is standard practice to include the proportional mode. There is little need to include the reset mode for the purposes of eliminating offset since the set point for the inner controller will be reset continuously by the outer or master controller. For the outer loop, the controller should contain the proportional mode and, if the loop is sufficiently important to merit cascade control, it is probably true that reset should be included to eliminate offset in the outer loop.

The use of rate or derivative control in either loop should be undertaken only if the loop has a very large amount of lag.

The tuning of cascade controllers is the same as the tuning of all feedback controllers, but the loop must be tuned from the inside out. The master controller should be put on manual, i.e., the loop broken, and then the inner loop can be tuned. Once the inner loop is properly tuned, then the outer loop may be tuned. In doing so, the outer loop "sees" the tuned inner loop functioning as part of the total process or the "all else" that is being controlled by the master controller. If one follows this general inside-first principle in tuning cascade controllers, no special problems should be encountered.

**Ratio Control Loops**    Another common type of multiple-loop feedback control system is *ratio control*. When one looks at only the hardware, ratio control is quite often confused with cascade control, because in ratio control one loop adjusts another. But basically, the operation of ratio control is quite different.

Ratio control is often associated with process operations in which it is necessary to mix two or more streams together continuously to maintain a steady composition in the resulting mixture. A practical way to do this is to use a conventional flow controller on one stream and to control the other stream with a ratio controller that maintains flow in some preset ratio or fraction to the primary stream flow.

A ratio control system for regulating the composition of a feed stream to a reactor is shown in Figure 2-25.

The design of a ratio control system poses no special problem because each of the loops is designed individually and the general principles presented earlier still apply.

It is also possible to implement a ratio control system if the primary instrument is not a controller but rather a transmitter. In such a situation, the set point of the controller is set in direct relation to the magnitude of the primary controlled variable. An example of this is shown in Figure 2-26.

Basically, the general principles are very similar to other ratio control systems except one of the streams is uncontrolled and the other is maintained in ratio to it.

**Feedforward Control**    In feedforward control a sensor is used to detect a process disturbance as it enters the system, and the sensor sends this information to a feedforward controller as shown in Figure 2-27.

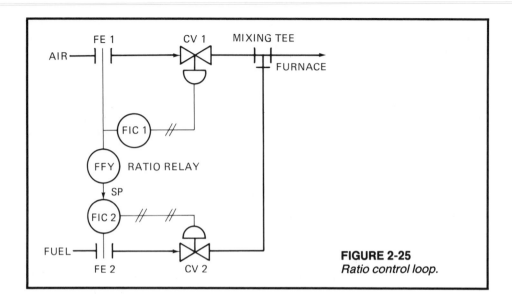

**FIGURE 2-25**
*Ratio control loop.*

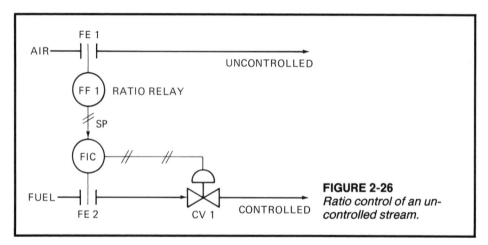

**FIGURE 2-26**
*Ratio control of an un-
controlled stream.*

The feedforward controller determines the required change in the manipulated variable so that, when the effect of the disturbance is combined with the
change in the manipulated variable, there is no change in the controlled variable.
This perfect correction is difficult to obtain.

There are some significant problems with feedforward control. The configuration of feedforward control assumes that the disturbances are known in advance, that the disturbances will have sensors associated with them, and that there
will be no important undetected disturbances.

## Tuning Control Loops
To tune a control loop, we need to determine the
optimum values of the controller gain $K_c$ (or proportional band PB), the reset time

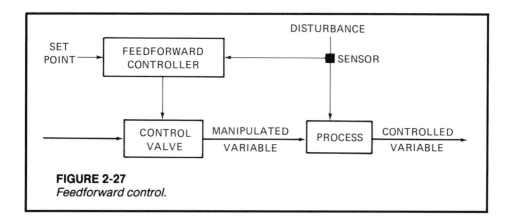

**FIGURE 2-27**
*Feedforward control.*

$t_r$ (or the reset rate as repeats per minute), and the derivative time $t_d$. The adjustment of these tuning parameters on feedback controllers is one of the least understood and most poorly practiced aspects of automatic control theory.

The first problem encountered in tuning controllers is to decide what sufficient control is and, as might be expected, how it differs from one process to the next. The most common criterion employed is to adjust the controller in order that the system's response curve has an amplitude ratio or *decay ratio* of one-quarter. A decay ratio of one-quarter means that the ratio of the overshoot of the first peak in the process response curve to the overshoot of the second peak is 4:1. This is illustrated in Figure 2-28.

Basically, there is no direct mathematical justification for requiring a decay ratio of one-quarter, but it represents a compromise between a rapid initial response and a fast line-out time. In many cases, this criterion is not sufficient to specify a unique combination of controller settings (i.e., in two-mode or three-mode controllers an infinite number of settings will yield a decay ratio of one quarter) each with a different period. This illustrates the problem of defining what constitutes sufficient control.

In some cases, it is important to tune the system so that there is no overshoot; in other cases, a slow and smooth response is desired; some cases warrant fast response and significant oscillations are no problem, and so on. The point is that you must determine what control is sufficient for each specific loop.

The feedback controller is only one piece of hardware in the entire loop; many other hardware items are connected to form the balance of the loop. For the purposes of adjusting the feedback controller, it is convenient and sufficient to view everything else within the feedback loop as being one unit. Actually, this is the way in which the feedback controller detects the balance of the loop, as illustrated in Figure 2-29.

The one parameter to adjust in a single-mode controller is the proportional gain $K_c$. There are two parameters to adjust in a two-mode controller, e.g., the proportional gain $K_c$ and the integral time $t_i$ in a PI controller. Three parameters must be adjusted in a PID controller: the controller gain $K_c$ for the proportional mode,

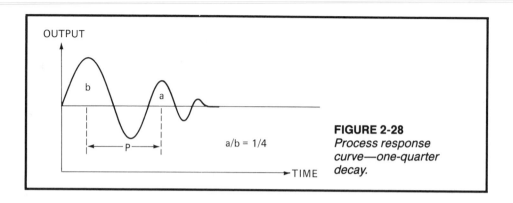

**FIGURE 2-28**
*Process response curve—one-quarter decay.*

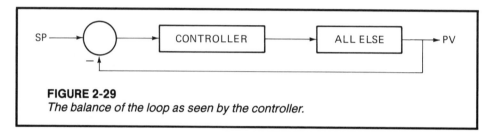

**FIGURE 2-29**
*The balance of the loop as seen by the controller.*

the integral time $t_i$ for the integral mode, and the $t_d$ for the derivative mode. In adjusting the controller, the gains around the loop will tend to dictate what the optimum gain in the controller should be. Similarly, the time constants and dead times that characterize the lag dynamics of the *all else* will tend to dictate what will be the optimum value of the reset time and what the derivative time in the controller should be. Stating this differently, before one can calculate or select the best values for the tuning parameters in the controller, one must obtain some quantitative information about the overall gain and the process lags that are present in the balance of the feedback loop. This illustrates quite clearly why controllers cannot be preset at the factory but must instead be individually tuned at the process plant.

**Ziegler-Nichols Tuning Method**   Techniques for adjusting controllers may be classified as either open-loop or closed-loop methods. One of the first methods proposed for tuning feedback controllers was the *ultimate* method proposed by Ziegler and Nichols in 1942. The term ultimate was attached to this method because its use required the determination of the ultimate gain (sensitivity) and the ultimate period for the loop. The ultimate gain is the maximum allowable value of gain (for a controller with only a proportional mode in operation) for which the closed-loop system shows a stable sine wave.

For any feedback control system, if the loop is closed (if the controller is on automatic), one can increase the controller gain and, as one does so, the loop will tend to oscillate more and more. As one continues to increase the gain farther, continuous cycling or oscillation in the controlled variable will be observable. This is the maximum gain at which the system may be operated before it becomes unstable; therefore, this is the ultimate gain. The period of these sustained oscillations is the ultimate period. If you increase the gain further still, the system will become unstable. These general situations are illustrated in Figure 2-30a, b, and c.

To determine the ultimate gain and the ultimate period, take the following steps:

1. Tune out all the reset and derivative action from the controller, leaving only the proportional mode.

2. Maintain the controller on automatic (i.e., leave the loop closed).

3. With the gain of the proportional mode of the controller at 1, impose an upset on the process and observe the response. (One easy method for imposing the upset is to change the set point.)

4. If the response curve from Step 3 does not damp out (as in the response curve in Figure 2-30a), the gain is too high (proportional band setting too low). The gain should be decreased (proportional band setting should be increased), and Step 3 repeated.

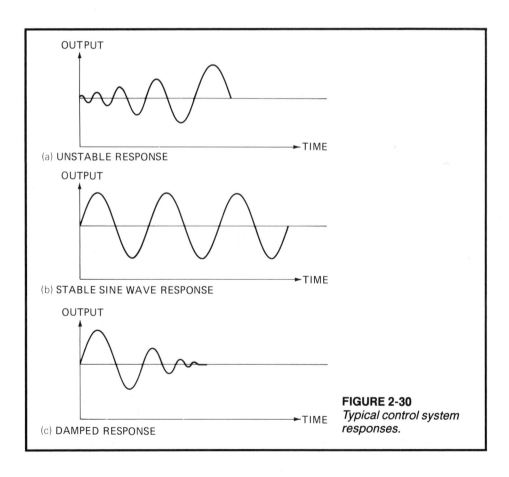

(a) UNSTABLE RESPONSE

(b) STABLE SINE WAVE RESPONSE

(c) DAMPED RESPONSE

**FIGURE 2-30**
*Typical control system responses.*

5.  If the response curve in Step 3 damps out (as in curve of Figure 2-30c), the gain is too low (proportional band is too high). The gain should be increased (proportional band setting should be decreased), and Step 3 repeated.

6.  When a response curve similar to the curve in Figure 2-30b is obtained, the values of the ultimate gain (or ultimate proportional band) setting and the ultimate period of the associated response curve are noted.

This ultimate gain at which the sustained oscillations are encountered is the ultimate sensitivity $S_u$ and the ultimate period is $P_u$.

The ultimate sensitivity ($S_u$) and the ultimate period ($P_u$) are then used to calculate controller settings. Ziegler and Nichols decided in the case of proportional controllers that a value of operating gain equal to one-half of the ultimate gain would often give a decay ratio of one-quarter; therefore they propose a tuning rule of thumb for a proportional controller:

$$K_u = 0.5S_u$$

By similar reasoning and testing, the following equations were found to represent good rules of thumb for controller settings for more complex controllers.

Proportional-plus-integral:

$$K_c = 0.45S_u$$
$$t_i = P_u/1.2$$

Proportional-plus-derivative:

$$K_c = 0.6S_u$$
$$t_d = P_u/8$$

Proportional-plus-integral-plus-derivative:

$$K_c = 0.6S_u$$
$$t_i = 0.5P_u$$
$$t_d = P_u/8$$

Again, it should be noted that the above equations are empirical and exceptions are common. They generally are intended to achieve a decay ratio of one quarter, i.e., this is the inherent definition of acceptable control.

**The Process Reaction Curve**  Generally speaking, open-loop methods require only that a single upset be imposed on the process. These methods give more precise data about the dynamics of a feedback control system and usually they give slightly better tuning results, although the variation in satisfaction from loop to loop can be quite significant.

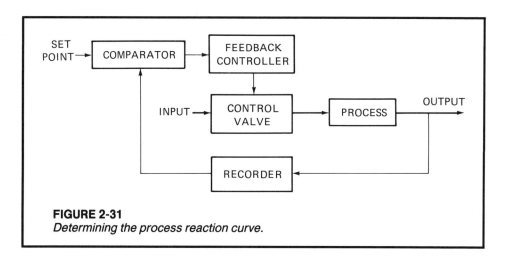

**FIGURE 2-31**
*Determining the process reaction curve.*

The process reaction curve is basically the *reaction* of the process to a step change in its input signal. The process reaction curve is the reaction of the "all else" viewed in Figure 2-29. It is important to get a complete picture of exactly what this process reaction curve will represent in a feedback loop, and this is shown in some detail in Figure 2-31.

Note that the control valve can be used to introduce the step change to the overall process, and the dedicated trend recorder on the feedback loop can be used to record the process reaction curve. In general, a process reaction curve can be determined as follows:

1. Let the system come to steady state.

2. Place the controller on manual operation.

3. Manually set the controller output signal at the value at which it was operating automatically.

4. Allow the system to reach steady state.

5. With the controller still in manual operation, impose a step change in the controller output signal.

6. Record the response of the controlled variable.

7. Return the controller output signal to its previous value and return the controller to automatic operation.

Once the steps listed above are completed, the recorded process reaction curve can be used to give information about the overall dynamics and parameters for the *all else* of the process loop. This information may be used to calculate needed tuning parameters of the feedback controller.

Another method utilizing the process reaction curve for tuning controllers was also proposed by Ziegler and Nichols: the ultimate method. To use this process reaction curve method, only the parameters $R_r$ and $L_r$ must be determined. A sample determination of these parameters for a control loop is illustrated in Figure 2-32.

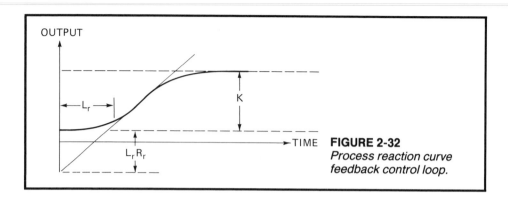

**FIGURE 2-32**
*Process reaction curve
feedback control loop.*

To obtain process information parameters in the process reaction curve method, a tangent is drawn to the process reaction curve at its point of maximum slope. This slope $R_r$ is the process reaction rate. Where this tangent line intersects the original baseline gives an indication of $L_r$, the process lag. $L_r$ is really a measure of equivalent dead time for the process. If this tangent drawn at the point of maximum slope is extrapolated to a vertical axis drawn at the time when the step was imposed, then the amount by which this is below the horizontal baseline will represent the product $L_rR_r$. Using these parameters, Ziegler and Nichols proposed a series of rules of thumb that can be used to calculate appropriate controller settings.

Proportional only:

$$K_c = 1/L_rR_r$$

Proportional-plus-integral:

$$K_c = 0.9/L_rR_r$$
$$t_i = 3.33\ L_r$$

Proportional-plus-integral-plus-derivative:

$$K_c = 1.2/L_rR_r$$
$$t_i = 2.0L_r$$
$$t_d = 0.5L_r$$

Ziegler and Nichols indicated these rules of thumb should give a decay ratio of one-quarter, i.e., this is the inherent definition of good control.

## EXERCISES

2.1 Explain the purpose and function of each component in a single feedback control loop.

2.2 Define the term process gain.

2.3 Prove that the time constant ($\tau$) in a thermal system has the units of time.

2.4 For the liquid system shown below, write differential equations where $A_1$ and $A_2$ are the liquid surface areas, $q_1$ is the input flow, and $h_2$ is the response.

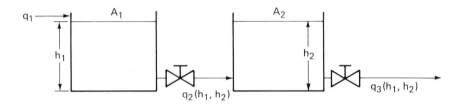

2.5 The tank shown in Figure 2-12 has an operating head (h) of 5 ft and a normal output flow of 0.2 ft³/s. The cross-sectional area of the tank is 10 ft². Find the system time constant ($\tau$).

2.6 Explain the concept of dead time.

2.7 Design a control system to pump down the liquid in the tank shown, using relay ladder logic.

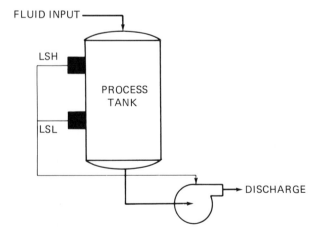

## BIBLIOGRAPHY

1. Considine, Douglas M. (ed.), *Handbook of Applied Instrumentation*, McGraw-Hill Book Company, 1964.

2. Murrill, P.W., *Fundamentals of Process Control Theory*, Instrument Society of America, 1981.

3. The Staff of Chemical Engineering (Ed.), *Practical Process Instrumentation and Control*, Chemical Engineering McGraw-Hill Publications Co., 1980.

4. Kirk, F.W; Rimboi, N.R; *Instrumentation*, American Technical Publishers, Inc., Third Edition, 1975.

5. Johnson, C.D., *Process Control Instrumentation Technology*, John Wiley & Sons, Second Edition, 1982.

6. Ogata, K., *Modern Control Engineering*, Prentice-Hall, Inc., 1970.

7. Weyrick, R.C., *Fundamentals of Automatic Control*, McGraw-Hill Book Company, 1975.

# 3
# Electronics Fundamentals

**Introduction**   The design of process control systems requires knowledge of the basic principles of electronics and electronic devices. This chapter will briefly discuss direct current (dc) circuit theory and then investigate the electronic circuits that are commonly used in the instrumentation and control field, such as power supplies, voltage regulators, operational amplifiers, and analog computers. The section on operational amplifiers is very important because of their extensive use in the transmitter and receiver instruments used in process control system applications.

**Direct Current Circuit Theory**   This section will cover the basic principles of direct current circuits. The subjects to be covered are:

1. Conductivity, resistivity and Ohm's Law
2. Series dc resistance circuits
3. Parallel dc resistance circuits
4. Wheatstone bridge circuit
5. Instrumentation current loops

**Conductivity, Resistivity and Ohm's Law**   An important physical property of some material is called conductivity, i.e., the ability to pass electric current. Suppose we have an electric wire (conductor) of length L and cross-sectional area A, and we apply a voltage V between the ends of the wire. If V is in volts and L is in meters, we can define the voltage gradient, E , as

$$E = \frac{V}{L} \text{ (volts/meter)} \tag{3-1}$$

Now if a current I in amperes flows through a wire of area A in meters², we can define the current density J as

$$J = \frac{I}{A} \text{ (amps/meters}^2) \tag{3-2}$$

The conductivity C is defined as the current density per unit voltage gradient E or, in equation form, we have

$$C = \frac{J}{E} \text{ (amps/meter}^2)/(\text{volts/meter})$$

or
$$C = \frac{I/A}{V/L} \tag{3-3}$$

Resistivity (r) is defined as the inverse of conductivity, or

$$r = \frac{1}{C}$$

The fact that resistivity is a natural property of certain materials leads to the basic principle of current flow called Ohm's Law.

Consider a wire of length L and area A. If it has resistivity, r, then its resistance R is

$$R = r \frac{L}{A} \tag{3-4}$$

The units of resistance are ohms. Since the resistivity, r, is the reciprocal of conductivity, we obtain the following:

$$r = \frac{V/L}{I/A} \tag{3-5}$$

When Equation 3-5 is substituted into Equation 3-4, we obtain

$$R = \frac{V}{I} \tag{3-6}$$

This relationship, R = V/I or V = IR, is called Ohm's Law, which assumes that the resistance of the material used to carry the current flow is linear, i.e., if the voltage across the resistance is doubled, the current through it also doubles. The resistance of materials like carbon, aluminum, copper, silver, gold, and iron is linear.

**Series DC Resistance Circuits**    When the components in a circuit are connected in successive order with the end of a component joined to the end of the next element, they form a series circuit. An example of a series circuit is shown in Figure 3-1.

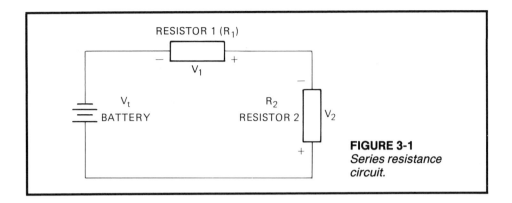

RESISTOR 1 ($R_1$)

$V_1$

$V_t$
BATTERY

$R_2$
RESISTOR 2   $V_2$

**FIGURE 3-1**
*Series resistance
circuit.*

In this circuit the current (I) flows from the negative terminal of the battery through the two resistors ($R_1$ and $R_2$) and back to the positive terminal. According to Ohm's Law, the amount of current (I) flowing between two points in a circuit equals the potential difference (V) divided by the resistance (R) between these points. If $V_1$ is the voltage drop across $R_1$, $V_2$ is defined as the voltage drop across $R_2$, and the current (I) flows through both $R_1$ and $R_2$, we obtain from Ohm's Law

$$V_1 = IR_1 \text{ and } V_2 = IR_2, \qquad \text{so that}$$

$$V_t = IR_1 + IR_2 \qquad \text{or}$$

$$V_t/I = R_1 + R_2$$

Since $V_t/I = R_t$, we obtain the total resistance of the series circuit of Figure 3-1:

$$R_t = R_1 + R_2$$

We can derive a more general equation for any number of resistors in series by using the classical law of conservation of energy. According to this law, the energy or power supplied to a series circuit must equal the power dissipated in the resistors in the circuit.

Thus,

$$P_t = P_1 + P_2 + P_3 + \ldots + P_n \qquad\qquad \text{or}$$

since $P = I^2R$

$$I^2R_t = I^2R_1 + I^2R_2 + I^2R_3 + \ldots + I^2R_n$$

If we divide this equation by I, we obtain the series resistance formula

$$R_t = R_1 + R_2 + R_3 + \ldots + R_n \qquad\qquad (3\text{-}7)$$

## EXAMPLE 3-1

**Problem:** Assume that the battery voltage in the series circuit of Figure 3-2 is 6 V dc and that resistor $R_1 = 1$ k$\Omega$ and resistor $R_2 = 2$ k$\Omega$. Find the total current flow $(I_t)$ in the circuit and the voltage across $R_1$ and $R_2$.

**Solution:** To calculate the circuit current $I_t$, first find the total circuit resistance $R_t$ using Equation 3-7:

$$R_t = R_1 + R_2$$
$$= 1\text{ k}\Omega + 2\text{ k}\Omega$$
$$= 3\text{ k}\Omega$$

Now according to Ohm's Law:

$$I_t = \frac{V_t}{R_t}$$

$$I_t = \frac{6V}{3\text{ k}\Omega} = 2\text{ mA}$$

The voltage across $R_1$ (i.e., $V_1$) is given by

$$V_1 = R_1 I_t$$
$$= (1\text{ k}\Omega)(2\text{ mA}) = 2\text{ V}$$

The voltage across $R_2$ (i.e., $V_2$) is obtained as follows:

$$V_2 = R_2 I_t$$
$$= (2\text{ k}\Omega)(2\text{ mA}) = 4\text{ V}$$

**Parallel Circuits**   When two or more components are connected across a power source, they form a parallel circuit. Each parallel path is called a branch, and each has its own current. In other words, parallel circuits have one common voltage across all the branches, but individual branch currents. These characteristics are opposite to series circuits that have one common current, but individual voltage drops.

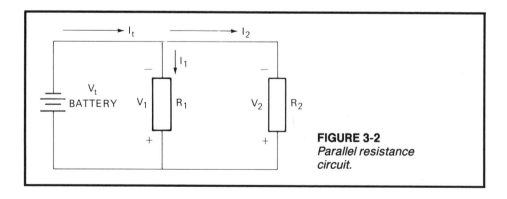

**FIGURE 3-2**
*Parallel resistance circuit.*

A parallel circuit with two resistors across a battery is shown in Figure 3-2. The total resistance ($R_t$) across the power supply can be found by Ohm's Law as follows: Divide the voltage across the parallel resistances by the total current of all the branches. In the circuit of Figure 3-2, $I_t = I_1 + I_2$ and $I_1 = V_t/R_1$, $I_2 = V_t/R_2$, so that $I = V_t/R_1 + V_t/R_2$. Since $I_t = V_t/R_t$, we obtain

$$\frac{1}{R_t} = \frac{1}{R_1} + \frac{1}{R_2}$$

or

$$R_t = \frac{R_1 \times R_2}{R_1 + R_2} \tag{3-8}$$

We can derive the general reciprocal resistance formula for any number of resistors in parallel from the fact that the total current $I_t$ is the sum of all the branch currents, or

$$I_t = I_1 + I_2 + I_3 + \ldots + I_n$$

This is simply the law of electrical charge conservation,

$$dQ/dt = dQ_1/dt + dQ_2/dt + dQ_3/dt + \ldots dQ_n/dt$$

This law implies that, since no charge accumulates at any point in the circuit, the charge dQ from the power source in time dt must appear as charges $dQ_1$, $dQ_2$, $dQ_3$, .... $dQ_n$ through the resistors $R_1$, $R_2$, $R_3$, ..., $R_n$ at the same time.

To illustrate the basic concepts of a parallel circuit, let's look at an example problem.

## EXAMPLE 3-2

**Problem:** Assume that the voltage for the parallel circuit shown in Figure 3-2 is 12 V and we need to find the currents $I_t$, $I_1$ and $I_2$ and the parallel resistance $R_t$, given that $R_1 = 30$ k$\Omega$ and $R_2 = 30$ k$\Omega$.

**Solution:** We can find the parallel circuit resistance $R_t$ by using Equation 3-8:

$$R_t = \frac{R_1 \times R_2}{R_1 + R_2} \tag{3-8}$$

$$R_t = \frac{(30\ \text{k})(30\ \text{k})}{30\ \text{k} + 30\ \text{k}}\ \Omega = 15\ \text{k}\Omega$$

The total current flow is given by

$$I_t = \frac{V_t}{R_t} = \frac{12\ \text{V}}{15\ \text{k}\Omega} = 0.8\ \text{mA}$$

The current in branch 1 ($I_1$) is obtained as follows:

$$R_1 = \frac{V_t}{R_1} = \frac{12\ V}{30\ k\Omega} = 0.4\ mA$$

Since $I_t = I_1 + I_2$, the current flow in branch 2 is given by

$$I_2 = I_t - I_1 = 0.8\ mA - 0.4\ mA = 0.4\ mA$$

**Wheatstone Bridge Circuit**  The Wheatstone bridge circuit, named for English physicist and inventor Sir Charles Wheatstone (1802-1875), was one of the first electrical measuring instruments invented to accurately measure resistance. The bridge circuit is shown in Figure 3.3. The circuit has two parallel resistance branches with two series resistors in each branch and a galvanometer (G) connected across the branches. The purpose of the circuit is to have the voltage drops balanced across the two parallel branches to obtain zero volts across the meter. In the Wheatstone bridge, the unknown resistance $R_x$ is balanced against a standard accurate resistor $R_s$ for precise measurement of resistance.

In the circuit shown, the switch $S_1$ is closed to apply the voltage $V_t$ to the four resistors in the bridge. To balance the circuit, the value of $R_s$ is varied until a zero reading is obtained on the meter with switch $S_2$ closed.

A typical application of the Wheatstone bridge circuit is to replace the unknown resistor $R_x$ with a temperature bulb. A temperature bulb is a device that varies its resistance with a change in temperature, so that the balancing resistor dial can be calibrated to read out a process temperature.

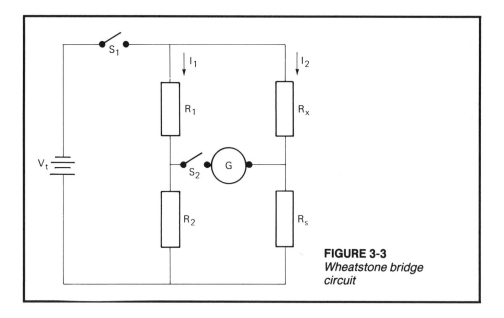

**FIGURE 3-3**
*Wheatstone bridge circuit*

When the bridge circuit is balanced (i.e., no current through galvanometer G), the circuit can be analyzed as two series resistance strings in parallel. The equal voltage ratios in the two branches of the Wheatstone bridge can be stated as

$$\frac{I_2 R_x}{I_2 R_s} = \frac{I_1 R_1}{I_1 R_2} \quad \text{or} \quad \frac{R_x}{R_s} = \frac{R_1}{R_2}$$

Note that $I_1$ and $I_2$ can be canceled out in the equation above, so we can invert $R_s$ to the right side of the equation to find $R_x$ as follows:

$$R_x = R_s \ \frac{R_1}{R_2} \tag{3-9}$$

To illustrate the use of a Wheatstone bridge, let's consider the following example.

**EXAMPLE 3-3**

**Problem:** Assume a Wheatstone bridge is balanced and $R_1 = 1$ k$\Omega$ and $R_2 = 10$ k$\Omega$. If $R_s$ is adjusted to read 50 $\Omega$ when the bridge is balanced, calculate the value of $R_x$.

**Solution:** We can use Equation 3-9 to determine $R_x$:

$$R_x = R_s \ \frac{R_1}{R_2} \tag{3-9}$$

$$R_x = 50 \ \Omega \ \frac{1 \text{ k}\Omega}{10 \text{ k}\Omega} = 5 \ \Omega$$

**Instrumentation Current Loop**   The brief discussion on dc circuit theory to this point was leading to this discussion on instrumentation current loops. The dc current loop shown in Figure 3-4 is used extensively in the instrumentation field to transmit process variables to indicators and/or controllers, and also to send control signals to field devices to manipulate process variables such as temperature, level, and flow. The normal current range used is 4 to 20 mA, and this value is converted to 1 to 5 V dc by a 250-$\Omega$ resistor at the input to controllers and indicators that are normally high input impedance ($Z_{in} > 10$ M$\Omega$) electronic amplifiers that draw virtually no current.

There are two main advantages to using the 4- to 20-mA current loop. First, only two wires are required for each remotely mounted field transmitter, so a cost savings is realized on both labor and wire in installing field devices. The second advantage is that the current loop is not affected by electrical noise.

## Power Supplies and Regulators   A basic understanding of the design and operation of dc power supplies is important in instrumentation and control because of their wide use in electronic control systems. DC power supplies use either half-wave or full-wave rectification depending on the power supply applica-

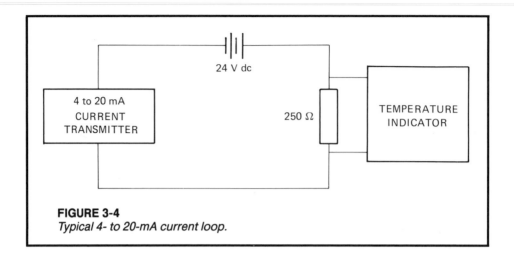

**FIGURE 3-4**
*Typical 4- to 20-mA current loop.*

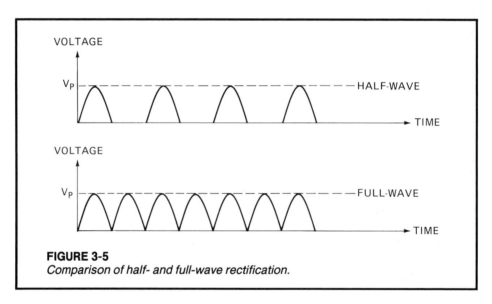

**FIGURE 3-5**
*Comparison of half- and full-wave rectification.*

tion. Figure 3-5 shows the output waveforms produced by half-wave and full-wave rectification. A schematic diagram of a half-wave rectifier is shown in Figure 3-6. In this circuit, the primary input voltage is 120 volts rms, and the secondary is given as 25 volts rms. The positive and negative cycles of the ac voltage across the secondary winding are in phase with the signal at the primary.

If we assume that the top of the transformer secondary is positive and the bottom is negative during a positive cycle of the input, then the diode is forward-biased and current flow is permitted through the load resistor, $R_L$, as indicated. The slight difference in output is due to the resistance of the diode. A silicon diode will produce a 0.7 volt drop, so the output is reduced by this amount.

During the negative input cycle, the top of the transformer will be negative and the bottom will be positive. This voltage polarity reverse biases the diode. A reverse-biased diode represents an extremely high resistance and serves as an open circuit. Therefore, with no current flowing through $R_L$, the output voltage will be zero for this cycle.

To calculate the dc voltage of the half-wave rectifier, we first determine the peak voltage of one cycle. This is obtained by multiplying the rms input voltage by 1.414. The average value is then determined by multiplying the peak value by 0.637. Since only one cycle of the two input cycles appears in the output, this value must be divided by 2. Combining these values, we find that 1.414 times 0.637 divided by 2 equals 0.45, or 45% of the rms input voltage. Therefore, the dc output of the half-wave rectifier is 45% of the rms ac value minus the diode voltage drop of 0.7 volt. A dc voltmeter would read this value across the load resistor, $R_L$, in the simple half-wave rectifier shown in Figure 3-6.

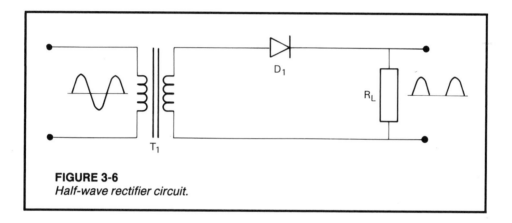

**FIGURE 3-6**
*Half-wave rectifier circuit.*

Peak voltage $(V_P) = 1.414 \times V$ rms

$V_P = 1.414 \times 25\ V = 35.35\ V$

Average voltage $(V_{av}) = 0.367 \times V_P$

$V_{av} = 0.367 \times 35.35\ V = 22.5\ V$

DC output $(V_{dc}) = (V_{ac}/2) - V_{diode}$

$V_{dc} = (22.5\ V/2) - V_{diode}$

$V_{dc} = (11.25 - 0.7)V = 10.55\ V$

The basic full-wave rectifier using two diodes is shown in Figure 3-7. The cathodes of both diodes are connected to obtain a positive output. The anodes of each diode are connected to opposite ends of the transformer secondary winding. The load resistor $(R_L)$ and the transformer center are connected to ground to complete the circuit.

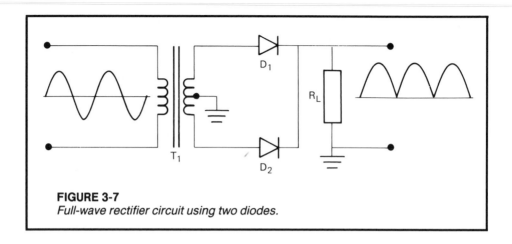

**FIGURE 3-7**
*Full-wave rectifier circuit using two diodes.*

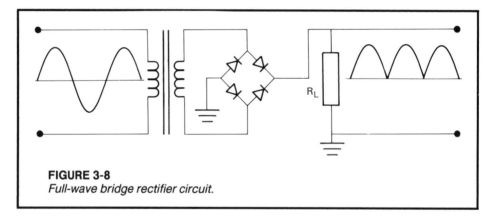

**FIGURE 3-8**
*Full-wave bridge rectifier circuit.*

In a full-wave rectifier, the current through $R_L$ is in the same direction for each alteration of the input, so that we obtain dc output for both halves of the sine-wave input, or full-wave rectification.

The dc output voltage of a full-wave rectifier is 90% of the ac rms voltage appearing between the center tap and the other ends of the transformer. This voltage is determined by calculating the peak value ($V_P$) of the rms voltage, then multiplying it by the average value ($V_{av}$). Since 1.414 times 0.637 equals 0.900, the potential dc output is 90% of the rms input. The dc output voltage appearing across $R_L$ of the circuit will be slightly less than 90% of the rms value because each diode has a voltage drop of 0.7 volt. This means that a dc voltmeter would read the rms value times 90% minus 0.7 volt across $R_L$.

The ripple frequency of the full-wave rectifier is also different from that of a half-wave circuit. Since each cycle of the input produces an output across $R_L$, the ripple frequency will be twice the input frequency. The higher ripple frequency and characteristic output of the full-wave rectifier are easier to filter than a similar half-wave output.

A bridge structure of four diodes is commonly used in power supplies to achieve full-wave rectification. In the rectifier shown in Figure 3-8, two diodes will conduct during the positive alteration and two will conduct during the negative alteration. A bridge rectifier does not require a center-tapped transformer as used in a two-diode full-wave rectifier.

The dc output appearing across $R_L$ of the bridge circuit has a ripple frequency of 120 Hz and will have a dc voltage a little less than 90% of the secondary rms value. Since each diode produces a 0.7 volt drop, the two diodes that conduct will reduce the output by 2 times 0.7, or 1.4 volts. The resulting dc output will be 90% of the rms value less 1.4 volts, so that in the circuit shown in Figure 3-8, the dc output voltage ($V_o$) will be

$$V_o = 0.9 \times 25 \text{ V} - 1.4 \text{ V} = 21.1 \text{ V dc}$$

Bridge rectifiers are commonly used in electronic power supplies for instruments because of their simple operation and desirable output. The diode bridge is generally housed in a single enclosure that has two input and two output connections. However, the output from a bridge rectifier still needs to be filtered to produce the smooth dc signal needed by most instrumentation circuits and devices.

**Capacitor Filter for DC Supply**   A dc rectifier circuit is necessary to convert an ac signal having zero average value to one that has a nonzero average value. However, the resulting pulsating dc signal is not pure enough for most applications. Therefore, the output of the bridge circuit needs to be filtered. A popular filter circuit is the single capacitor filter shown in Figure 3-9. The capacitor is connected across the rectifier output, and the dc output voltage is available across the capacitor.

Figure 3-10 shows a full-wave rectifier output signal before the signal is filtered, and Figure 3-11 shows the resulting waveform after the capacitor is connected across the rectifier.

As shown, this filtered output voltage has a dc level with some ripple voltage riding on it.

**Zener Diode Voltage Regulators**   In the process control applications, it is sometimes useful to know how to use an existing dc voltage to obtain a lower fixed

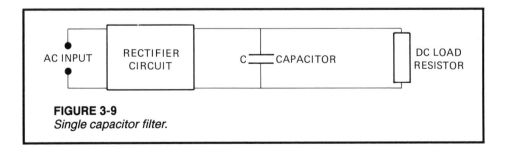

**FIGURE 3-9**
*Single capacitor filter.*

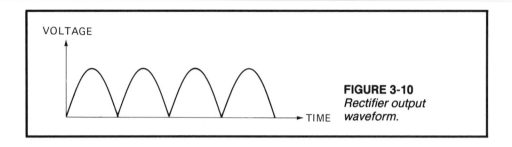

**FIGURE 3-10**
*Rectifier output waveform.*

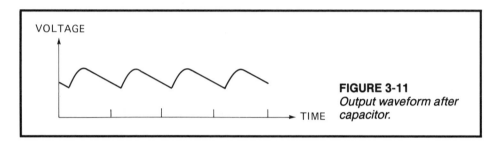

**FIGURE 3-11**
*Output waveform after capacitor.*

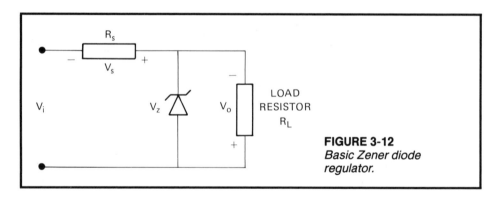

**FIGURE 3-12**
*Basic Zener diode regulator.*

voltage. Zener diodes can be used for this purpose. A typical Zener diode circuit is shown in Figure 3-12.

In the design of a Zener diode regulator, the designer must know the input voltage variations and the output load requirements. The input may be constant or have maximum and minimum values depending upon the form of the supply source. The output voltage will be determined by the designer's choice of the Zener diode voltage ($V_z$) and the circuit requirements.

The design objective of the circuit in Figure 3-12 is to determine the proper values of the series resistance, $R_s$, and the Zener power dissipation, $P_z$. A general solution for these values can be developed, if the following are known:

1. Input voltage range; $V_i$ (min) to $V_i$ (max)

2. Output voltage required; $V_o$

3. Load current $I_o$ range; $I_o$ (min) to $I_o$ (max)

The value of $R_s$ must be selected so that the Zener current does not drop below a minimum value ($I_z$ [min]). This minimum Zener current is required to keep the device in the breakover region in order to maintain the Zener voltage (see Figure 3-13). The minimum current can be found in manufacturer's data sheets.

The basic voltage loop equation for the circuit in Figure 3-12 is given by:

$$V_i - (I_z + I_o)R_s - V_o = O \qquad \text{or}$$
$$V_i = (I_z + I_o)R_s + V_o \tag{3.10}$$

The minimum Zener current will occur when $V_i$ is minimum and $I_o$ is maximum, so that $R_s$ is given by:

$$R_s = \frac{V_i(\text{min}) - V_z(\text{max})}{I_z(\text{min}) + I_o(\text{max})} \tag{3.11}$$

Having found $R_s$, the maximum power dissipation $P_z$ (max ) for the Zener diode is given by:

$$P_z(\text{max}) = I_z(\text{max}) V_z(\text{max})$$

where:
$$I_z(\text{max}) = \frac{V_i(\text{max}) - V_z(\text{min})}{R_s} - I_o(\text{min}) \tag{3.12}$$

so that the maximum power dissipated by the Zener diode is

$$P_z(\text{max}) = \left[ \frac{V_i(\text{max}) - V_z(\text{min})}{R_s} - I_o(\text{min}) \right] V_z \tag{3.13}$$

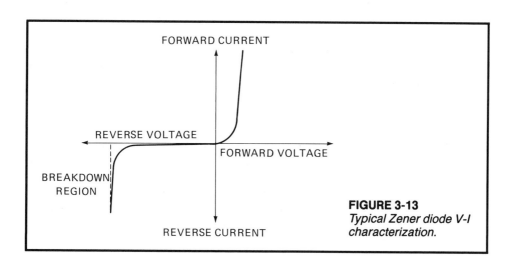

**FIGURE 3-13**
*Typical Zener diode V-I characterization.*

An example calculation to obtain +12 V from a +15 V supply is given below.

**EXAMPLE 3-4**

**Problem:** We need a dc voltage source with the following specifications: $V_o = 12$ V, $I_o$ (max) = 50 mA, and $I_z$ (min) = 10 mA with $V_i = 15$ V.

**Solution:** We need to select a 12 V Zener diode with the correct power rating, but first we need to find $R_s$.
Using Equation 3.11,

$$R_s = \frac{V_i \text{ (min)} - V_z \text{ (max)}}{I_z \text{ (min)} + I_o \text{ (max)}} = \frac{15 \text{ V} - 12 \text{ V}}{10 \text{ mA} + 50 \text{ mA}} = 50 \ \Omega$$

Now, we find $P_z$ (max), using $P_z$ (max) = $I_z$ (max)$V_o$

where:     $$I_z \text{ (max)} = \frac{V_i \text{ (max)} - V_z \text{ (min)}}{R_s} - I_o \text{ (min)}$$

so that

$$I_z \text{ (max)} = \frac{15 \text{ V} - 12 \text{ V}}{50 \ \Omega} - 10 \text{ mA} = 50 \text{ mA}$$

$$P_z \text{ (max)} = (50 \text{ mA})(12 \text{ V}) = 600 \text{ mwatts}$$

Therefore, we need to select a 12 V Zener with a power rating of 600 mW.

The Zener diode is an inexpensive method to obtain good voltage regulation. However, if better regulation is required at a reasonable cost, some excellent integrated circuit voltage regulators are available.

**Integrated Circuit (IC) Voltage Regulators**   The IC voltage regulators contain all the circuitry needed for excellent voltage regulation in a single IC chip. We will discuss the operation of a popular group of 3-terminal fixed-voltage regulators for both positive and negative voltages.

An excellent power supply can be built using a transformer connected to an ac source to step the voltage to a desired level, then rectifying with a half- or full-wave circuit, filtering the voltage using a capacitor filter, and finally regulating the dc voltage using an IC voltage regulator.

A group of fixed-positive-voltage IC regulators, designated by the IC manufacturers as series 78, provides fixed voltages from 5 V to 24 V. Figure 3-14 shows how these regulators are connected, and Table 3-1 lists some typical data. A rectified and filtered unregulated dc voltage is the input, $V_{in}$, to pin 1 of the IC regulator. The output voltage ($V_{out}$) from pin 2 is then available to connect to the load. Pin 3 is the IC circuit reference or ground. When selecting the desired fixed regulated output voltage, the two digits after the 78 prefix indicate the regulator output voltage.

Negative-voltage regulator ICs are available in the 79 series, as shown in Figure 3-15 and listed in Table 3-2. These regulators provide a series of ICs similar to the 78 series but operate on negative voltages, providing a regulated negative output voltage.

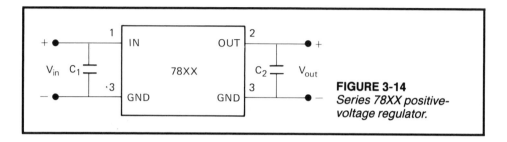

**FIGURE 3-14**
*Series 78XX positive-voltage regulator.*

**TABLE 3-1**
**Positive Series 78XX Voltage Regulator ICs**

| IC Part Number | Output Voltage | Minimum $V_i$ |
|---|---|---|
| 7805 | + 5 V | 7.3 V |
| 7806 | + 6 V | 8.35 V |
| 7808 | + 8 V | 10.5 V |
| 7810 | +10 V | 12.5 V |
| 7812 | +12 V | 14.6 V |
| 7815 | +15 V | 17.7 V |
| 7818 | +18 V | 21.0 V |
| 7824 | +24 V | 27.1 V |

**TABLE 3-2**
**Negative Series 79XX Voltage Regulator ICs**

| IC Part Number | Output Voltage | Minimum $V_i$ |
|---|---|---|
| 7905 | − 5 V | 7.3 V |
| 7906 | − 6 V | 8.35 V |
| 7908 | − 8 V | 10.5 V |
| 7910 | −10 V | 12.5 V |
| 7912 | −12 V | 14.6 V |
| 7915 | −15 V | 17.7 V |
| 7918 | −18 V | 21.0 V |
| 7924 | −24 V | 27.1 V |

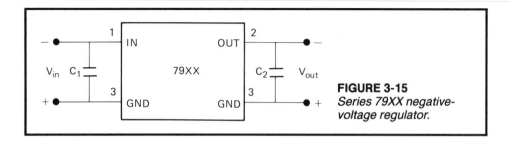

**FIGURE 3-15**
*Series 79XX negative-voltage regulator.*

## Operational Amplifiers

The operational amplifier derives its name from its early association with precision analog computing circuits to simulate various mathematical "operations". The early versions of operational amplifiers were bulky vacuum tube types with limited applications. The present IC (integrated circuit) versions, because of their very small size, cost, and low power requirements, find very extensive use in analog circuits used in process instruments. Its instrumentation circuit applications include analog scaling and signal conditioning, sample-hold, precision voltage comparisons, current-to-voltage (I/V) conversion, voltage-to-current (V/I) conversion, active signal filters, and numerous other circuits.

We will assume for this discussion that we have an ideal operational amplifier, i.e., the gain is infinite, the input impedance is infinite, and the output impedance is zero. The schematic symbol for an op amp is shown in Figure 3-16. The op amp has two inputs, labeled inverting (–) and noninverting (+), and an output signal. A signal at the inverting input produces an output of opposite polarity, and a signal input to the noninverting terminal is not inverted. Feedback from the output terminal to one of the input terminals is generally used to stabilize the gain of the amplifier.

**Unity-Gain Follower**   The simplest feedback circuit that one might design using an "ideal" operational amplifier is the unity-gain follower of Figure 3-17. In this circuit 100% of the output voltage is fed back to the negative input. The input signal is connected directly to the noninverting input, and the output follows precisely. In the definition of an "ideal" op amp, the voltages at the input terminals are assumed to be equal or $V_1 = V_2$. Since the input signal $V_i$ equals the voltage at the noninverting terminal $V_1$ (i.e., $V_i = V_1$) and the output voltage $V_o$ equals the signal $V_2$ at the inverting terminals (i.e., $V_o = V_2$), we obtain $V_o = V_i$ or $V_o/V_i = 1$.

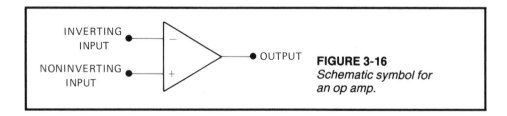

**FIGURE 3-16**
*Schematic symbol for an op amp.*

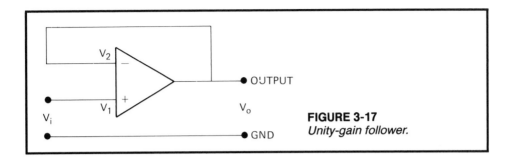

**FIGURE 3-17**
*Unity-gain follower.*

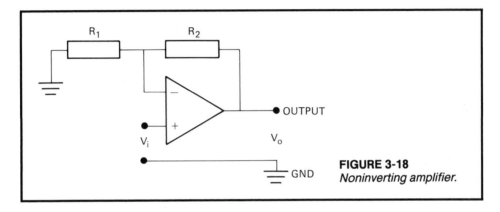

**FIGURE 3-18**
*Noninverting amplifier.*

Since gain of an amplifier is defined as the ratio of voltage out ($V_o$) over voltage in ($V_i$), the gain of the amplifier is given by

$$G = \frac{V_o}{V_i} = 1 \quad \text{(unity gain)}$$

**Noninverting Amplifier**   A noninverting amplifier can be designed by placing a voltage divider network in the feedback leg of the unity-gain amplifier, as shown in Figure 3-18. This is a resistive network consisting of $R_1$ and $R_2$, so that the circuit equation becomes:

$$\frac{V_i}{R_1} + \frac{(V_i - V_o)}{R_2} = 1$$

$$\frac{V_o}{V_i} = 1 + \frac{R_2}{R_1}$$

Since gain is defined as voltage out ($V_o$) divided by the voltage into the amplifier ($V_i$), the gain of the noninverting amplifier ($G_n$) is given by

$$G_n = 1 + \frac{R_2}{R_1} \tag{3-10}$$

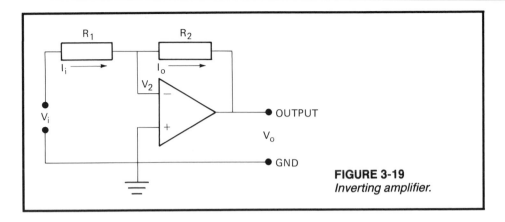

**FIGURE 3-19**
*Inverting amplifier.*

Because the op amp is assumed to be ideal, the gain is determined solely by the resistors used, and it must be equal to, or greater than, one.

**Inverting Amplifier**   The basic circuit for the inverting amplifier is shown in Figure 3-19. In this case, the plus (+) or noninverting input is connected directly to signal ground, and the input source is connected between $R_1$ and ground.

In this configuration, the voltage at the inverting terminal (–) of the op amp $V_2$ is constrained to zero by the internal circuits in the assumed ideal op amp; that is, $V_2$ will behave as a "virtual ground" (i.e., $V_2 = 0$).

The circuit analysis is straightforward, $I_i = (V_2 - V_i)/R_1$, and $I_o = (V_o - V_2)/R_2$; since $V_2 = 0$ and $I_i = I_o$ we have

$$-\frac{V_i}{R_1} = \frac{V_o}{R_2}$$

$$\text{Gain (G)} \;\; = \frac{V_o}{V_i} = -\frac{R_2}{R_1} \tag{3-11}$$

Again, the gain is determined solely by the resistors used to set the amount of feedback, but in this application the output is an inverted version of the input.

**Difference Amplifier**   To obtain the difference between two signals, $V_1$ and $V_2$, the op amp circuit shown in Figure 3-20 can be used. Note that the feedback is applied from $V_o$ to the negative terminal of the op amp. Since the noninverting gain $(G_n = 1 + [R_2/R_1])$ is always higher than the inverting gain $(G_i = -R_2/R_1)$, the signal at the positive terminal must be attenuated if subtraction is to take place. The resistor network consisting of $R_3$ and $R_4$ is used to perform this attenuation.

Using superposition and the gain expressions given by Equations 3-10 and 3-11, the output voltage $V_o$ can be written as

$$V_o = V_1 \left(-R_2/R_1\right) + V_3 \left(1 + R_2/R_1\right)$$

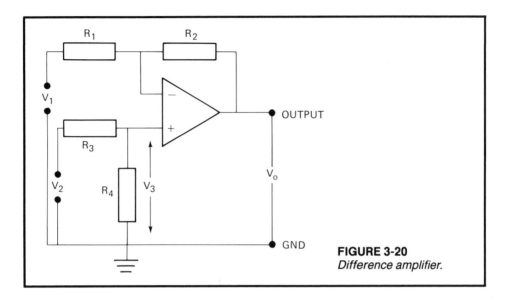

**FIGURE 3-20**
*Difference amplifier.*

However, we need an expression containing the input signals $V_1$ and $V_2$. Since

$$V_3 = (R_4/[R_3 + R_4])V_2,$$
$$V_o = V_1 (-R_2/R_1) + V_2 ([R_4/R_3+ R_4][1 + R_2/R_1])$$

To simplify the calculations, we can choose $R_1 = R_3$ and $R_2 = R_4$, so that $V_o = V_2(R_2/[R_1 + R_2])(1 + R_2/R_1) - V_1(R_2/R_1)$. This simplifies to:

$$V_o = (V_2 - V_1)\ \frac{R_2}{R_1}$$

Thus, the difference between $V_2$ and $V_1$ is amplified by $R_2/R_1$.

## Analog Computers

This section discusses the operation of electronic analog computers and the techniques for using analog computers to simulate real-time process control systems. The analog computers use the operational amplifiers discussed in previous sections for the analysis and simulation of linear differential equations.

Figure 3-21(a) shows a schematic diagram of a sign inverter, where the output voltage ($V_o$) is equal to the input voltage ($V_i$) times a constant($-R_2/R_1$), which is negative, so that the circuit produces a sign inversion. To simplify the drawing of analog computers, we normally use the symbol shown in Figure 3-21(b) to represent a sign inverter.

Another important mathematical operation in analog computers is summation. The addition of several inputs can be accomplished by placing resistors at the input to the high-gain op amp as shown in Figure 3-22, where 3-22(a) shows a schematic diagram of a summer that adds n inputs. The output $V_o$ is

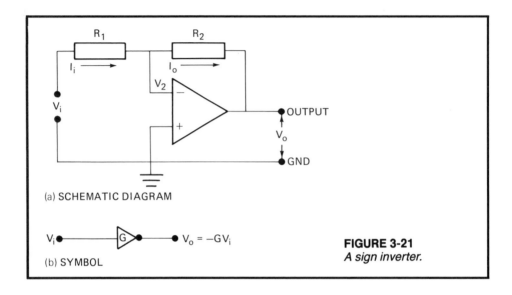

(a) SCHEMATIC DIAGRAM

$V_i \bullet \qquad \triangleright \qquad \bullet \quad V_o = -GV_i$

(b) SYMBOL

**FIGURE 3-21**
*A sign inverter.*

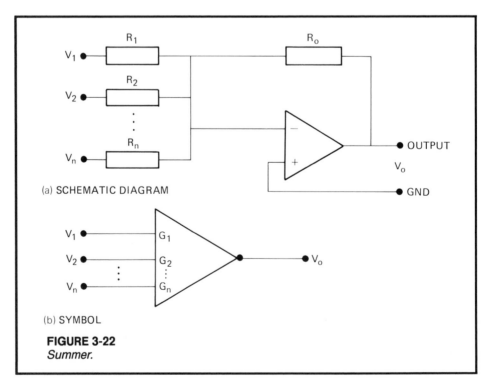

(a) SCHEMATIC DIAGRAM

(b) SYMBOL

**FIGURE 3-22**
*Summer.*

$$V_o = - \left[ \frac{R_o}{R_1} V_1 + \frac{R_o}{R_2} V_2 + \ldots + \frac{R_o}{R_n} V_n \right]$$

**EXAMPLE 3-4**

**Problem:** Find the voltage out of a three input summer with the following parameters:

$$R_o = 1 \text{ M}\Omega, R_1 = 200 \text{ k}\Omega, R_2 = 1 \text{ M}\Omega, \text{ and } R_3 = 100 \text{ k}\Omega.$$

**Solution:** $G_1 = 1 \text{ M}\Omega/200 \text{ k}\Omega = 5$, $G_2 = 1 \text{ M}\Omega/1 \text{ M}\Omega = 1$, and $G_3 = 1 \text{ M}\Omega/100 \text{ k}\Omega = 10$, so that

$$V_o = - (5V_1 + V_2 + 10V_3)$$

The analog computer symbol for this case is shown in Figure 3-23.

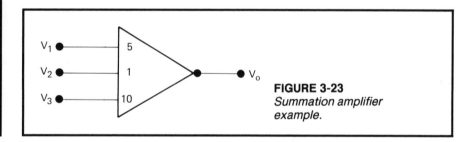

**FIGURE 3-23**
*Summation amplifier example.*

The most important math function that can be performed by op amps is integration. To obtain an integrator, we place a capacitor across a high gain, low drift op amp and use a resistor at the input, as shown in Figure 3-24. The equation for the output voltage ($V_o$) is given by:

$$V_o(s) = \frac{-1}{RCs} V_i(s) \qquad \text{(in s-transform notation)}$$

or $$V_o(t) = \frac{-1}{RC} \int V_i(t)dt \qquad \text{(in the time domain)}$$

Note that in integrating the input $V_i$ to obtain the output $V_o$, the initial conditions must be given. We can indicate the initial condition as $V_o(0)$, so the equation becomes

$$V_o = (-1/R_iC_o) \int V_i \, dt + V_o(0)$$

Figure 3-24a shows how the integrator is programmed for the initial conditions (I.C.). The operator first places switch $S_1$ in the I.C. position and the capacitor is charged to the initial voltage ($V_o$) desired. Then the integrator is switched to the operate position.

Figure 3-24b shows the commonly used symbol for an integrator. If, for example, $R_i = 250$ k$\Omega$ and $C_o = 1$ $\mu$F, then $1/(R_iC_o) = 4$. The initial condition $V_o$ (0) is listed above the integrator symbol.

Another simple but important function required in analog computers is multiplication by a fraction. The multiplication of an input voltage $V_i$ by a constant k, where $0 < k < 1$, can be accomplished by using a potentiometer as shown in Figure 3-25a. The output voltage $V_o$ is

$$V_o = \frac{R_o}{R_i} V_i$$

Figure 3-25(b) shows the commonly used symbol for a potentiometer in an analog computer diagram.

An important feature of analog computers is their ability to solve differential equations. For example, assume we need to solve the following equation:

$$\frac{d^2x}{dt^2} + 10 \frac{dx}{dt} + 4x = 0 \tag{3-12}$$

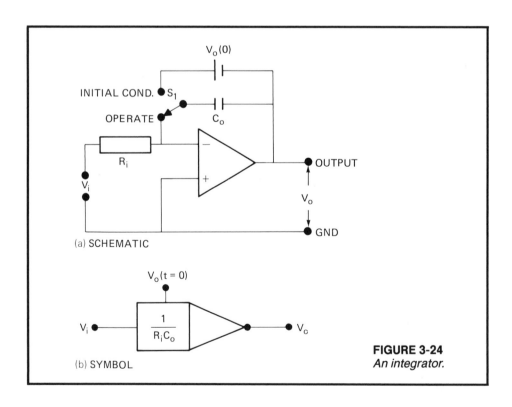

(a) SCHEMATIC

(b) SYMBOL

**FIGURE 3-24**
*An integrator.*

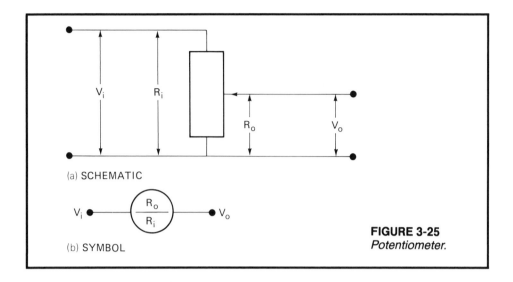

(a) SCHEMATIC

(b) SYMBOL

**FIGURE 3-25**
*Potentiometer.*

where the initial conditions are given as

$$\frac{dx(o)}{dt} = 0 \text{ and } x(o) = 0$$

The first step in setting up the analog computer is to assume that the highest-order derivative is available, then use the computer to solve for this highest-order derivative. In the present example the highest-order derivative is given as follows:

$$\frac{d^2x}{dt^2} = -10 \frac{dx}{dt} - 4x \qquad (3\text{-}12)$$

The variable $dx/dt$ can be obtained by integrating $d^2x/dt^2$, and $x$ can be obtained by integrating $dx/dt$. Figure 3-26 shows an analog computer diagram for this system. Note that the sum of the inputs to the first integrator is the highest derivative term that we assume was originally available.

It is important to note that there is a sign change associated with each operational amplifier. Thus, the number of op amps (integrators, inverters, etc.) must be odd to prevent saturation of the system. In the analog computer in Figure 3-26 there are three op amps in the diagram.

## Analog Computer Simulation of Processes     The simulation of dynamic processes is a very important application of an analog computer. Suppose we want to test the effect of a PID controller on a first-order process with time delay. We can simulate such a process with the analog computer setup shown in Figure 3-27.

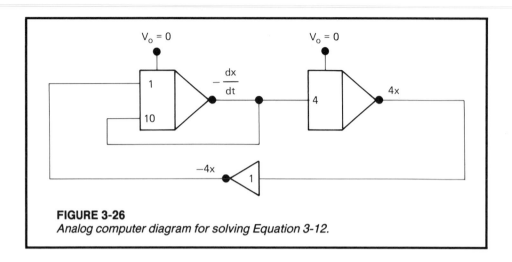

**FIGURE 3-26**
*Analog computer diagram for solving Equation 3-12.*

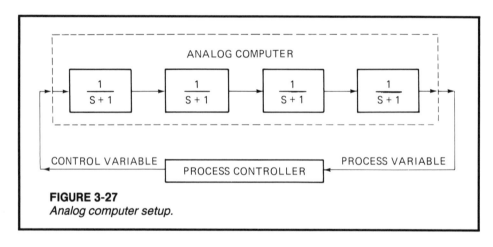

**FIGURE 3-27**
*Analog computer setup.*

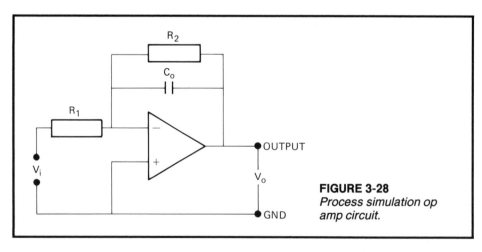

**FIGURE 3-28**
*Process simulation op amp circuit.*

The actual physical circuit used to obtain the $1/s+1$ transfer function is shown in Figure 3-28.

To derive the transfer function for this circuit, we can assume that the op amp shown is an "ideal amplifier" so that normal circuit analysis shows

$$i_1 = i_2 + i_3 \qquad \text{or}$$

$$\frac{V_i}{R} = -\frac{V_o}{R} - C\frac{dV_o}{dt}$$

$$V_i = -V_o - RC\frac{dV_o}{dt}$$

Since the circuit time constant is given by $\tau = RC$,

$$V_i = -V_o - \tau\frac{dV_o}{dt}$$

If we take the Laplace transform of this equation, assuming that the initial conditions are zero, we obtain

$$-V_i(s) = V_o(s) + \tau s V_o(s)$$

If we let $\tau = 1$, we have $-V_i(s) = V_o(s)(s+1)$

$$V_o = -\frac{1}{s+1}V_i \qquad \text{or} \qquad T(s) = -\frac{V_o(s)}{V_i(s)} = -\frac{1}{s+1}$$

As the block diagram in Figure 3-27 shows, we used four circuits in series to obtain the total transfer function:

$$T(s) = \frac{1}{(s+1)^4}$$

The reason we selected this particular transfer function is that it most closely resembles a first-order real-time process with time delay, which is the most common system encountered in process control.

$$T(s) = \frac{1}{(s+1)^4} \cong \frac{Ke^{-\theta s}}{(\tau s + 1)}$$

where:   $\theta$ = dead time
   $K$ = process gain
   $\tau$ = time constant

Analog computer simulation can be an important aid in the design of complicated process control systems. The effects of change in process system parameters on the performance of the system can be easily determined before the system is built. One advantage of analog simulation is that any convenient time scale may be used, so that processes that take hours or days to complete can be simulated and tested in a few minutes. Another advantage is that process control methods can be tested in the laboratory at very low cost.

However, the precise mathematical representation of complex components in a process control system can be very difficult, and it is possible that some of the important features of a system component may be overlooked in the simulation. This might cause serious errors in the process solution. In order to avoid such errors, the system setup might include actual system components, such as process controllers, control valves, or the like. If some of the process instrumentation is included, no important characteristics of the actual instruments are lost.

The analog computer is also quite versatile and convenient to use in simulating control systems that involve nonlinear components. Such nonlinear operations as multiplying two variables can be carried out easily with an analog computer. Electronic circuits are also available for simulating such commonly encountered nonlinearities as dead time, saturation, backlash, and friction.

## EXERCISES

3.1  In the series resistance circuit shown, find the total current $(I_t)$ in the circuit and the voltage drop, $V_1$, across resistor $R_1$ and the voltage drop, $V_2$, across $R_2$.

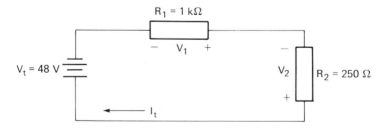

3.2  In the parallel resistance circuit of Figure 3-3, assume that $R_1 = 100 \ \Omega$, $R_2 = 200 \ \Omega$, and $V_t = 100$ V dc. Find $I_1$, $I_2$, and $I_t$.

3.3  Assume that the Wheatstone bridge circuit shown is balanced (i.e., $I_g = 0$). Calculate the value of $I_1$, $I_2$, and $R_x$.

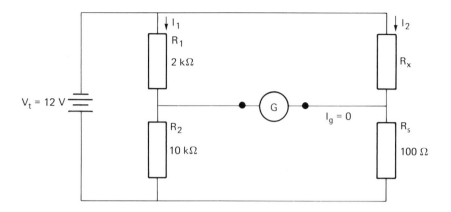

What are the voltage drops across $R_1$ and $R_2$?

3.4 Find the dc output voltage (V dc) for the half-wave rectifier circuit shown in Figure 3-6, if the peak voltage across the secondary of the transformer $T_1$ is 40 V.

3.5 Find the dc output voltage (V dc) for the full-wave rectifier circuit shown in Figure 3-8, if the peak voltage across the secondary of the transformer $T_1$ is 20 V.

3.6 Calculate the value of $R_s$ required for the Zener diode shunt regulator shown below, if $V_i = 10$ V, $V_o = 5$ V, $I_o$ (max) = 100 mA, $I_z$ (min) = 10 mA.

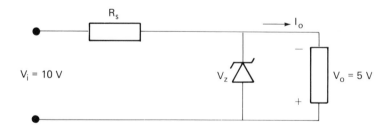

3.7 Design a +5-V power supply using a full-wave rectifier and a series 78 I.C. voltage regulator. Draw a schematic diagram for the power supply.

3.8 Design a noninverting amplifier using an ideal op amp to convert a 10-mV dc signal to a 1-V dc signal. Draw a schematic of the circuit.

3.9 Calculate the output voltage of the summing amplifier shown for the following sets of input voltages and resistors (Note $R_o = 1$ M$\Omega$ in all cases).

(a) $V_1 = +2$ V, $V_2 = +4$ V, $V_3 = +1$ V
$R_1 = 100$ k$\Omega$, $R_2 = 200$ k$\Omega$, $R_3 = 500$ k$\Omega$

(b) $V_1 = -1$ V, $V_2 = +2$ V, $V_3 = +4$ V
$R_1 = 1$ M$\Omega$, $R_2 = 500$ k$\Omega$, $R_3 = 200$ k$\Omega$

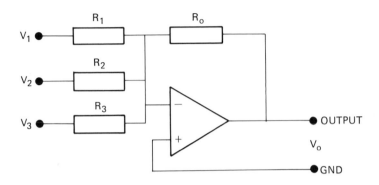

## BIBLIOGRAPHY

1. Malvino, A.P.; *Electronic Principles*, Second Edition, McGraw-Hill Book Co., 1979.

2. Grob, B.; *Basic Electronics*, Fifth Edition, McGraw-Hill Book Co., 1984.

3. Budak, A.; *Passive and Active Network Analysis and Synthesis*, Houghton Mifflin Co., 1974.

4. Motorola Semiconductor Products Inc., *Zener Diode Handbook*, May 1967.

5. Ogata, K.; *Modern Control Engineering*, Prentice-Hall, Inc., 1970.

# 4

# Digital System Fundamentals

**Introduction**   The application of digital techniques to process control requires an understanding of digital system fundamentals. A working knowledge of digital principles is also required in the design and implementation of logic systems and microcomputer-based control systems. In this chapter, the basic concepts of digital signals, digital devices and logic design will be discussed. The design of programmable logic controllers and computer control systems will be discussed in later chapters.

**Digital Signals**   The use of digital techniques in process control requires that the measurement and control signals be encoded into digital form. Digital signals are simply two-state (binary) signals (on/off, start/stop, high voltage/low voltage, etc.).

The simplest approach to encoding analog data into a digital word is provided by the American Standard Code for Information Interchange (ASCII). This method uses a pattern of seven bits (ones and zeros) to represent letters and numbers. Sometimes an extra bit (parity bit) is used to check that the correct pattern has been transmitted. Some examples of coding data using the ASCII standard are given below:

$$
\begin{aligned}
0 &= 011\ 0000 \\
1 &= 011\ 0001 \\
2 &= 011\ 0010 \\
&\quad\ \cdot \\
&\quad\ \cdot \\
A &= 100\ 0001 \\
B &= 100\ 0010 \\
&\ \text{etc.}
\end{aligned}
$$

The reader should refer to an ASCII Code Chart for a complete listing of conversions between binary strings and actual data.

Many methods are used for encoding digital numbers in logic circuits and computers. The most common method is the simple binary code. A review of number systems follows.

## Review of Numbering Systems

Many methods are used for encoding numbers in digital systems; however, the three most commonly used are the binary, the octal, and hexadecimal numbering systems. We will start first with a brief review of the familiar decimal numbering system, followed by coverage of the other three common numbering systems.

**Decimal Numbering System**   The decimal numbering system is in common use, probably because man started to count with his fingers. However, the decimal system is not easy to implement electronically. A ten-state electronic device would be quite costly and complex. It is much easier and more efficient to use the binary (two-state) numbering system when manipulating numbers using logic circuits.

A decimal number, $d_n \ldots d_2\, d_1\, d_0$ can be written mathematically as:

$$N_{10} = d_n R^n + \ldots d_2 R^2 + d_1 R^1 + d_0 R^0 \qquad (4\text{-}1)$$

where R is equal to the number of digit symbols used in the system. R is called the radix and is equal to 10 in the decimal system. The subscript 10 on the number N in Equation 2-1 indicates that it is a decimal number. However, it is common practice to omit this subscript in writing out decimal numbers.

For example, the decimal number 735 can be written as:

$$735 = (7 \times 10^2) + (3 \times 10^1) + (5 \times 10^0)$$

When written as 735, the powers of ten are implied by positional notation. The value of the decimal number is computed by multiplying each digit by the weight of its position and summing the result. As we will see this is true for all numbering systems; the decimal equivalent of any number can be calculated by multiplying the digit times its base raised to the power of the digit's position.

**Binary Numbering System**   The binary numbering system uses the number 2 as the base and the only allowable digits are 0 or 1. This is the basic numbering system for computers and programmable controllers, which are basically electronic devices that manipulate 0's and 1's to perform math and control functions. It was easier and more convenient to design digital computers that operate on two entities or numbers rather than the ten numbers used in the decimal world. Furthermore, most physical elements in the process environment have only two states, such as a pump on or off, a valve open or closed, a switch on or off, and so on.

A binary number follows the same format as a decimal number and it can be written as:

$$N_b = Z_n R^n + \ldots Z_2 R^2 + Z_1 R^1 + Z_0 R^0 \qquad (4\text{-}2)$$

where R is equal to 2 in the binary system and $Z_n$ (bit-n) can take on the values of 0 or 1. The binary number 10101 would be written

$$(1 \times 2^4) + (0 \times 2^3) + (1 \times 2^2) + (0 \times 2^1) + (1 \times 2^0)$$

or $(1 \times 16) + (0 \times 8) + (1 \times 4) + 0 \times 2) + (1 \times 1) = 21 \text{ (decimal)}$

**EXAMPLE 4-1**

**Problem:** Convert the binary number 101110 to its decimal equivalent.

**Solution:**

$$(1 \times 2^5) + (0 \times 2^4) + (1 \times 2^3) + (1 \times 2^2) + (1 \times 2^1) + (0 \times 2^0) =$$
$$(1 \times 32) + (0 \times 16) + (1 \times 8) + (1 \times 4) + (1 \times 2) + (0 \times 1) =$$
$$32 + 0 + 8 + 4 + 2 + 0 = 46$$

The addition of binary numbers is illustrated in Table 4-1.

**TABLE 4-1**
**Binary Addition**

| |
|---|
| 0 + 0 = 0 |
| 0 + 1 = 1 |
| 1 + 0 = 1 |
| 1 + 1 = 10 |

**EXAMPLE 4-2**

**Problem:** Perform binary addition on the following numbers: 1010 and 0110.

**Solution:** Using Table 4-1 as a guide, we obtain,

$$
\begin{array}{r}
1010 \\
+\ 0110 \\
\hline
10000
\end{array}
$$

The following example problem will help illustrate binary subtraction.

**EXAMPLE 4-3**

**Problem:** Subtract the binary number 0110 from the binary number 1001.

**Solution:**

$$
\begin{array}{r}
1001 \\
-0110 \\
\hline
11
\end{array}
$$

The subtraction of binary numbers is illustrated in Table 4-2.

**TABLE 4-2**
**Binary Subtraction**

$$1 - 0 = 1$$
$$0 - 0 = 0$$
$$1 - 1 = 0$$
$$*10 - 1 = 1$$

*Note: When subtracting 1 from 0 you must borrow a 1 from the next higher-order bit.

**Octal Numbering System**   It requires substantially more digits to express a number in binary form than in the decimal system. For example, $130_{10} = 10000010_2$. It is difficult for people to read and manipulate large numbers without making errors. To reduce errors in binary number manipulations, some computer companies started using the octal numbering system. This system uses the number 8 as a base with the eight digits of 0, 1, 2, 3, 4, 5, 6, 7. Like all other number systems, each digit in an octal number has a weighted value according to its position. For example:

$$1301_8 = (1 \times 8^3) + (3 \times 8^2) + (0 \times 8^1) + (1 \times 8^0)$$
$$= (1 \times 512) + (3 \times 64) + (0 \times 8) + (1 \times 1)$$

A binary number with a large number of 1's and 0's can be represented with an equivalent octal number with fewer digits. As shown in Table 4-3, one octal digit can be used to express three binary digits, so the number of digits is reduced by a factor of three. For example, the following binary number can be represented as octal by grouping binary bits in groups of three:

**TABLE 4-3**
**Binary and Octal**
**Equivalent Numbers**

| Binary | Octal |
|--------|-------|
| 000    | 0     |
| 001    | 1     |
| 010    | 2     |
| 011    | 3     |
| 100    | 4     |
| 101    | 5     |
| 110    | 6     |
| 111    | 7     |

| 1 | 1 | 0 | 0 | 0 | 1 | 1 | 0 | 1 | 0 | 1 | 0 | 1 | 0 | 1 | 0 | Binary Number |

| 1 | 1 | 0 | 0 | 0 | 1 | 1 | 0 | 1 | 0 | 1 | 0 | 1 | 0 | 1 | 0 | 3-Bit Groups |

| 1 | 4 | 3 | 2 | 5 | 2 | Octal Number |

**EXAMPLE 4-4**

**Problem:** Represent the binary number 101011010101111 in octal.

**Solution:**

| 1 | 0 | 1 | 0 | 1 | 1 | 0 | 1 | 0 | 1 | 0 | 1 | 1 | 1 | 1 | Binary Number |

| 1 | 0 | 1 | 0 | 1 | 1 | 0 | 1 | 0 | 1 | 0 | 1 | 1 | 1 | 1 | 3-Bit Groups |

| 5 | 3 | 2 | 5 | 7 | Octal Number |

Therefore, $101011010101111_2 = 53257_8$

**Hexadecimal Numbering System** The hexadecimal numbering system provides an even shorter notation than the octal system and is the most commonly used numbering system in computer applications. The hexadecimal system has a base of 16 and four binary bits are used to represent a single symbol. The sixteen symbols are 0, 1, 2, 3, 4, 5, 6, 7, 8, 9, A, B, C, D, and F. The letters A through F are used to represent the binary numbers 1010, 1011, 1100, 1101, 1110, and 1111, corresponding to the decimal numbers 10 through 15. The hexadecimal digits and their binary equivalents are given in Table 4-4.

To convert a binary number to a hexadecimal number, we use Table 4-4. For example, the binary number 0110 1111 1000 is simply the hex number 6F8.

Again, the hexadecimal numbers follows the standard convention:

$$N = Z_n 16^n + \ldots Z_2 16^2 + Z_1 16^1 + Z_0 16^0$$

The positional weights are powers of sixteen with 1, 16, 256, and 4096 being the first four decimal values.

**EXAMPLE 4-5**

**Problem:** Convert the hex number 1FA to its decimal equivalent.

**Solution:**

$$N = Z_n 16^n + \ldots Z_2 16^2 + Z_1 16^1 + Z_0 16^0$$

Since $Z_2 = 1$, $Z_1 = F_H = 15_{10}$, and $Z_0 = A_H = 10^{10}$

**TABLE 4-4**
**Hexadecimal and Binary**
**Equivalent Numbers**

| Hexadecimal | Binary |
|:-----------:|:------:|
| 0 | 0000 |
| 1 | 0001 |
| 2 | 0010 |
| 3 | 0011 |
| 4 | 0100 |
| 5 | 0101 |
| 6 | 0110 |
| 7 | 0111 |
| 8 | 1000 |
| 9 | 1001 |
| A | 1010 |
| B | 1011 |
| C | 1100 |
| D | 1101 |
| E | 1110 |
| F | 1111 |

we obtain
$$1 \times 16^2 + 15 \times 16^1 + 10 \times 16^0 = 256 + 240 + 10 = 506_{10}$$

The hexadecimal system is used for human convenience only and the computer system actually operates on binary numbers.

## Logic Gates
In most logic systems, binary numbers 1 and 0 are represented by voltage or current levels. For example, in transistor-transistor logic (TTL) gates, a binary 1 is represented by a voltage signal in the range of 2.0 to 5.0 volts, and a binary 0 is represented by a voltage level between 0 and 0.8 volt. Solid-state electronic circuits are available that can be used to manipulate digital signals to perform a variety of logical functions, such as AND, OR, NAND, NOR, NOT, and exclusive OR. These circuits are the building blocks used in logic system design.

It is beyond the scope of this book to examine the internal functions of these circuits in detail. In subsequent sections of this chapter, these logic circuits or gates are defined and a symbol is given for each. TTL hardware is also discussed for many common logic circuits.

**OR Gate** An OR gate, with two or more inputs and a single output, operates in accordance with the following definition: *the output of an OR gate assumes the 1 state if one or more inputs assume the 1 state.*

The inputs to a logic gate are designated by A, B, . . ., N and the output by Z. It is assumed that the inputs and outputs can take one of two possible values, either 0 or 1. A standard symbol for the OR gate is given in Figure 4-1 together with the logic expression for this gate (i.e, $Z = A + B + .. + N$). A truth table, which contains a tabulation of all possible input values and their corresponding outputs, is also given for a two-input OR gate.

An example of OR logic in process control: if the water level in a hot water heater is low, OR the temperature in the tank is too high, a logic system can be designed to turn off the heater in the system.

The following logic identities for OR gates can be easily verified.

$$A + B + C = (A + B) + C = A + (B + C) \tag{4-3}$$

$$A + B = B + A \tag{4-4}$$

$$A + A = A \tag{4-5}$$

$$A + 1 = 1 \tag{4-6}$$

$$A + 0 = A \tag{4-7}$$

Remember that A, B, and C can take on only the value of 0 or 1. Refer to the definition of the OR gate and to the truth table in Figure 4-1.

**AND Gate**  An AND gate has two or more inputs and a single output, and it operates in accordance with the following definition: *the output of an AND gate assumes the* 1 *state if and only if all the inputs assume the* 1 *state.*

A standard symbol for the AND gate is given in Figure 4-2 together with the logic expression and a two-input AND gate truth table.

The logic expressions for an AND gate are as follows:

$$ABC = (AB)C = A(BC) \tag{4-8}$$

$$AB = BA \tag{4-9}$$

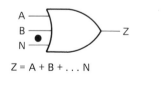

| | INPUTS | OUTPUT |
| A | B | Z |
|---|---|---|
| 0 | 0 | 0 |
| 0 | 1 | 1 |
| 1 | 0 | 1 |
| 1 | 1 | 1 |

$Z = A + B + \ldots N$

(a) SYMBOL AND EQUATION    (b) 2-INPUT TRUTH TABLE

**FIGURE 4-1**
*OR gate—symbol, equation, and truth table.*

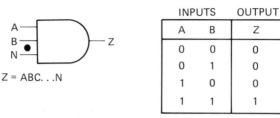

(a) SYMBOL AND EQUATION    (b) 2-INPUT TRUTH TABLE

**FIGURE 4-2**
*AND gate—symbol, equation, and truth table.*

$$AA = A \tag{4-10}$$

$$A1 = A \tag{4-11}$$

$$A0 = 0 \tag{4-12}$$

These identities can be verified by reference to the definitions of the AND gate and by using a truth table for the AND Gate.

For example, Equation 4-11 ($A1 = A$) can be verified. Let $B = 1$ and tabulate $AB = Z$ in a truth table.

| A | B | Z |
|---|---|---|
| 0 | 1 | 0 |
| 1 | 1 | 1 |

Note that $A = Z$, so that $A \cdot 1 = A$ for both values (0 and 1) of A.
Some important auxiliary identities used in logic design are as follows:

$$A + AB = A \tag{4-13}$$

$$A + \overline{A}B = A + B \tag{4-14}$$

$$(A + B)(A + C) = A + BC \tag{4-15}$$

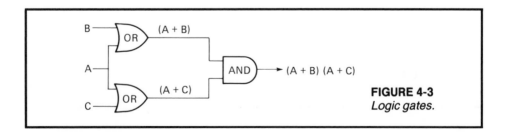

**FIGURE 4-3**
*Logic gates.*

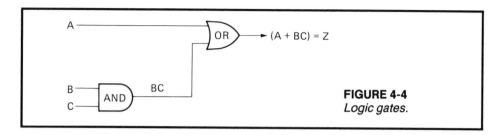

**FIGURE 4-4**
*Logic gates.*

These identities are important because they reduce the number of logic gates required to synthesize a logic function. For example, in Equation 4-15, the left side $(A + B)(A + C)$ can be synthesized using the three logic gates shown in Figure 4-3.

However, if the reduced form on the right side of the equation is used $(A + BC)$, only two gates are required to produce the output Z, as shown in Figure 4-4.

**NAND Gate**   A third logic operation of interest is the NAND gate; its operations are summarized in Figure 4-5. Note that the NAND gate output is the exact opposite of the AND gate output. When all the inputs to a NAND are 1, the output is 0. In all other configurations, the NAND output has a logic value of 1.

**NOR Gate**   Another logic gate in common use is the NOR gate. Figure 4-6 shows its operations. It produces a logic 1 result if and only if all inputs are logic 0. The truth table shown is for a two-input NOR gate.

**NOT and Exclusive OR Gates**   Two other helpful logic devices are the NOT and Exclusive OR gates. The NOT, or inverter gate, produces an output opposite the input. Figure 4-7 shows the operation of the NOT gate.

The Exclusive OR gate provides a logic 1 output if and only if the input signals are not identical. The function of the Exclusive OR (XOR) is illustrated in Figure 4-8.

The logic operator symbol is normally used for the Exclusive OR operation.

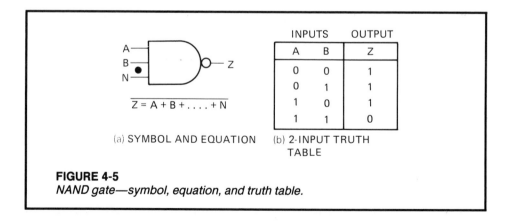

**FIGURE 4-5**
*NAND gate—symbol, equation, and truth table.*

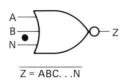

| INPUTS | | OUTPUT |
| --- | --- | --- |
| A | B | Z |
| 0 | 0 | 1 |
| 0 | 1 | 0 |
| 1 | 0 | 0 |
| 1 | 1 | 0 |

$\overline{Z} = \overline{ABC...N}$

(a) SYMBOL AND EQUATION

(b) 2-INPUT TRUTH TABLE

**FIGURE 4-6**
*NOR gate—symbol, equation, and truth table.*

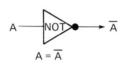

$A = \overline{A}$

| INPUT | OUTPUT |
| --- | --- |
| A | $\overline{A}$ |
| 0 | 1 |
| 1 | 0 |

(a) SYMBOL AND EQUATION

(b) NOT GATE TRUTH TABLE

**FIGURE 4-7**
*Symbol and truth table for NOT gate.*

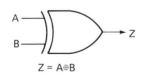

$Z = A \oplus B$

| INPUTS | | OUTPUT |
| --- | --- | --- |
| A | B | Z |
| 0 | 0 | 0 |
| 0 | 1 | 1 |
| 1 | 0 | 1 |
| 1 | 1 | 0 |

(a) SYMBOL AND EQUATION

(b) 2-INPUT XOR TRUTH TABLE

**FIGURE 4-8**
*Symbol, equation, and truth table for XOR gate.*

## DeMorgan's Theorem

**DeMorgan's Theorem**    A great deal of logic design is based upon a set of rules called DeMorgan's Theorem. This theorem demonstrates that any logic equation can be synthesized from AND, NOT, and NAND gates or from OR, NOT, and NOR gates. DeMorgan's theorem can be summarized: *if the inversion bar (NOT function) is broken between two logic variables, the logic symbol connecting the variable can be changed.*

The reverse is also true: *if the inversion bar is joined between two variables, the logic symbol connecting the variables can be changed.*

In equation form, DeMorgan's Theorem is:

$$\overline{(A + B + \ldots N)} = \overline{A} \cdot \overline{B} \ldots \overline{N} \qquad (4\text{-}16)$$

$$\overline{(AB \ldots N)} = \overline{A} + \overline{B} \ldots \overline{N} \qquad (4\text{-}17)$$

DeMorgan's Theorem and some other basic logic laws and identities have been summarized in Table 4-5 for easy reference.

---

**TABLE 4-5**
**Logic Laws**

**Fundamental Laws**

| OR | AND | NOT |
|---|---|---|
| $A + 0 = A$ | $A0 = 0$ | $A + \overline{A} = 1$ |
| $A + 1 = 1$ | $A1 = A$ | $A\overline{A} = 0$ |
| $A + A = A$ | $AA = A$ | $\overline{\overline{A}} = A$ (involution) |
| $A + \overline{A} = 1$ | $A\overline{A} = 0$ | |

Associative Laws

$$(A + B) + C = A + (B + C), (AB)C = A(BC)$$

Commutative Laws

$$A + B = B + A, AB = BA$$

Distributive Laws

$$A(B + C) = AB + AC$$

DeMorgan's Theorem

$$\overline{A + B + \ldots N)} = \overline{A} \cdot \overline{B} \ldots, \overline{N} \text{ and } \overline{AB\,N} = \overline{A} + \overline{B} + \overline{N}$$

Auxiliary Identities

$$A + AB = A \text{ and } A + \overline{A}B = A + B$$
$$(A + B)(A + C) = A + BC$$

Three laws are very useful in logic design: distributive, involution ($\overline{\overline{A}} = A$), and DeMorgan's Theorem. Distribution is essentially equivalent to factoring. Involution and DeMorgan's Theorem work together to interchange AND and OR functions.

In applying these laws to logic design, the least complex gate realization is found by factoring out all common terms. The application of these rules to logic circuit design can be demonstrated by the following examples.

### EXAMPLE 4-6

**Problem:** Synthesize $(A + \overline{B})(C + \overline{D})$ with NAND gates only.

**Solution:**

$(A + \overline{B}) \times (C + \overline{D}) = \overline{\overline{(A + \overline{B}) \times (C + \overline{D})}}$      by involution

$= \overline{(\overline{A \times B})} \times \overline{(\overline{C \times D})}$      by DeMorgan's Theorem

### EXAMPLE 4-7

**Problem:** Synthesize $\overline{A} + (B \times (\overline{C} + D))$ with two levels of NAND gates.

**Solution:**

$\overline{A} + (B \times (\overline{C} + D)) = \overline{A} + ((B \times \overline{C}) + (B \times D))$      by distributive law

$= \overline{A} + (B \times \overline{C}) + (B \times D)$      by associative law

$= \overline{A \times \overline{\overline{B \times \overline{C}}} \times \overline{B \times D}}$

## Logic Hardware

Many logic devices are available to the designer today. One of the most widely used general purpose devices is the 74XX TTL (transistor-transistor logic) series of integrated circuits. These logic elements have been incorporated into 14, 16, and larger pin (input/output connection) packages. The six most common types are shown in Figure 4-9.

The pin numbering of the 74XX series ICs is as follows: the pin 1 end of the package is indicated by an indentation or other representative mark. Pin 1 is the first pin counterclockwise (CCW) from the mark when viewed from the top. The other pins are numbered CCW from pin 1.

## Synthesis of Logic Circuits
We have discussed the synthesis of a logic equation by first reducing it using logic expressions. In this section, the simplification of logic listings using logic maps will be discussed. The method will be based on the synthesizing of two special logic outputs called the minterm and the maxterm.

### The Minterm
The minterm is a logic item in an output list (truth table) having a 1. An example is shown in the truth table in Figure 4-10. The third output $Z_3$ is the only term with a logic 1.

A minterm is defined as a logic item in a logic list with a minimum number of 1's, short of none at all. The minterm can be synthesized with an AND operation

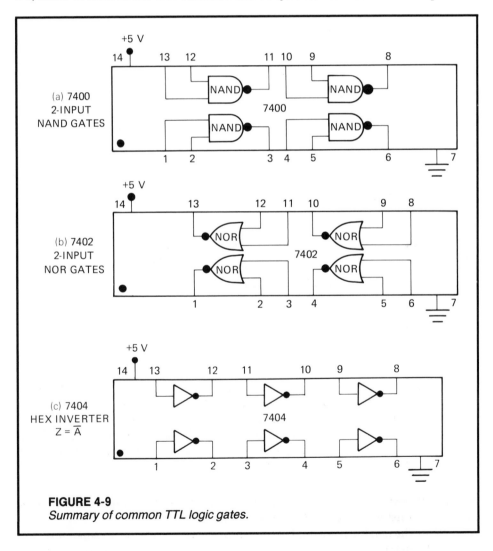

**FIGURE 4-9**
*Summary of common TTL logic gates.*

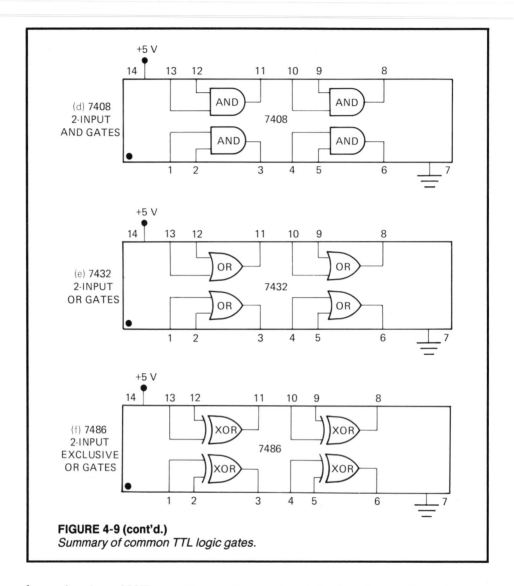

**FIGURE 4-9 (cont'd.)**
*Summary of common TTL logic gates.*

by performing a NOT operation on the zero inputs in the column where the minterm 1 resides. Then the minterm $Z_3$ is given by $Z_3 = \overline{A}B\overline{C}$. It can be verified that the output Z for the entire truth table is given by $Z = Z_3 = \overline{A}B\overline{C}$. A general rule can be stated: *a minterm is synthesized through an AND operation operating on the inputs to the minterm, with a NOT operation applied to those inputs having the value 0 in the truth table when the output is 1.*

**The Maxterm**   The maxterm is defined as the dual of the minterm and consists of an output list with a single 0 as shown in Figure 4-11.

Since the maxterm is a dual of the minterm, a general rule for a maxterm can be stated: *a maxterm is synthesized through an OR operation operating on the inputs to the maxterm with a NOT operation applied to a given input, if it has the value 1 when the output is 0.*

We are now ready to synthesize the logic expression for any truth table with more than one maxterm or minterm by using methods called sum-of-minterms and product-of-maxterms.

**Sum-of-Minterms**  To develop the idea of sum-of-minterms, consider the truth table in Figure 4-12. In this example, we have two minterms $Z_2$ and $Z_3$, where $Z_2 = A\overline{B}$ and $Z_3 = \overline{A}B$. If we compute the logical sum of $Z_2$ and $Z_3$ we have:

$$
\begin{array}{rl}
Z_2 & 0100 \\
Z_2 & 0010 \\
\hline
Z_2 + Z_3 = & 0110
\end{array}
$$

Comparing this logic sum to the original truth table (Figure 4-12), we see that

$$Z = Z_2 + Z_3$$

or

$$Z = A\overline{B} + \overline{A}B$$

It can be verified that any logic truth table can be synthesized as a logic sum-of-minterms, where a minterm is written for each 1 in the output of the truth table.

**Product-of Maxterms**  It would be expected, based on the principle of duality, that an alternate general logic synthesis expression based on maxterms could be found. Refer to the truth table in Figure 4-12 where there are two maxterms $Z_1$ and $Z_4$, where $Z_1 = A + B$ and $Z_4 = \overline{A} + \overline{B}$. If the logic product were calculated, then

$$
\begin{array}{rl}
Z_1 & 0111 \\
Z_4 & 1110 \\
\hline
Z_1 \cdot Z_4 = & 0110
\end{array}
$$

or $Z = Z_1 Z_4 = (A + B)(\overline{A} + \overline{B})$, which is an alternate solution for Z.

It can be concluded that any truth table can be synthesized as a logic product-of-maxterms, where a maxterm is written for each 0 in the truth table.

**Redundant Logic**  The use of minterms and maxterms to synthesize logic operations does not always produce the simplest logic equation. For example, assume that the logic shown in Figure 4-13 needs to be synthesized.

If the sum-of-minterm method is used to synthesize the table, the result is:

$$Z = ABC + \overline{A}BC + A \cdot \overline{B}C + \overline{A}BC \tag{4-18}$$

However, a much simpler function for the table is given by

$$Z = AB + \overline{A}C \tag{4-19}$$

| INPUTS | | | OUTPUT |
|:---:|:---:|:---:|:---:|
| $A$ | $B$ | $C$ | $Z$ |
| 0 | 0 | 0 | 0 |
| 1 | 0 | 0 | 0 |
| 0 | 1 | 0 | 1 |
| 1 | 1 | 0 | 0 |
| 0 | 0 | 1 | 0 |
| 1 | 0 | 1 | 0 |
| 0 | 1 | 1 | 0 |
| 1 | 1 | 1 | 0 |

◄——— MINTERM $Z_3$

**FIGURE 4-10**
*Minterm example—truth table.*

| INPUTS | | | OUTPUT |
|:---:|:---:|:---:|:---:|
| $A$ | $B$ | $C$ | $Z$ |
| 0 | 0 | 0 | 1 |
| 1 | 0 | 0 | 1 |
| 0 | 1 | 0 | 0 |
| 1 | 1 | 0 | 1 |
| 0 | 0 | 1 | 1 |
| 1 | 0 | 1 | 1 |
| 0 | 1 | 1 | 1 |
| 1 | 1 | 1 | 1 |

◄——— MAXTERM $Z_3$

**FIGURE 4-11**
*Maxterm example—truth table.*

| INPUTS | | OUTPUT |
|:---:|:---:|:---:|
| $A$ | $B$ | $Z$ |
| 0 | 0 | 0 |
| 1 | 0 | 1 |
| 0 | 1 | 1 |
| 1 | 1 | 0 |

◄——— $Z_1$ MAXTERM
◄——— $Z_2$ MINTERM
◄——— $Z_3$ MINTERM
◄——— $Z_4$ MAXTERM

**FIGURE 4-12**
*Sum-of-minterms examples.*

| INPUTS | | | OUTPUT | TERMS |
|---|---|---|---|---|
| A | B | C | Z | |
| 1 | 1 | 1 | 1 | $Z_1$ |
| 0 | 1 | 1 | 1 | $Z_2$ |
| 1 | 0 | 1 | 0 | $Z_3$ |
| 0 | 0 | 1 | 1 | $Z_4$ |
| 1 | 1 | 0 | 1 | $Z_5$ |
| 0 | 1 | 0 | 0 | $Z_6$ |
| 1 | 0 | 0 | 0 | $Z_7$ |
| 0 | 0 | 0 | 0 | $Z_8$ |

**FIGURE 4-13**
*Example truth table—redundant logic.*

This simpler function can be obtained using logic laws and identities as follows:

$$Z = ABC + AB\overline{C} + \overline{A}CB + \overline{A}C\overline{B} \quad \text{by associative laws}$$

$$Z = AB(C + \overline{C}) + \overline{A}C(B + \overline{B}) \quad \text{by distributive laws}$$

$$Z = AB(1) + \overline{A}C(1) \quad \text{by identities } C + \overline{C} = 1 \text{ and } B + \overline{B} = 1$$

$$Z = AB + \overline{A}C \quad \text{by identity } A(1) = A$$

This shows that although a logic output can always be synthesized by a standard sum-of-minterms or products-of-maxterms expression, the function can be more complex than is actually required (i.e., more logic gates required in the circuit). Thus, there are terms that add to the logic complexity without contributing to the logic behavior; or there is redundant logic.

The main indicator of redundant logic is an input, or a group of inputs, that appears with all its possible logic values in a set of otherwise identical terms.

In the example of Equation 4-18, this redundancy appeared twice. C is redundant in $ABC + AB\overline{C}$ because it appears with all its possible values (i.e., C and $\overline{C}$) with the term AB. This redundancy in a truth table can be made more apparent by grouping those rows with a logic 1 output. For example, the truth table in Figure 4-13 can be rearranged as shown in Figure 4-14.

It is evident from the table that in area 1, A and B are constant and C appears with all possible values. Furthermore, in area 2, A and C are constant and B appears with two values (0 and 1). The areas shown might be called redundancy areas, and a rule of logic simplification can be stated: *the logic value of a redundancy area can be specified by the inputs that are constant in the area.*

**The Logic Map** The logic map description is a special form of truth table arranged in such a way that redundancy areas are easily recognized. Only three- and four-input maps will be discussed because these two types are adequate for most logic map design applications.

|  | INPUTS | | | OUTPUT | |
|---|---|---|---|---|---|
|  | $A$ | $B$ | $C$ | $Z$ | |
| **AREA 1** | 1 | 1 | 1 | 1 | $Z_1$ |
|  | 1 | 1 | 0 | 1 | $Z_5$ $\rightarrow$ AB |
| **AREA 2** | 0 | 1 | 1 | 1 | $Z_2$ |
|  | 0 | 0 | 1 | 1 | $Z_4$ $\rightarrow \overline{A}C$ |
|  | 1 | 0 | 1 | 0 | $Z_3$ |
|  | 0 | 1 | 0 | 0 | $Z_6$ |
|  | 1 | 0 | 0 | 0 | $Z_7$ |
|  | 0 | 0 | 0 | 0 | $Z_8$ |

**FIGURE 4-14**
*Redundant grouping.*

The three-input map is based on the eight-position truth table. For example, given the truth table of Figure 4-14, a three-input map as shown in Figure 4-15 can be generated.

This logic map has been designed to have the following property: areas that are adjacent or symmetrical around a central axis of the map represent redundant areas. There are two redundant areas ($A_1$ and $A_2$) as shown in Figure 4-16 (a mark-up of the logic map in Figure 4-15).

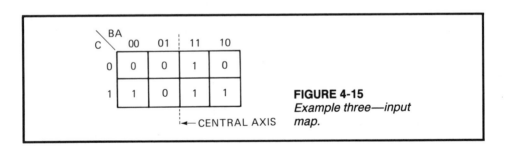

**FIGURE 4-15**
*Example three—input map.*

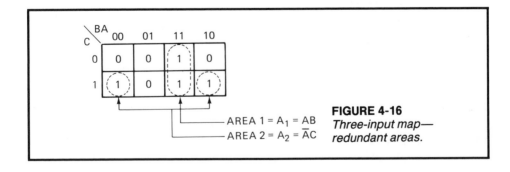

AREA 1 = $A_1$ = AB
AREA 2 = $A_2$ = $\overline{A}C$

**FIGURE 4-16**
*Three-input map— redundant areas.*

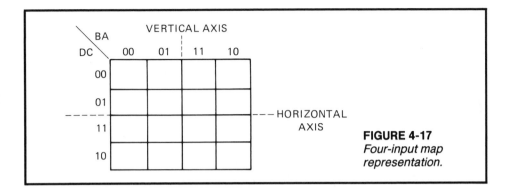

**FIGURE 4-17**
*Four-input map representation.*

The resulting logic expression $Z = AREA\ 1 + AREA\ 2 = AB + \overline{A}C$ is the minimum sum-of-minterm synthesis for the logic function.

A four-input map is formed from a sixteen-position truth table, as shown in Figure 4-17. The pattern of the inputs is designed to produce redundant areas based on symmetry around two central axes, similar to a three-input map.

To illustrate the utility of a four-input map, a logic function will be synthesized from a truth table in Example 4-8.

## EXAMPLE 4-8

**Problem:** Synthesize the logic function Z in the truth table given below, using a four-input map and sum-of-minterms.

| INPUTS | | | | OUTPUT |
|---|---|---|---|---|
| *A* | *B* | *C* | *D* | *Z* |
| 0 | 0 | 0 | 0 | 1 |
| 1 | 0 | 0 | 0 | 0 |
| 0 | 1 | 0 | 0 | 1 |
| 1 | 1 | 0 | 0 | 1 |
| 0 | 0 | 1 | 0 | 1 |
| 1 | 0 | 1 | 0 | 1 |
| 0 | 1 | 1 | 0 | 1 |
| 1 | 1 | 1 | 0 | 1 |
| 0 | 0 | 0 | 1 | 0 |
| 1 | 0 | 0 | 1 | 1 |
| 0 | 1 | 0 | 1 | 1 |
| 1 | 1 | 0 | 1 | 1 |
| 0 | 0 | 1 | 1 | 1 |
| 1 | 0 | 1 | 1 | 1 |
| 0 | 1 | 1 | 1 | 1 |
| 1 | 1 | 1 | 1 | 1 |

**Solution:**

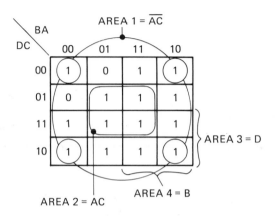

Four redundant areas are found and the logic function Z is given by

$$Z = \overline{A} \cdot \overline{C} + AC + B + D$$

Notice that the redundant areas overlapped to further reduce the final equation.

## Limitations of Logic Map Design Approach
The logic map design approach is, in theory, capable of implementing any logic system that can be written in truth table format. However, when this method is used for practical applications, the unthinking or "brute force" approach is quite impractical in many cases. For example, take the problem of designing a parity bit generator. A very practical logic circuit, the parity generator is used typically as a check on the transmission of binary data, such as over a telephone line. Parity generation consists of basing the logic output upon whether the number of 1's in the transmitted data is odd or even.

Assume a design is needed for a four-input parity bit generator as shown in Figure 4-18. This circuit will produce a logic 1 output when there are an odd num-

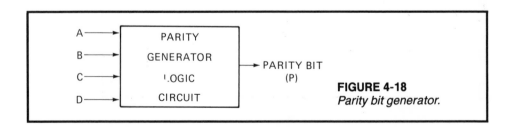

**FIGURE 4-18**
*Parity bit generator.*

| INPUTS | | | | PARITY BIT |
|---|---|---|---|---|
| A | B | C | D | P |
| 0 | 0 | 0 | 0 | 0 |
| 1 | 0 | 0 | 0 | 1 |
| 0 | 1 | 0 | 0 | 1 |
| 1 | 1 | 0 | 0 | 0 |
| 0 | 0 | 1 | 0 | 1 |
| 1 | 0 | 1 | 0 | 0 |
| 0 | 1 | 1 | 0 | 0 |
| 1 | 1 | 1 | 0 | 1 |
| 0 | 0 | 0 | 1 | 1 |
| 1 | 0 | 0 | 1 | 0 |
| 0 | 1 | 0 | 1 | 0 |
| 1 | 1 | 0 | 1 | 1 |
| 0 | 0 | 1 | 1 | 0 |
| 1 | 0 | 1 | 1 | 1 |
| 0 | 1 | 1 | 1 | 1 |
| 1 | 1 | 1 | 1 | 0 |

**FIGURE 4-19**
*Truth table for parity bit generator.*

ber of 1's in the input to the circuit. The truth table for this parity generator is given in Figure 4-19.

When this table is applied to a logic map, it may be seen at a glance that there is no chance for simplification.

Another conclusion can be arrived at by considering the problem again with two inputs. The truth table for a parity bit generator with two inputs is given in Figure 4-20.

Examination of this table reveals that it is the truth table for the Exclusive OR logic operation. Thus, the logic equation for parity bit generator, if the total of the two input bits is odd is:

$$P = A \oplus B$$

| INPUTS | | PARITY BIT |
|---|---|---|
| A | B | P |
| 0 | 0 | 0 |
| 0 | 1 | 1 |
| 1 | 0 | 1 |
| 1 | 1 | 0 |

**FIGURE 4-20**
*Two-input even parity generator truth table.*

Now consider the result of the application of an additional Exclusive OR operation on P and a new input C.

$$
\begin{array}{rl}
A & \quad 0101 \quad 0101 \\
B & \quad 0011 \quad 0011 \\
C & \quad \underline{0000 \quad 1111} \\
P = A \oplus B \quad = & \quad 0110 \quad 0110 \\
P \oplus C \quad = & \quad 0110 \quad 1001
\end{array}
$$

It can be seen that the result is that a new parity bit is produced if there is an odd number of bits at the input. It may be concluded that an even parity generator can be based on the cascading of Exclusive OR operations. Therefore, a four-input even parity generator can easily be synthesized as shown in Figure 4-21 using only three logic gates. Note that the circuit is called a even parity generator because the parity bit is attached to the string of input bits to produce a data string with an even number of 1 bits.

Another limitation to the logic map or truth table approach is that it applies only to logic functions that can be implemented using standard logic gates (AND, OR, NOT, etc.). However, most logic applications include such items as solid-state timing and latching devices. The discussion of digital system fundamentals will be completed by covering these types of solid-state digital devices.

## Timing Devices

Timing devices are used in process industrial control systems to provide a repeatable and predictable sequence of events. Many processes require timing of the events in the system; for example, painting metal parts on an assembly line might require precise timing of the application of each coat of paint.

This section will discuss methods for developing a single pulse and a train of pulses for initiation and timing control in digital systems. The solid-state circuits that perform these tasks are called monostable and astable multivibrators. The monostable device provides a single pulse with adjustable pulse width while the astable device produces a pulse train with variable duty cycle and frequency.

**Astable Multivibrator**   The manufacturer's model number 555 integrated circuit (IC) is the most popular IC used to produce timing pulses for a digital system. This device requires an external resistor and capacitor network to set the output frequency and the duty cycle. Figure 4-22 gives the IC pin identification as well as astable multivibrator circuitry for a 555.

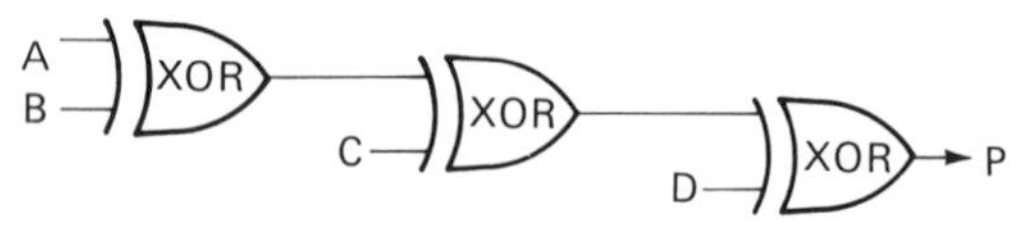

**FIGURE 4-21**
*Four-input even parity generator.*

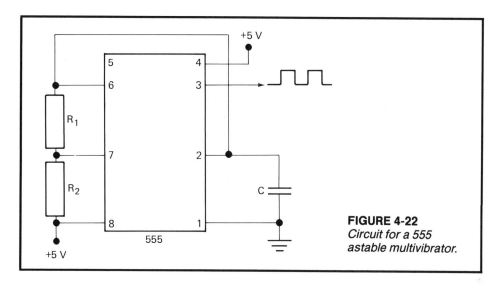

**FIGURE 4-22**
*Circuit for a 555 astable multivibrator.*

The clock frequency ($f_c$) for a 555 astable multivibrator is calculated using the following equation:

$$f_c = 1.44/(R_2 + 2R_1)C \qquad (4\text{-}20)$$

The duty cycle, which is the ratio of the time spent in the logic zero state to the sum of the time spent in the logic 0 and 1 states, is given by

$$D = R_1/(R_1 + R_2) \qquad (4\text{-}21)$$

Thus a duty cycle of 0.5 produces a square wave and is obtained when $R_1 = R_2$.

**Monostable Multivibrator**   The most common integrated circuit used to produce a single pulse for timing is the 74121. This monostable device, or one-shot, provides precisely timed intervals for use in digital circuits. It is generally used to modify the duration of a digital signal by either stretching (increasing pulse width) or shortening the signal (decreasing pulse width).

Figure 4-23 gives a typical circuit for a one-shot using the 74121 and the circuit waveform.

The pulse width of the output signal is controlled in the circuit by the external feedback components (resistor-capacitor network). If no external feedback components are used, the circuit yields a pulse width output of 30 to 50 ns. The pulse width can be determined from Equation 4-22.

$$T \cong 0.7\,RC \qquad (4\text{-}22)$$

where:   $T$ = pulse width in seconds
$R$ = resistance in ohms
$C$ = capacitance in farads

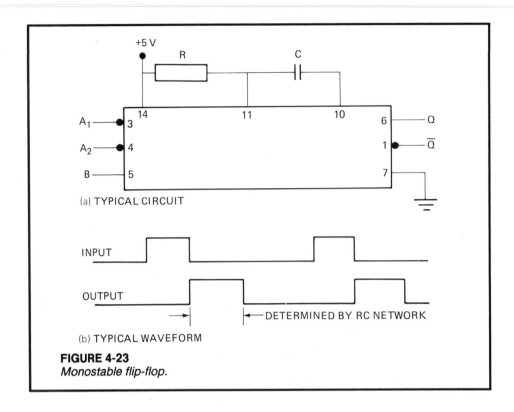

(a) TYPICAL CIRCUIT

(b) TYPICAL WAVEFORM

**FIGURE 4-23**
*Monostable flip-flop.*

The manufacturer's data sheet for the 74121 one-shot should be consulted for limitations on the values of R and C.

## Latching Devices and Flip-Flops

In logic gates (AND, OR, NOT, etc.) discussed so far, the output responded immediately to changes at the input. Several digital circuit applications require devices that do not respond to every input logic change.

Latches belong to one class of digital devices whose outputs may or may not follow the input. The latch output does not return to a predetermined logic level but holds its output until the controlling input is altered in an allowable manner.

The flip-flop is another digital device that does not respond to every input change. The difference between a latch and a flip-flop is that a latch is asynchronous to a correct input logic change immediately, while the flip-flop device does not respond to the input logic change until a clock input signal is sent to the device. This section will discuss general characteristics of R-S latches, D latches, and the J-K flip-flop.

**R-S Latch** The R-S (reset-set) latch is a logic circuit having two possible states. It is designed such that an enabling level on the S (set) input, with R in the opposite state, yields a Q = high output. An enabling level on the R (reset) input, with S in the opposite state, yields a Q = low output. Figure 4-24(a) shows the logic symbol

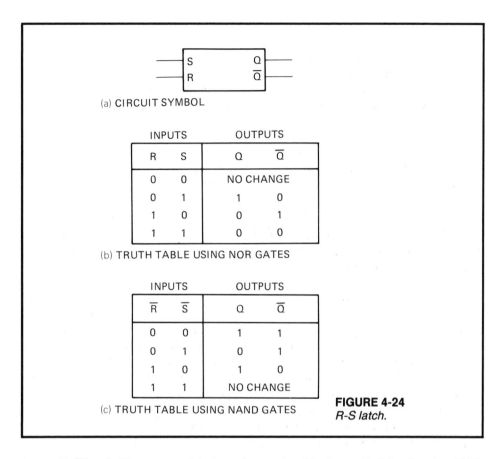

(a) CIRCUIT SYMBOL

| INPUTS | | OUTPUTS | |
|---|---|---|---|
| R | S | Q | $\overline{Q}$ |
| 0 | 0 | NO CHANGE | |
| 0 | 1 | 1 | 0 |
| 1 | 0 | 0 | 1 |
| 1 | 1 | 0 | 0 |

(b) TRUTH TABLE USING NOR GATES

| INPUTS | | OUTPUTS | |
|---|---|---|---|
| $\overline{R}$ | $\overline{S}$ | Q | $\overline{Q}$ |
| 0 | 0 | 1 | 1 |
| 0 | 1 | 0 | 1 |
| 1 | 0 | 1 | 0 |
| 1 | 1 | NO CHANGE | |

(c) TRUTH TABLE USING NAND GATES

**FIGURE 4-24**
*R-S latch.*

for an R-S latch. Figure 4-24(b) gives the truth table for an R-S latch using NOR gates, and Figure 4-24(c) gives the truth table for an R-S latch using NAND gates.

**EXAMPLE 4-9**

**Problem:** Design a R-S latch using TTL NOR gates.

**Solution:** If the 7402 quadruple two-input NOR gates are used, the circuit can be designed as follows:

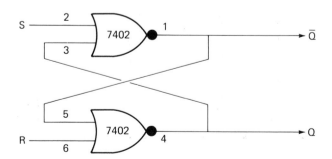

**D-Latch**   The D-latch is the most common gated latch in use. It is a bistable device with a single data input (D), This single input is obtained by adding an inverter to the basic R-S circuit inputs to ensure that R and S are always in the opposite state, thus eliminating the possibility of a race condition. A race condition occurs when two inputs are switched at the same time and the resulting output is unpredictable. Race situations need to be avoided if the digital system is to function reliably.

In the D-latch, a change in the data input will be transferred to the output whenever the proper logic level is present on the enable input (G); i.e., as long as the latch is enabled, the output (Q) will follow the input. Figure 4-25 shows the standard symbol and function table for a D-latch.

**J-K Latch**   The symbol and function table for a J-K latch are given in Figure 4-26. The J-K latch is similar to the R-S latch with one exception: if two high inputs occur simultaneously, the J-K latch outputs will reverse their output states. This eliminates the undefined state found in the R-S latch.

**J-K Flip-Flop**   The symbol and function table for a J-K flip-flop are shown in Figure 4-27. The two basic types of triggering methods employed when using a J-K flip-flop circuit are edge and master-slave. Edge triggering transfers input data to the output on a predetermined clock transition. In master-slave triggering, input data is sampled when the clock input is high and transferred to the output on the trailing edge of the clock. When using master-slave triggering, the input data must not change during the period of time the clock is high.

The J-K flip-flop is the basic building block of most digital computers. Normally, computers are based on 8-bit, 16-bit, or 32-bit words and the single bit in the computer word is generally a flip-flop circuit that can assume a value of 0 or 1.

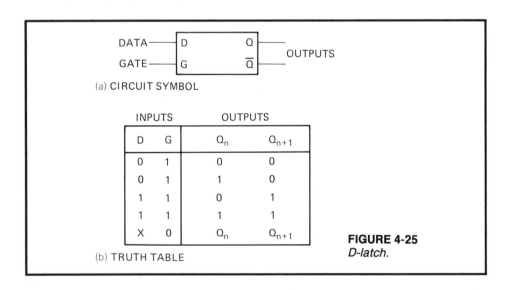

(a) CIRCUIT SYMBOL

| INPUTS | | OUTPUTS | |
|---|---|---|---|
| D | G | $Q_n$ | $Q_{n+1}$ |
| 0 | 1 | 0 | 0 |
| 0 | 1 | 1 | 0 |
| 1 | 1 | 0 | 1 |
| 1 | 1 | 1 | 1 |
| X | 0 | $Q_n$ | $Q_{n+1}$ |

(b) TRUTH TABLE

**FIGURE 4-25**
*D-latch.*

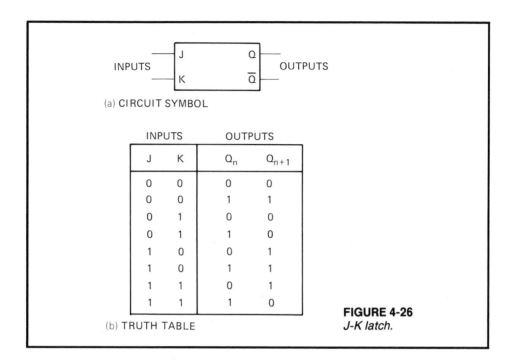

(a) CIRCUIT SYMBOL

| INPUTS | | OUTPUTS | |
|---|---|---|---|
| J | K | $Q_n$ | $Q_{n+1}$ |
| 0 | 0 | 0 | 0 |
| 0 | 0 | 1 | 1 |
| 0 | 1 | 0 | 0 |
| 0 | 1 | 1 | 0 |
| 1 | 0 | 0 | 1 |
| 1 | 0 | 1 | 1 |
| 1 | 1 | 0 | 1 |
| 1 | 1 | 1 | 0 |

(b) TRUTH TABLE

**FIGURE 4-26**
*J-K latch.*

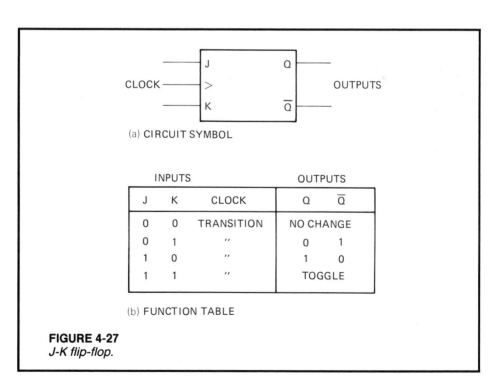

(a) CIRCUIT SYMBOL

| INPUTS | | | OUTPUTS | |
|---|---|---|---|---|
| J | K | CLOCK | Q | $\overline{Q}$ |
| 0 | 0 | TRANSITION | NO CHANGE | |
| 0 | 1 | ′′ | 0 | 1 |
| 1 | 0 | ′′ | 1 | 0 |
| 1 | 1 | ′′ | TOGGLE | |

(b) FUNCTION TABLE

**FIGURE 4-27**
*J-K flip-flop.*

## EXERCISES

4.1  Convert the binary number 10010 to a decimal number.

4.2  Find the binary equivalent to the decimal number 115.

4.3  Add the binary number, 10101, to the binary number 1101 and find the decimal result.

4.4  Convert the octal number 707 to a binary number.

4.5  Convert the binary number 1000111 to an octal number.

4.6  Convert the hexadecimal number 2D9 to its binary and decimal equivalent numbers.

4.7  Verify the logic identity $A + B = B + A$.

4.8  Verify the logic identity $A + AB = A$.

4.9  Synthesize $ABC + A\overline{B}D + DC + A\overline{D}$ with two-input NOR and two-input NAND gates.

4.10  Synthesize $A\overline{C} + B \times (C + D)$ with two-input NAND gates.

4.11  Design a 7-input odd parity generator using XOR and NOT gates.

4.12  Design an astable multivibrator using a 555 IC and a 1 µfarad capacitor to produce a square wave with a frequency of 480 Hz (cycles per second).

4.13  Design an R-S latch using TTL-7400 IC NAND gates and show IC pin numbers on the logic drawing.

## BIBLIOGRAPHY

1.  Kintner, P.M., *Electronic Digital Techniques*, McGraw-Hill Book Company, 1968.

2.  Floyd, T.L., *Digital Logic Fundamentals*, Charles E. Merrill Publishing Company, 1977.

3.  Malvino, A.P., *Digital Computer Electronics - An Introduction to Microcomputers*, Second Edition, McGraw-Hill Book Company, 1983.

4.  Grob, B., *Basic Electronics*, Fifth Edition, McGraw-Hill Book Company,1984

5.  Budak, A., *Passive and Active Network Analysis and Synthesis*, Houghton Mifflin Co., 1974.

6.  Boylestad, R.L. and Nashelsky, L., *Electronic Devices and Circuit Theory*, Third Edition, Prentice-Hall, Inc., 1982.

7.  Clare, C.R., *Designing Logic Systems Using State Machines,* McGraw-Hill Book Company, 1973.

# 5

# Level and Pressure Measurement

**Introduction**   The purpose of this chapter is to discuss the principles of level and pressure measurement in industrial processes. Pressure measurement is discussed first because of the process values that are inferred by measuring pressure. Liquid level, fluid flow, temperature, and pressure are process values that can be derived from pressure measurement. Since level measurement is in some cases closely related to pressure, it will be discussed in this chapter.

**Pressure Measurement Basics**   Many methods are used to measure pressure. The choice of a particular method depends upon many factors, including the specific requirements of the measuring system, the accuracy required, and the static, dynamic, and physical properties of the process. A pressure element or transducer is always used to convert pressure to a mechanical or electrical signal. This signal is then used for process indication or to generate a scaled transmitted signal.

**Definition of Pressure**   Pressure is force applied to, or distributed over, a surface. The relationship between pressure, force, and area is expressed as:

$$P = \frac{F}{A} \qquad (5\text{-}1)$$

where   P   = pressure
F   = force
A   = area

In this discussion of pressure, the term "fluid" will refer to both liquids and gases. Both will occupy the container in which they are placed; but a liquid, if it does not completely fill the container, will have a free liquid surface, whereas a gas will always fill the volume of its container. If a gas is confined in a container, the molecules of the gas strike the walls of the container. This collision of molecules against the walls results in a force against the surface area of the container. The pressure is equal to the force applied to the walls divided by the area that is perpendicular to the force. For a liquid at rest, the pressure exerted by the fluid at any point will be perpendicular to the boundary of the fluid.

Pascal's Law is important in understanding pressure measurement. This law states that whenever an external pressure is applied to any confined fluid at rest, the pressure is increased at every point in the fluid by the amount of the external pressure.

A practical application of Pascal's law is the hydraulic press shown in Figure 5-1.

A small force ($F_1$) is applied to the small piston (area $A_1$). The following relationship exists in the hydraulic press because according to Pascal's Law the pressure at every point is equal.

Since $$P_1 = P_2 \tag{5-2}$$

$$P_1 = \frac{F_1}{A_1}$$

and $$P_2 = \frac{F_2}{A_2}$$

then $$\frac{F_1}{A_1} = \frac{F_2}{A_2}$$

or $$F_2 = \frac{A_2}{A_1} \, F_1 \tag{5-3}$$

The hydraulic press is a force amplifier where the gain of the amplifier is given by $A_2/A_1$.

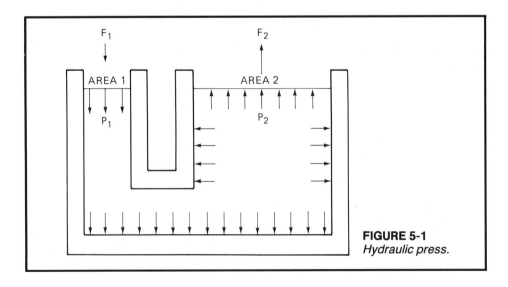

**FIGURE 5-1**
*Hydraulic press.*

Example 5-1 will illustrate how the concept expressed by Pascal's Law can be utilized in practical applications.

**EXAMPLE 5-1**

**Problem:** Find the force $F_2$, given the following specification for the hydraulic press in Figure 5-1:

$$A_1 = 0.5 \text{ square inch}$$
$$A_2 = 5 \text{ square inches}$$
$$F_1 = 100 \text{ pounds}$$

**Solution:** By using Equation 5-3,

$$F_2 = \frac{A_2}{A_1} F_1 \tag{5-3}$$

$$F_2 = [5 \text{ in.}^2/0.5 \text{ in.}^2](100 \text{ pounds})$$

$$F_2 = 1000 \text{ pounds}$$

The most common application of this principle is in automobile hydraulic brakes. It is also used extensively in pneumatic and hydraulic instrument applications.

**Pressure Units**   The standard unit of pressure in the English or foot-pounds-second (fps) system is in pounds per square inch or psi, where the force is in pounds and the area is in square inches. In International System of Units (SI), pressure is measured as newtons per square meter or pascals (Pa). Table 5-1 lists several pressure-unit conversion factors.

**Gage and Absolute Pressure**   Absolute pressure is the pressure measured above total vacuum or zero absolute, where zero absolute represents total lack of pressure. Gage pressure is the pressure measured above atmospheric or barometric pressure; it represents the positive difference between measured pressure and existing atmospheric pressure.

Most pressure gages, transmitters, and other pressure-measuring devices indicate a zero reading when the measuring point is exposed to the atmosphere; this

---

**TABLE 5-1**
**Pressure Unit Conversion Factors**

---

1 in. of water = 0.0360 psi = 0.0737 in. mercury
1 ft of water = 0.4320 psi = 0.8844 in. mercury
1 psi = 27.7417 in. water = 2.0441 in. mercury
1 kg per sq cm = 14.22 psi = 98.067 kilopascals

---

(All fluids at a temperature of 22°C)

point is called zero psig. However, some instruments are designed to produce a reading referenced to absolute zero and indicate a reading near 14.7 psi when the measuring point is exposed to atmospheric pressure. This reading is generally termed 14.7 psia. Figure 5-2 helps to explain the relationship between absolute and gage pressure.

The equation used to convert from gage pressure ($P_g$) in psig to absolute pressure ($P_a$) in psia is given by:

$$P_a = P_g + P_{atm}, \text{ when } P_g > P_{atm} \tag{5-4}$$

or

$$P_a = P_{atm} - P_g, \text{ when } P_g < P_{atm} \tag{5-4a}$$

where $P_{atm}$ is atmospheric pressure and $P_g$ is gage pressure.

It should be noted that a change in atmospheric pressure will cause a change in absolute pressure. Therefore, a change in barometric pressure would cause a change in reading of an absolute pressure-measuring instrument but not in a gage pressure instrument.

**EXAMPLE 5-2**

**Problem:** Find the absolute pressure corresponding to a pressure gage reading of 30 psig, if the local barometric reading is 14.6 psi.

**Solution:** From Equation 5-4,

$$P_a = P_g + P_{aim}$$

$$P_a = 30 + 14.6$$

$$P_a = 44.6 \text{ psia}$$

**EXAMPLE 5-3**

**Problem:** Find the absolute pressure if a vacuum gage reads 11.5 psig and the atmospheric pressure is 14.6 psia.

**Solution:** When dealing with pressure below atmospheric pressure, Equation 5-4a must be used, so that $P_a = P_{atm} - P_g$ or $P_a = 14.6 - 11.5 = 3.1$ psia.

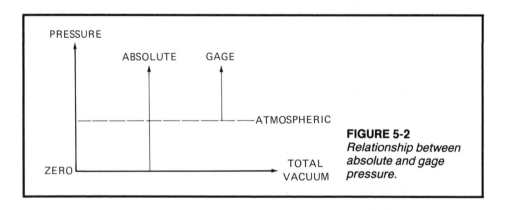

**FIGURE 5-2**
*Relationship between absolute and gage pressure.*

**Manometers**   A manometer is one of the most common devices used to measure pressure in the laboratory. They are used extensively to calibrate pressure-measuring instruments in the process industries. Figure 5-3 explains the basic principle of a manometer. The weight of one (1) cubic foot of water is 62.3 pounds, and this weight is exerted over the surface area of one square foot or 144 square inches. Since pressure is defined as P = F/A (Equation 5-1) the total pressure on the surface area of 1 square foot is:

$$P = \frac{F}{A} = \frac{62.3 \text{ lbs}}{144 \text{ in.}^2} = 0.433 \text{ psi}$$

This means a 1-foot column of water exerts a pressure of 0.433 pound per square inch. Conversely, a pressure of 0.433 psi will cause a column of water to be raised 1 foot.

A manometer is a device with one or two transparent tubes and two liquid surfaces, where pressure applied to the surface in one tube causes an elevation of the liquid surface in the other tube. The amount of elevation is read from a scale that is usually calibrated to read directly in pressure units.

In general, an unknown pressure is applied to one tube and a reference (known) pressure is applied to the other tube. The difference between the known pressure and the unknown pressure is balanced by weight per unit area of the displaced manometer liquid. Mercury and water are the most commonly used liquids in manometers; however, any fluid can be used. The formula for the pressure reading of a manometer is given by Equation 5-5:

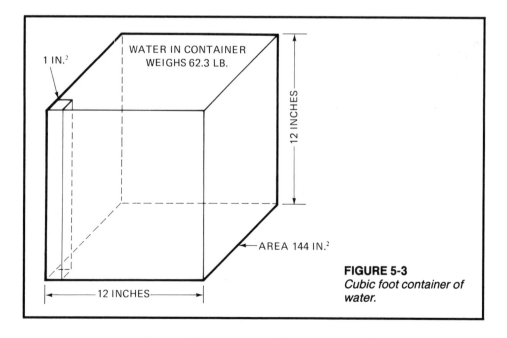

WATER IN CONTAINER WEIGHS 62.3 LB.

1 IN.²

12 INCHES

AREA 144 IN.²

12 INCHES

**FIGURE 5-3**
*Cubic foot container of water.*

$$P = h(0.03606)G \qquad (5\text{-}5)$$

where:    P    = pressure in psi
          h    = the amount of displaced liquid in inches
          G    = specific gravity of the manometer liquid
    0.03606    = pressure of a 1-inch displacement of a column of water

Manometers can provide a very accurate pressure measurement and are often used as calibration standards for other pressure measurement devices. The pressure measurement range of most manometers is usually from a few inches to about 30 inches. The range depends on the physical length and arrangement of the tubes and the specific gravity of the fill fluid.

The four most common types of manometers are: (1) U-tube, (2) well or reservoir, (3) inclined, and (4) float type.

**U-Tube Manometer**    The U-tube manometer shown in Figure 5-4 has two transparent tubes connected together to form a U shape. The pressure to be measured (P) is applied to the left side of the tube, and the other side of the tube is normally open to the atmosphere so that the amount of elevation can be read from a pressure scale engraved on the right hand tube.

### EXAMPLE 5-4

**Problem:** Find the pressure in psi if a pressure applied to a water-filled manometer causes a water displacement of 30 inches.

**Solution:** From Table 5-1, 1 inch of water = 0.0360 psi; therefore, 30 inches WC × 0.0360 psi/1 inch of WC = 1.08 psi, where WC is water column.

**Well (Reservoir) Manometer**    A well or reservoir manometer is shown in Figure 5-5. In this application, the pressure to be measured is applied to the gage reservoir and the other tube is open to the atmosphere. The pressure is given by the difference in height between levels 1 and 2.

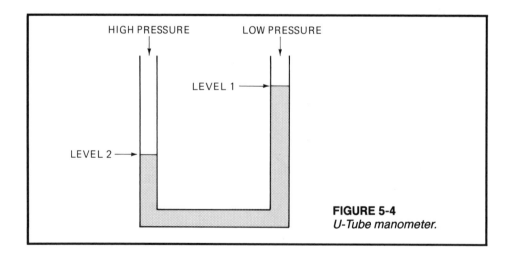

HIGH PRESSURE    LOW PRESSURE

LEVEL 1

LEVEL 2

**FIGURE 5-4**
*U-Tube manometer.*

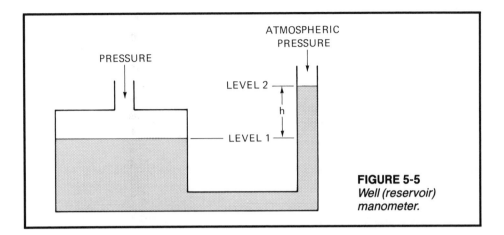

**FIGURE 5-5**
*Well (reservoir) manometer.*

Let's look at an example problem, assuming the reservoir in Figure 5-5 is filled with mercury.

**EXAMPLE 5-5**

**Problem:** Find the displacement of liquid in a mercury manometer if a pressure of 15 psig is applied. The specific gravity of mercury is 13.62.

**Solution:** Using Equation 5.5,

$$P = h(0.03606)G$$

Therefore,   $h = \dfrac{P}{(0.03606)G} = \dfrac{15 \text{ psig}}{(0.03606 \text{ psig/in.})(13.62)}$

$$h = 30.54 \text{ inches}$$

**Inclined Manometers**   The inclined manometer in Figure 5-6 is designed to measure low pressures. The inclined tube has an open end while the pressure being measured is applied to the reservoir.

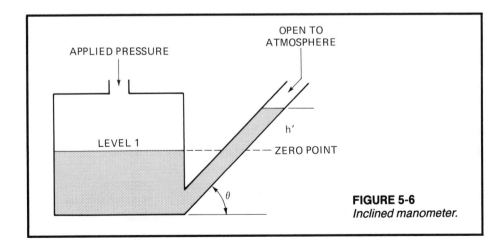

**FIGURE 5-6**
*Inclined manometer.*

Since the angle of inclination is fixed, there is an exact relationship between the liquid movement along the tube and the vertical displacement. This relationship is:

$$h = h' \sin \theta \qquad (5\text{-}6)$$

where:  h  = vertical displacement of the manometer liquid
        h' = distance traveled by the liquid up the tube
        θ  = angle of inclination from the horizontal

**Float Manometer**   The final manometer to be discussed is the float type shown in Figure 5-7. In this instrument a float is placed in the reservoir and connected to a pointer. This pointer moves up and down a calibrated scale on a dial that gives a direct pressure reading as the pressure applied to the instrument changes.

## Pressure Gages and Transmitters   Pressure gages are used for local indication and are the most common type of pressure measurement instrument used in the process industries. Pressure gages consist of a dial or indicator and a pressure element. A pressure element converts pressure into a mechanical motion.

Most mechanical pressure elements rely on the pressure acting on a surface area inside the element to produce a force that causes a mechanical deflection. The common elements used are diaphragms, bellows elements, and Bourdon tubes.

The most common device used to convert pressure into a physical movement is the diaphragm shown in Figure 5-8.

In this device, we apply a pressure $P_1$ to one side of the diaphragm and pressure $P_2$ to the other side, so the net force is

$$F_1 = (P_2 - P_1)A$$

where A = diaphragm area in m² and $P_1$, $P_2$ = pressure in N/m²

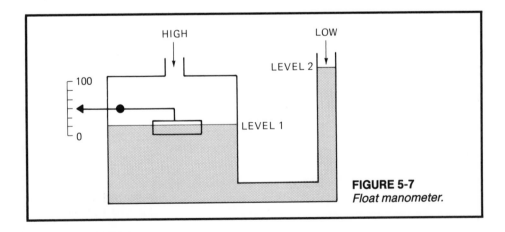

**FIGURE 5-7**
*Float manometer.*

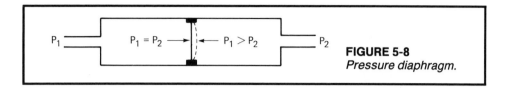

**FIGURE 5-8**
*Pressure diaphragm.*

A diaphragm acts like a spring and will extend or contract until a force is developed that balances the pressure difference force.

The bellows pressure element shown in Figure 5-9, a device much like the diaphragm, converts a pressure difference into a physical displacement. The difference is that the movement in a bellows is much more a straight-line expansion.

Another device used to measure pressure is the Bourdon tube shown in Figure 5-10. In this device a section of tubing closed at one end is partially flattened and coiled as shown. When a pressure is applied to the open end, the tube uncoils. This movement provides a displacement proportional to the applied pressure. In a pressure gage the tube is mechanically linked to a pointer on a pressure dial to give a calibrated reading.

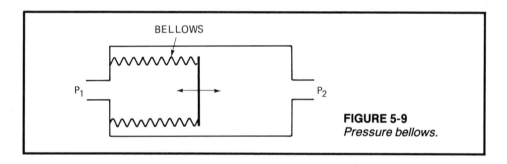

**FIGURE 5-9**
*Pressure bellows.*

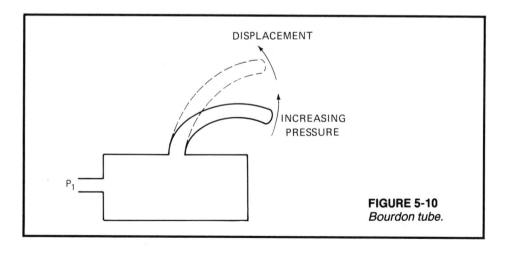

**FIGURE 5-10**
*Bourdon tube.*

The fact that a pressure gage can be used only for local indication sometimes limits its capability in process measurement and control. Some control applications require that the pressure value be transmitted some distance, such as to a central control room, and then be converted to a usable pressure reading. Pressure transmitters are designed to convert a pressure value to a scaled signal, either electric, pneumatic, or mechanical. A block diagram of a pressure transmitter is given in Figure 5-11.

In a typical pneumatic transmitter, the pressure to be measured is applied across a pair of metal diaphragms welded to opposite sides of a chamber. The force developed on the diaphragm is brought out of the chamber by a rigid rod passing through the diaphragm. This force is opposed by a balancing force developed by a pneumatic bellows. Imbalance between the capsule force and the bellows force is sensed by a pneumatic nozzle-baffle. This simple pneumatic servomechanism is responsive to nozzle pressure and re-establishes the balance. As a result, pneumatic pressure is maintained exactly proportional to applied pressure and is used as an output signal (usually 3 to 15 psi).

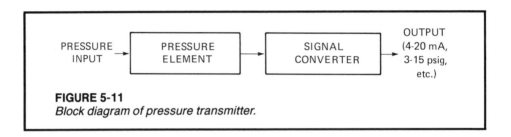

**FIGURE 5-11**
*Block diagram of pressure transmitter.*

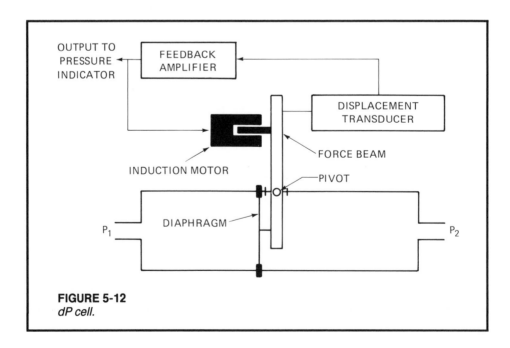

**FIGURE 5-12**
*dP cell.*

The electrical principles used to measure pressure displacement are numerous and varied. Most electronic pressure transmitters employ capacitive, differential transformer, force balance, photoelectric, piezoelectric, potentiometric, resistive, strain gage, or thermoelectric means of measurement.

A typical example of an electronic pressure transmitter is the differential pressure cell (dP) shown in Figure 5-12. In this device, a differential pressure is applied to a diaphragm, but the diaphragm is effectively kept from moving by an electronic feedback system. In this feedback system, any movement of the diaphragm is transmitted via a force beam to a displacement transducer, which then sends an electronic signal to an amplifier. The amplifier then sends an error signal to an induction motor to correct for the movement of the diaphragm. This error signal also provides an electrical measurement of the differential pressure applied to the cell.

It should be noted that the pneumatic transmitter actually measures a differential pressure (dP) applied to the high and low inputs of the transmitter. Pressure measurement is always made with respect to a reference point. Gage pressure is referenced to atmospheric pressure. Absolute pressure measurement represents a pressure level above a complete vacuum, which is the absence of pressure or 0 psia. In either case, a measurement represents the difference in pressure between a value and the reference level. In a strict sense, all pressure measurements are differential pressure measurements.

## Level Measurement by Differential Pressure
A very common and practical application for pressure or dP transmitters is level measurement. In this application the actual level value is inferred from a pressure measurement. Consider the example shown in Figure 5-13. As was seen earlier in this chapter, there is a direct relationship between the hydrostatic pressure caused by a column of liquid, the specific gravity of the liquid, and the height of the vertical column of liquid. In most cases, the specific gravity of a fluid is constant, so that pressure (P) is directly proportional to liquid level (h), giving

$$P = kh \qquad (5\text{-}7)$$

where k is the proportionality constant.

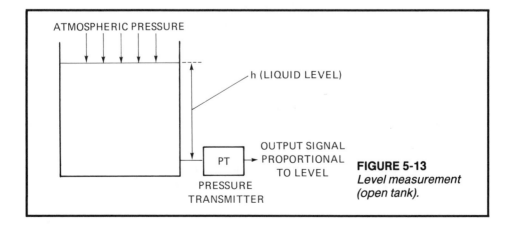

**FIGURE 5-13**
*Level measurement (open tank).*

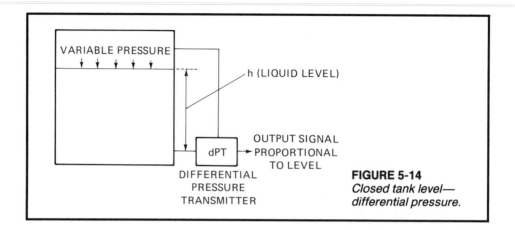

VARIABLE PRESSURE

h (LIQUID LEVEL)

OUTPUT SIGNAL
dPT → PROPORTIONAL
TO LEVEL

DIFFERENTIAL
PRESSURE
TRANSMITTER

**FIGURE 5-14**
*Closed tank level—
differential pressure.*

Another common example is the closed tank level measurement shown in Figure 5-14. In this example, if the pressure in the closed tank changes, an equal force is applied to both sides of the dP transmitter. Since the dP cell responds only to changes in differential pressure, a change in static pressure on the liquid surface will not change the output of the transmitter. Thus, the dP cell responds only to changes in liquid level when the specific gravity of the liquid is constant.

## Use of Bubblers in Level Measurement

In the use of bubblers to measure liquid level, a dip tube is installed in a tank with its open end a few inches from the bottom. A gas is forced through the tube, and, when gas bubbles escape from the open end, the gas pressure in the tube equals the hydrostatic head of the liquid. As liquid level (head) varies, the gas pressure in the dip tube changes correspondingly. This pressure can be detected by pressure gages or detectors for continuous indication of level or by pressure switches for ON/OFF level control of the tank. Figure 5-15 illustrates an air bubbler installation for an open (atmospheric) tank.

The purge supply pressure should be at least 10 psi higher than the highest hydrostatic pressure to be measured. The purge rate should be kept small, about 1 scfh, so that there is no significant pressure drop in the dip tube. Usually the purge media is air or nitrogen, although liquids can be used.

For tanks that operate under pressure or vacuum, the installation of a bubbler system becomes slightly more complex because the liquid level measurement is a function of the difference between the purge gas pressure and the vapor pressure above the liquid. Because we now have differential pressure involved, the transducer used is normally a dP cell.

There are some definite disadvantages to using bubblers. In addition to limited accuracy, another disadvantage is that bubblers must introduce foreign matter into the process. Liquid purges can upset the material balance of the process, and gas purges can overload the vent system on vacuum processes. If the purge media fails, not only is the level indication on the tank lost, but the system is exposed to process material, which can cause plugging, corrosion, freezing, or safety hazards.

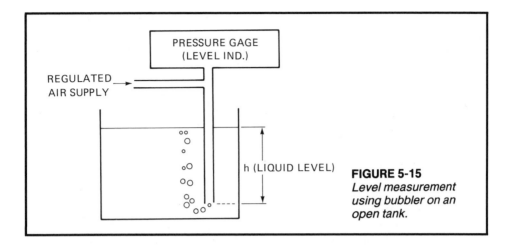

**FIGURE 5-15**
*Level measurement using bubbler on an open tank.*

## Capacitance Probes

A capacitor consists of two conductors separated by an insulator. The conductors are called plates and the insulator is referred to as the dielectric. The basic nature of a capacitor is its ability to accept and store an electric charge. When a capacitor is connected to a battery, as shown in Figure 5-16, electrons will flow from the negative terminal of the battery to the capacitor, and the electrons on the opposite plate of the capacitor will flow to the positive terminal of the battery. This electron flow will continue until the voltage across the capacitor equals the applied voltage.

Capacitor size is measured in farads. A capacitor has the capacitance of one farad if it stores a charge of one coulomb when connected to a one-volt supply. Because this is a very large unit, one millionth of it, noted as the microfarad ($\mu$F), is commonly used. The electric size in farads of a capacitor is dependent on its physical dimensions and on the type of material (dielectric) between the capacitor plates. The equation for a parallel plate capacitor is given by the following:

$$C = E_0 K\varepsilon \ \frac{A}{d} \qquad\qquad (5\text{-}8)$$

where A is the area in square meters of either plate, d is the distance in meters between plates, and K$\varepsilon$ is the dielectric constant, or relative permittivity, as listed in

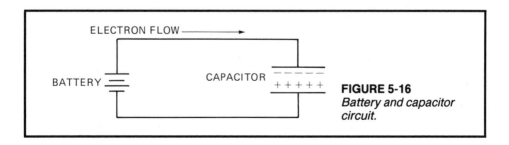

**FIGURE 5-16**
*Battery and capacitor circuit.*

Table 5-2. The constant $E_0 = 8.85 \times 10^{-12}$ farads/meter is the absolute permittivity of air or vacuum in SI units.

For pure substances, the dielectric constant is a fundamental property. The dielectric constant of any mixture of substances can be established experimentally.

Several laws for capacitive circuits are worth noting. One is that the capacitance of two or more capacitors connected in parallel is equal to the sum of the individual capacitances (i.e., $C_t = C_1 + C_2 + \ldots + C_n$). The second law is that for capacitors connected in series, the reciprocal of the total capacitance $(1/C_t)$ equals the sum of the reciprocals of the individual capacitors (i.e., $1/C_t = 1/C_1 + 1/C_2 + \ldots + 1/C_n$).

A change in the characteristics of the material between the plates will cause a change in dielectric constant, which is often larger and more easily measured than changes in other properties. This makes the dielectric measurement suitable for detection of the level of material in vessels, because changes in process level change the dielectric constant. While these changes are helpful in measuring the level of the material, they also influence the accuracy of level measurement and, therefore, must be evaluated carefully.

As material temperature increases, its dielectric constant tends to decrease. Temperature coefficients are in the order of 0.1 percent per degree Celsius. Automatic temperature compensator circuits can be installed to cancel the effect of temperature variations. Chemical and physical composition and structure changes affect the dielectric constant. When the dielectric constant of solids is to be measured, it should be noted that variations in average particle size and changes in packing density will affect the dielectric constant. Current flow to ground through material resistance tends to short out the capacitor. This shorting of the measured capacitance with a variable resistance can make the dielectric measurement very inaccurate if the resistance is low compared to the capacitive reactance.

Variations in process level cause changes in capacitance that can be measured with an electronic circuit in the level instrument. As shown in Figure 5-17, the probe is insulated from the vessel and forms one plate of the capacitor; the ves-

**TABLE 5-2**
**Dielectric Constants**

| Material | Dielectric constant $K\varepsilon$ |
|---|---|
| Air or Vacuum | 1 |
| Aluminum Oxide | 7 |
| Ceramics | 80-1200 |
| Glass | 8 |
| Mica | 3-8 |
| Oil | 2-5 |

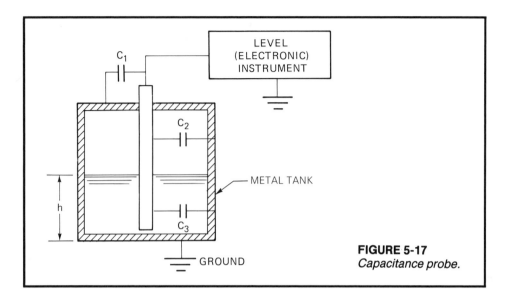

**FIGURE 5-17**
*Capacitance probe.*

sel forms the other. The material between the two plates is the dielectric. As level rises, vapors with low dielectric constant (1.0) are displaced by the higher dielectric process materials. Capacitance changes are detected with an electronic instrument calibrated in units of level.

In Figure 5-17, $C_1$ is the "stray capacitance" of the system, which is unaffected by level changes. $C_2$ is the capacitance in the vapor above the liquid and $C_3$ is the capacitance of the process material. The total capacitance $C_e$ is given by $C_e = C_1 + C_2 + C_3$.

For measuring the level of conductive materials, insulated (normally Teflon™ coated) probes are used. This measurement is largely unaffected by the effective resistance, and, therefore, this probe design is applicable to both conductive and nonconductive processes.

If the process material adheres to the probe, a level reduction in the vessel will leave a layer of fluid on the probe. When this layer is conductive, the wet portion of the probe will be coupled to ground, and the instrument will not read the new level but will register the level to which the probe is coated. Other than the changes in process material dielectric constant, this represents one of the most serious limitations of capacitance installations. It should be noted that if the probe coating is nonconductive, the interference with measurement accuracy is much less pronounced.

## Conductivity Probes   Conductivity probes use the fact that most liquids will conduct electricity. Figure 5-18 illustrates the operation of the conductivity level probe.

An electrode is shown above the liquid level on the left side of the sketch. The circuit, therefore, is open and no current is flowing through the level switch to energize it. When the liquid level rises as shown on the right side of the sketch, a con-

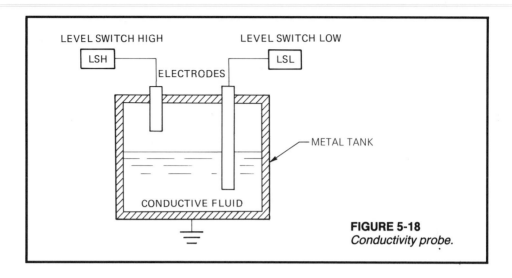

**FIGURE 5-18**
*Conductivity probe.*

ductive path between the electrode and the grounded tank is established, closing the high level switch. Energization of the switch closes the load relays: operating pumps, solenoid valves, or other processing equipment.

If the tank is fabricated of fiberglass or other insulating material, the conducting circuit can be made between the sensing probe and a reference probe.

Because these switches are available in a variety of configurations, they can be used for on-off control of one piece of equipment or for control of several pieces of equipment. A typical application would be the control of the liquid level in a sump. The relay ladder diagram in Figure 5-19 shows how two conductivity probes can be used in conjunction with an electromechanical control relay (CR1) to control a sump pump.

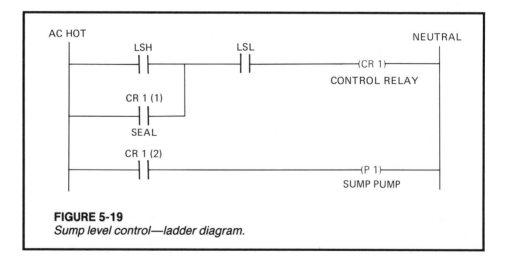

**FIGURE 5-19**
*Sump level control—ladder diagram.*

As level rises, LSL will close since this is the switch operated by the lower probe. The control relay CR1 remains de-energized. When the level rises further, LSH closes, thereby energizing CR1 and closing contact CR1(1). This is a seal-in circuit, so that CR1 will remain energized after LSH drops out. With CR1 energized, the second set of relay contacts CR1(2) closes and energizes pump P1. When the liquid level is pumped down below LSH, it will open the switch, but control relay CR1 will remain ON because the seal contacts are still closed. When the level falls below LSL, that switch opens, de-energizes CR1, and turns off the pump. The pump will remain off until the sump fills up to the high level again.

## Diaphragm Level Detectors
All diaphragm detectors operate on the simple principle of detecting the pressure exerted by the process material against the diaphragm. The designs discussed below include diaphragm switches for liquid and solid materials services and diaphragm devices for continuous liquid level detection.

For solid materials service, diaphragm switches can be selected from a number of design variations. Devices with mercury switches can be used with materials having a high bulk density, while units with microswitches are used for lower density services.

Figure 5-20 shows how diaphragm switches can be used to detect liquid level by sensing the pressure of a captive air column in a riser pipe beneath the diaphragm.

A head of liquid above the inlet of the riser pipe compresses the air sufficiently for switch actuation. The diaphragm is in contact with the captive air but not with the process. These units are limited in application to atmospheric tanks.

Two versions of the continuous level detection, both limited to atmospheric tanks, are shown in Figure 5-21. The diaphragm box instrument shown on the left side of the sketch is quite similar in operation to the previously discussed riser pipe diaphragm switches except that the diaphragm isolates the captive air from the

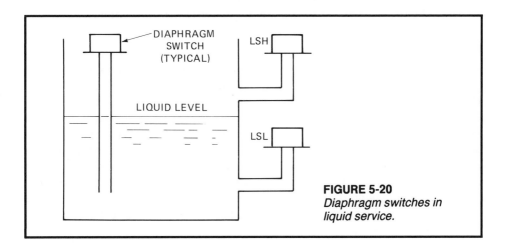

**FIGURE 5-20**
*Diaphragm switches in liquid service.*

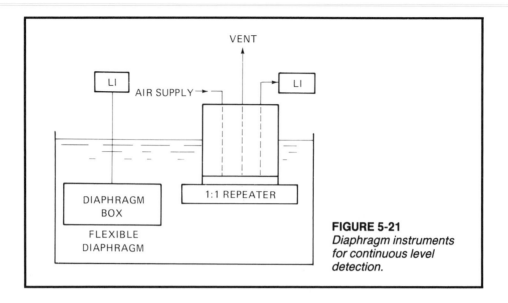

**FIGURE 5-21**
*Diaphragm instruments
for continuous level
detection.*

process fluid. The unit consists of an air-filled diaphragm connected to a pressure detector via air tubing. As the level rises above the diaphragm, the liquid head pressure compresses the captive air inside. The air pressure in the tubing is sensed by a pressure element and displayed as level.

The one-to-one pressure repeater is illustrated on the right side of Figure 5-21. This instrument is submerged in the vessel; the static head of the liquid exerts an upward force on the diaphragm, which increases as the level rises. The upward force is opposed by the air supply pressure on the other side of the diaphragm. The force due to rising level moves the diaphragm toward a bleed orifice, thus restricting its flow to atmosphere and causing the air pressure to build up until it equals the static head pressure. When the forces on the two sides of the diaphragm are equal, the unit is in equilibrium. Air supply to the unit can be regulated at a pressure slightly in excess of the maximum pressure to be measured.

## Displacer Level Detectors
Archimedes' Principle states that a body fully or partially immersed in a fluid is buoyed up by a force equal to the weight of the fluid displaced. By measurement of the apparent weight of an immersed displacer, a level instrument can be devised. If the cross-sectional area of the displacer and the density of the liquid are constant, then a unit change in level will result in a reproducible unit change in displacer weight. The simplest level device of this type involves a displacer that is heavier than the process liquid and is suspended from a spring scale. When the liquid level is below the displacer, the scale shows the full weight of the displacer. As the level rises, the apparent weight of the displacer decreases, thereby yielding a linear and proportional relationship between spring tension and level. The spring scale can be calibrated 0 to 100 percent, or in other level units.

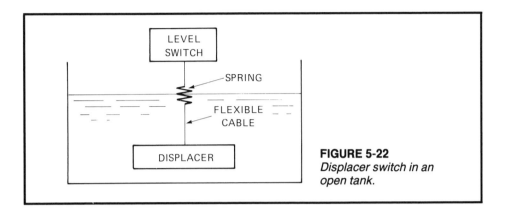

**FIGURE 5-22**
*Displacer switch in an
open tank.*

This simple device is limited to applications in open tanks. In actual industrial measurement, the basic problem is to seal the process from the spring scale or other force-detecting mechanism. This seal has to be frictionless and useful over a wide range of pressures, temperatures, and corrosion conditions.

The major difference between a float level switch and a displacer level switch is that a float stays on the surface and a displacer is partially or totally immersed. As shown in Figure 5-22, the displacer is mounted on a flexible cable attached to a support spring. When the tank is empty, the spring is loaded with the full weight of the displacer. Changing buoyancy, resulting from immersion of the displacer, unloads the downward force on the support spring and provides the small stem movement required for switch action.

## Float Level Instruments
Float level switches and indicators incorporate in their designs a float that follows the liquid level or the interface level between liquids of differing specific gravities. Standard floats are normally spherical or cylindrical for top-mounted designs and spherical or oblong for side-mounted designs. Small diameter floats are used in higher density materials; larger floats are used for liquid-liquid interface detection or for lower density materials.

One of the most direct and simple methods of float level measurement is shown in Figure 5-23. In the unit shown, a tape is connected to a float on one end and to a counterweight on the other to keep the tape under constant tension. The float motion results in the counterweight riding up and down a direct reading gage board, thereby indicating the level in the tank.

A second device for level indication or switching in atmospheric tanks or sumps is a side-mounted float. The float has a rod connected to it. Rod motion may be used to indicate level on a gage board or it may be used to trip high and low level switches for alarm or automatic pump control.

Float switches used in pressurized tanks require a seal between the process and the switch. In the majority of cases the float motion is transferred to the switch or indicator mechanism by magnetic coupling. Figure 5-24 shows a typical example of a magnetically activated level switch. In this configuration a reed switch is posi-

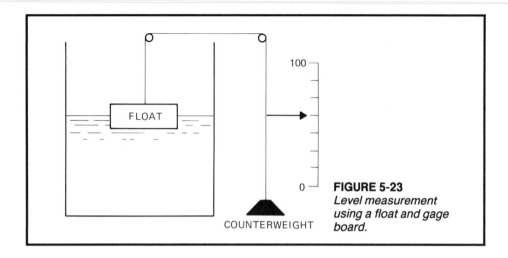

**FIGURE 5-23**
*Level measurement using a float and gage board.*

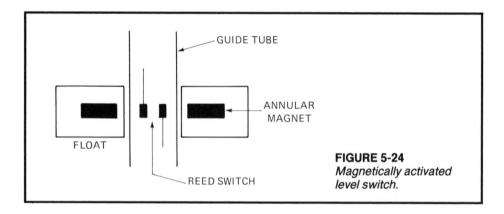

**FIGURE 5-24**
*Magnetically activated level switch.*

tioned inside a sealed and nonmagnetic guide tube at a point where rising or falling liquid level should activate the switch. The float, which contains an annular magnet, rises or falls with liquid level and is guided by the tube.

In the example shown, the switch is normally closed and will open when the float and magnet are at the same level as the reed switch. The switch opening can be used, for example, to sound an alarm or stop a pump. The switch can also be designed to close when activated by the magnet.

## EXERCISES

5.1 Find the force $F_2$, given the following specifications for the hydraulic press shown below:

   $A_1$ = 1.0 square inch
   $A_2$ = 10 square inches
   $F_1$ = 100 pounds

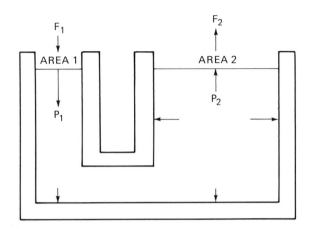

5.2 Find the absolute pressure corresponding to a pressure gage reading of 28 psig if the local barometric reading is 14.5 psi.

5.3 Find the absolute pressure if a vacuum gage reads 9.5 psig and the atmospheric pressure is 14.6 psia.

5.4 If a pressure applied to a water-filled manometer causes a water displacement of 20 inches, find the pressure in psi.

5.5 Find the displacement of liquid in a mercury manometer if a pressure of 10 psig is applied. The specific gravity of mercury is 13.619.

## BIBLIOGRAPHY

1. Murrill, P.W., *Fundamentals of Process Control Theory*, Instrument Society of America, 1981.

2. Kirk, F.W., and Rimboi, N.R., *Instrumentation*, American Technical Publishers, Inc. Third Edition, 1975.

3. Johnson, C.D., *Process Control Instrumentation Technology*, John Wiley & Sons, Second Edition, 1982.

4. Ogata, K., *Modern Control Engineering*, Prentice-Hall, Inc., 1970.

5. Weyrick, R.C., *Fundamentals of Automatic Control*, McGraw-Hill Book Company, 1975.

6. Liptak, B.G., and Kriszta, V., (ed.), *Process Control—Instrument Engineers' Handbook*, Chilton Book Company, Revised Edition, 1982.

# 6

# Temperature Measurements

**Introduction**  The purpose of this chapter is to explore the more common temperature-measuring techniques and transducers used in process control. The common temperature-measuring devices are filled-system thermometers, bimetallic thermometers, thermocouples, resistance temperature detectors (RTDs), thermistors, and integrated circuit (IC) temperature sensors. Each transducer type will be discussed in detail, but first we will cover the history of temperature measurement, temperature scales, and reference temperatures.

**Brief History of Temperature Measurement**  The first known temperature-measuring device was invented by Galileo in about 1592. It consisted of an open container filled with colored alcohol and a long narrow-throated glass tube with a hollow sphere at the upper end suspended in the alcohol. When it was heated, the air in the sphere expanded and bubbled through the liquid. Cooling the sphere caused the liquid to move up the tube. Changes in the temperature of the sphere and the surrounding area could then be observed by the position of the liquid inside the tube. This "upside-down" thermometer was a poor indicator since the level changed with atmospheric pressure and the tube had no scale. Some improvements were made in temperature measurement accuracy with the development of the Florentine thermometer, which had sealed construction and a graduated scale.

In the period that followed, many thermometric scales were designed, all based on two or more fixed points; however, no scale was universally recognized until the early 1700's when Gabriel Fahrenheit, a Dutch instrument maker, designed and made accurate and repeatable mercury thermometers. For the fixed point on the low end of his temperature scale, Fahrenheit used a mixture of ice water and salt. This was the lowest temperature he could reproduce, and he labeled it "zero degrees". The high end of his scale was more imaginative: he chose the body temperature of a healthy person and called it 96 degrees.

**131**

The upper temperature of 96 degrees was selected instead of 100 degrees because at the time it was the custom to divide things into twelve parts. Fahrenheit, with the apparent goal of obtaining more resolution, divided the scale into 24, then 48 and eventually 96 parts. It was later decided to use the symbol °F for degrees of temperature in the Fahrenheit scale, in honor of Fahrenheit. The Fahrenheit scale gained popularity primarily because of the repeatability and quality of the thermometers that Fahrenheit built.

Around 1742, Anders Celsius proposed that the melting point of ice and the boiling point of water be used for the two fixed temperature points. Celsius selected zero degrees as the boiling point and 100 degrees as the melting point. Later, the end points were reversed and the centigrade scale was born. In 1948, the name was officially changed to the Celsius scale and the symbol °C was chosen to represent degrees Celsius or centigrade of temperature.

## Temperature Scales

It has been experimentally determined that the lowest possible temperature is –273.15°C. The Kelvin Temperature Scale was chosen so that its zero is at –273.15, and the size of the kelvin was the same as the Celsius degree. Kelvin temperature is given by

$$T = T_c + 273.15°$$

Another scale, the Rankine scale (°R), defined in the same manner and simply the Fahrenheit equivalent of the Kelvin scale, was named after an early pioneer in the field of thermodynamics, W.J.M. Rankine.

The conversion equations for the four modern temperature scales are:

$$T°C = \frac{5}{9}(T°F - 32°) \qquad T°F = \frac{9}{5}T°C + 32°$$

$$T = T°C + 273.15° \qquad T°R = T°F + 459.67°$$

### EXAMPLE 6-1

**Problem:** Given a temperature of 125°C, express this temperature in (a) degrees °F and (b) kelvins.

**Solution:** (a) $\qquad T°F = \frac{9}{5}T°C + 32°$

$$T(°F) = \frac{9}{5}(125°C) + 32°$$

$$T = 257°F$$

(b) $\qquad T = T°C + 273.15°$

$$T = 125°C + 273.15°$$

$$T = 398.15 \text{ kelvins}$$

## Reference Temperatures
We cannot build a temperature divider as we can a voltage divider, nor can we add temperatures as we would add lengths to measure distance. We must rely upon temperatures established by physical phenomena that are easily observed and consistent in nature.

The International Practical Temperature Scale (IPTS) is based on such phenomena. Revised in 1968, it established the eleven reference temperatures listed in Table 6-1.

Since we have only these fixed temperatures to use as a reference, we must use instruments to interpolate between them, but accurately interpolating between these temperatures can require some fairly exotic transducers, many of which are too complicated or expensive to use in process control applications.

## Filled-System Thermometers
Many physical properties change with temperature. Among these are the volume of a liquid, the length of a metal rod, the electrical resistance of a wire, the pressure of a gas kept at constant volume, and the volume of a gas kept at constant pressure. Filled-system thermometers use the phenomenon of thermal expansion, either volumetric or linear.

The filled thermal device consists of a primary element in the form of a reservoir or bulb, a flexible capillary tube, and a hollow Bourdon tube that actuates a signal-transmitting device and/or a local indicating temperature dial. A typical filled-system thermometer is shown in Figure 6-1. In this system the filling fluid, either liquid or gas, expands as temperature increases and causes the Bourdon tube to uncoil and indicate the temperature on a calibrated dial.

The filling or transmitting medium is either a vapor, a gas, mercury, or another liquid. The liquid-filled system is the most common because it requires the smallest volume bulb or permits a smaller instrument.

**TABLE 6-1**
**IPTS-68 Reference Temperatures**

| Equilibrium Point | K | °C |
|---|---|---|
| Triple point of hydrogen | 13.81 | −259.34 |
| Liquid/vapor phase of hydrogen at std. atmosphere pressure | 17.042 | −256.108 |
| Boiling point of hydrogen | 20.28 | −252.87 |
| Boiling point of neon | 27.102 | −246.048 |
| Triple point of oxygen | 54.361 | −218.789 |
| Boiling point of oxygen | 90.188 | −182.962 |
| Triple point of water | 273.16 | 000.01 |
| Boiling point of water | 373.15 | 100.0 |
| Freezing point of zinc | 692.73 | 419.58 |
| Freezing point of silver | 1235.08 | 961.93 |
| Freezing point of gold | 1337.58 | 1064.43 |

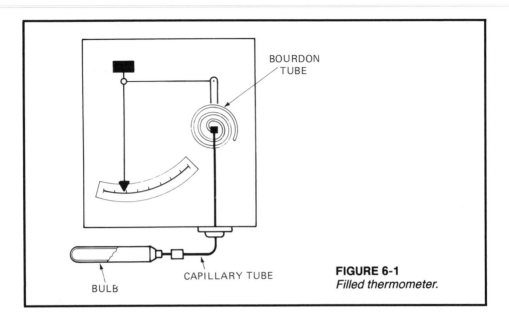

BOURDON TUBE

CAPILLARY TUBE

BULB

**FIGURE 6-1**
*Filled thermometer.*

The gas-filled system uses the perfect gas law, which states for an ideal gas:

$$T = kPV$$

where: T = temperature
k = constant
P = pressure
V = volume

If volume is constant and the gas is ideal, the pressure in the filled system is proportional to temperature. However, the system volume is not constant, since it varies with Bourdon tube deflection, and neither is the gas ideal. The two most nearly perfect gases, hydrogen and helium, tend to transpire through the metal parts in the system. Nitrogen is more widely used in gas-filled systems because it does not readily escape from the instrument. But it is not an ideal gas, so the instrument is not as accurate as a hydrogen- or helium-filled instrument.

## Bimetallic Thermometers

The bimetallic thermometer consists of two materials with grossly different thermal expansion coefficients bonded together as shown in Figure 6-2. It is a low cost thermometer but has the disadvantages of being relatively inaccurate, having hysteresis, and having a relatively slow response time. It is normally used only in ON/OFF control applications or control systems that do not require accurate or responsive control.

This transducer uses the change in size of material with temperature or thermal expansion. To understand thermal expansion, consider a simple model of a solid, where the atoms in the solid are held together in a regular array of forces of electrical origin. The forces between atoms are like the forces that would be ex-

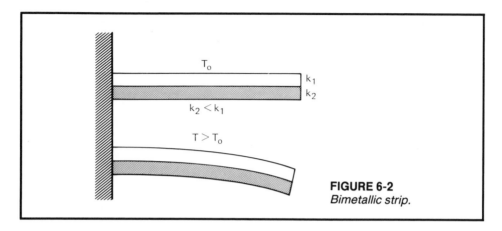

**FIGURE 6-2**
*Bimetallic strip.*

erted by an array of springs connecting the atoms together. At any temperature above absolute zero (−273.15°C), the atoms of the solid are vibrating. When the temperature is increased, the amplitude of the vibrations increases and the average distance between atoms increases. This leads to an expansion of the whole body as the temperature is increased. The change in any linear dimension of the solid is called a *linear* expansion. If the length of this linear dimension is l, the change in length, arising from a change in temperature $\Delta T$, can be designated by $\Delta l$. From experimentation, we find that the change in length ($\Delta l$) is proportional to the change in temperature ($\Delta T$) and the original length l. So, we can write

$$\Delta l = \kappa l\, \Delta T$$

where $\kappa$ is called the *coefficient of linear expansion.*

This coefficient has different values for different materials, and Table 6-2 lists the experimentally determined values for the average coefficient of linear expansion of several common solids in the temperature range of 0°C to 100°C.

A bimetallic strip will curve when exposed to a temperature change, as shown in Figure 6-2, because of the different thermal expansion coefficients of the metals. This effect can be used to close switch contacts, or to actuate an ON/OFF device when the temperature changes to some selected set point. The bimetallic strip is also used in dial thermometers.

**TABLE 6-2**
**Thermal Expansion Coefficients**

| Material | Expansion Coefficient ($\kappa$) |
| --- | --- |
| Aluminum | $25 \times 10^{-6}$/°C |
| Copper | $16.6 \times 10^{-6}$/°C |
| Steel | $6.7 \times 10^{-6}$/C |
| Beryllium/copper | $9.3 \times 10^{-6}$/°C |

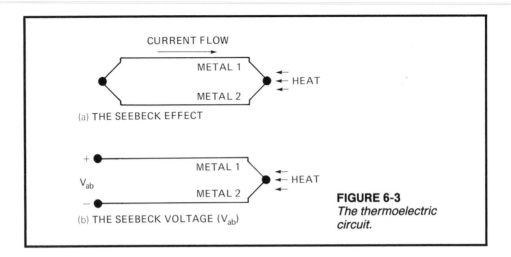

CURRENT FLOW

METAL 1

HEAT

METAL 2

(a) THE SEEBECK EFFECT

+

$V_{ab}$

METAL 1

HEAT

METAL 2

−

(b) THE SEEBECK VOLTAGE ($V_{ab}$)

**FIGURE 6-3**
*The thermoelectric circuit.*

## Thermocouples

**Thermoelectric Circuit**   When two wires composed of dissimilar metals are joined at both ends and one of the ends is heated, a continuous current flows in the "thermoelectric" circuit. Thomas Seebeck made this discovery in 1821. This circuit is shown is Figure 6-3(a).

If this circuit is broken at the center, as shown in Figure 6-3(b), the net open circuit voltage (the Seebeck voltage) is a function of the junction temperature and the composition of the two metals.

All dissimilar metals exhibit this effect, and this configuration of two dissimilar metals joined together is called a *thermocouple* or TC. The most common TC's and their normal temperature ranges are listed in Table 6-3.

For small changes in temperature, the Seebeck voltage is linearly proportional to temperature:

$$V_{ab} = \alpha \, (T_1 - T_2)$$

where $\alpha$, the Seebeck coefficient, is the constant of proportionality.

**TABLE 6-3**
**Standard Thermocouple Types and Ranges**

| Type | Materials | Normal Range |
|------|-----------|--------------|
| J | Iron-constantan | −190°C to 760°C |
| T | Copper-constantan | −200°C to 371°C |
| K | Chromel-alumel | −190°C to 1260°C |
| E | Chromel-constantan | −100°C to 1260°C |
| S | 90% platinum + 10% rhodium-platinum | 0°C to 1482°C |
| R | 87% platinum + 13% rhodium-platinum | 0°C to 1482°C |

**EXAMPLE 6-2**

**Problem:** Find the Seebeck voltage for a thermocouple with $\alpha = 40\,\mu V/°C$ if the junction temperatures are 40°C and 80°C.

**Solution:** The Seebeck voltage can be found as follows:

$$V_{ab} = \alpha(T_1 - T_2)$$
$$V_{ab} = (40\,\mu V/°C)(80°C - 40°C) = 1.6\,mV$$

**Thermocouple Tables**   To take advantage of the voltage produced by thermocouples, comprehensive tables of voltage versus temperature have been determined for many types of thermocouples, as shown in Appendix A at the end of this chapter.

The tables give the voltage that results for a particular type of thermocouple when the reference junctions are at 0°C, and the measurement junction is at a given temperature. For example, we see that for a type K thermocouple at 200°C with a 0°C reference the voltage produced is:

$$V(200°C) = 8.13\,mV \qquad (type\ K,\ 0°C)$$

Conversely, if we measure a voltage of 29.14 mV with a type K thermocouple and a 0°C reference, we find from the K TC table that

$$T(29.14\,mV) = 700°C \qquad (type\ K,\ 0°C)$$

However, in most cases the TC voltage does not fall exactly on a table value as in the case above. When this happens, it is necessary to interpolate between table values that bracket the desired value. An approximate value of temperature can be found using the following interpolation equation:

$$T_m = T_l + \left[\ \frac{T_h - T_l}{V_h - V_l}\ \right](V_m - V_l)$$

In this equation, the measured voltage $V_m$ lies between a higher voltage $V_h$ and lower voltage $V_l$, which are in the tables. The temperatures corresponding to these voltages are $T_h$ and $T_l$, respectively. An example problem will help to explain this concept.

**EXAMPLE 6-3**

**Problem:** A voltage of 6.22 mV is measured with a type J TC at a 0°C reference. Find the temperature of the measurement junction.

**Solution:** From the table we see that $V_m = 6.22\,mV$ lies between $V_l = 6.08\,mV$ and $V_h = 6.36\,mV$, with corresponding temperatures of $T_l = 115°C$ and $T_h = 120°C$, respectively. Therefore, the junction temperature is found as follows:

$$T_m = 115°C + \frac{(120°C - 115°C)}{(6.36 \text{ mV} - 6.08 \text{ mV})} (6.22 \text{ mV} - 6.08 \text{ mV})$$

$$T_m = 115°C + \frac{5°C}{0.28 \text{ mV}} 0.14 \text{ mV}$$

$$T_m = 117.5°C$$

**Measuring Thermocouple Voltage**  We cannot measure the Seebeck voltage directly because we must first connect a voltmeter to the thermocouple, and the voltmeter leads themselves create a new thermoelectric circuit.

Let us connect a digital voltmeter (DVM) across a copper-constantan (type T) thermocouple and look at the voltage output as shown in Figure 6-4.

We would like the voltmeter to read only $V_1$, but by connecting the voltmeter in an attempt to measure the output of junction J1, we have created two more metallic junctions: J2 and J3. Since J3 is a copper-to-copper junction, it creates no thermal voltage ($V_3 = 0$); but J2 is a copper-to-constantan junction, which will add a voltage ($V_2$) in opposition to $V_1$. The resultant voltmeter reading V will be proportional to the temperature difference between J1 and J2. This indicates that we cannot find the temperature at J1 unless we first find the temperature of J2.

One way to determine the temperature of J2 is to physically put the junction into an ice bath, forcing its temperature to be 0°C and establishing J2 as the "reference junction," shown in Figure 6-5. Since both voltmeter terminal junctions are now copper-copper, they create no thermal voltage, and the reading "V" on the voltmeter is proportional to the temperature difference between J1 and J2.

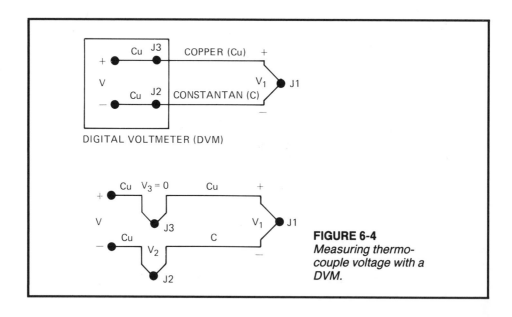

**FIGURE 6-4**
*Measuring thermo-couple voltage with a DVM.*

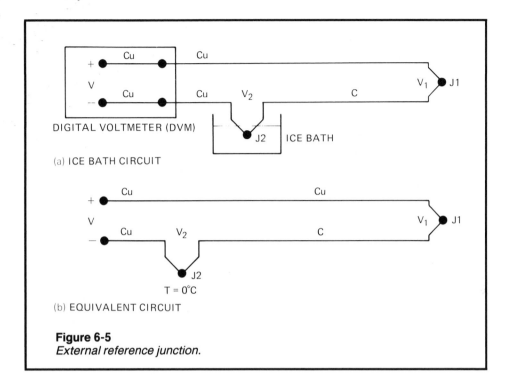

(a) ICE BATH CIRCUIT

(b) EQUIVALENT CIRCUIT

**Figure 6-5**
*External reference junction.*

Now the voltmeter reading is:

$$V = (V_1 - V_2) \cong \alpha\,(T_{J1} - T_{J2})$$

If we specify $T_{J1}$ in degrees Celsius:

$$T_{J1}\,(^\circ C) + 273.15 = T_{J1}\,(\text{kelvins})$$

then V becomes:

$$V = V_1 - V_2$$
$$V = \alpha\,(T_{J1} + 273.15) - (T_{J2} + 273.15)$$
$$V = \alpha\,(T_{J1} - T_{J2})$$
$$V = \alpha\,(T_{J1} - 0)$$
$$V = \alpha\,T_{J1}$$

We used this involved discussion to emphasize that the ice bath junction output, $V_2$, is not zero volts; it is a function of absolute temperature.

By adding the voltage of the ice point reference junction, we have now referenced the TC voltage reading (V) to 0°C. This method is very accurate because the ice point temperature can be precisely controlled. The ice point is used by the National Bureau of Standards (NBS) as the fundamental reference point for their thermocouple tables, so we can now look at the thermocouple tables in Appendix A and directly convert from voltage V to temperature.

The copper-constantan thermocouple shown in Figure 6-5 is a unique example because the copper wire is the same metal as the voltmeter terminals. Let us use an iron-constantan thermocouple (type J) instead of the copper-constantan (Figure 6-6). The iron wire increases the number of dissimilar metal junctions in the circuit, as both voltmeter terminals become Cu-Fe thermocouple junctions.

This circuit will still provide moderately accurate measurements as long as the voltmeter (+) and (–) terminals (J3 and J4) are at the same temperature, because the thermoelectric effects of J3 and J4 act in opposition:

$$V_1 = V$$

if                                    $$V_3 = V_4$$

i.e., if                              $$T_{J3} = T_{J4}$$

If both front panel terminals are not at the same temperature, there will be an error. For a more precise measurement, the copper voltmeter leads should be extended so the copper-to-iron junctions are made on an "isothermal" (same temperature) block as shown in Figure 6-7.

The isothermal block is not only a good electrical insulator but a good heat conductor, and this helps hold J3 and J4 at the same temperature. The absolute block temperature is unimportant because the two Cu-Fe junctions act in opposition. We still have

$$V = \alpha (T_1 - T_{ref})$$

The circuit in Figure 6-7 will give us accurate readings, but it would be nice to eliminate the ice bath, if possible. One way to do this is to replace the ice bath with another isothermal block, as shown in Figure 6-8.

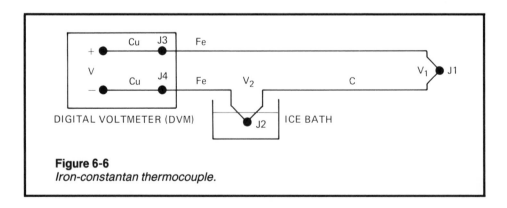

**Figure 6-6**
*Iron-constantan thermocouple.*

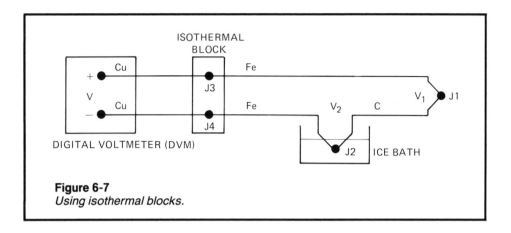

**Figure 6-7**
*Using isothermal blocks.*

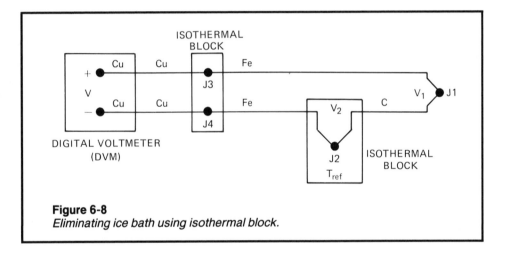

**Figure 6-8**
*Eliminating ice bath using isothermal block.*

The new block is at reference temperature $T_{ref}$, and because J3 and J4 are still at the same temperature, we can again show that

$$V = \alpha \, (T_{J1} - T_{ref})$$

This is still a complicated circuit, because we have to connect two thermocouples. Let us eliminate the extra Fe wire in the negative (−) lead by combining the Cu-Fe junction (J4) and the Fe-C junction ($J_{ref}$).

We can do this by first joining the two isothermal blocks (Figure 6-9).

We have not changed the output voltage V. It is still

$$V = \alpha \, (T_{J1} - T_{Jref})$$

Now we call upon the law of intermediate metals to eliminate the extra junction. This empirical "law" states that a third metal (in this case, iron) inserted be-

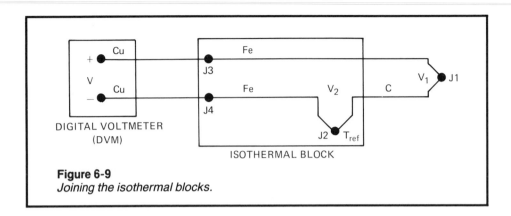

**Figure 6-9**
*Joining the isothermal blocks.*

tween the two dissimilar metals of a thermocouple junction will have no effect upon the output voltage as long as the two junctions formed by the additional metal are at the same temperature (see Figure 6-10).

This is a useful conclusion, as it completely eliminates the need for the iron (Fe) wire in the negative lead. This can be seen in Figure 6-11, where again, $V = \alpha$ $(T_{J1} - T_{ref})$, where $\alpha$ is the Seebeck coefficient for an Fe-C thermocouple.

Junctions J3 and J4 take the place of the ice bath. These two junctions now become the "reference junction".

Now we can proceed to the next logical step: Directly measure the temperature of the isothermal block (the reference junction) and use that information to compute the unknown temperature, $T_{J1}$.

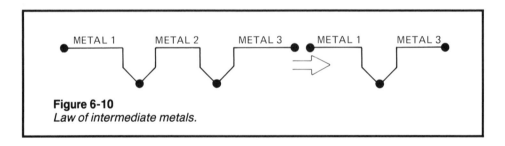

**Figure 6-10**
*Law of intermediate metals.*

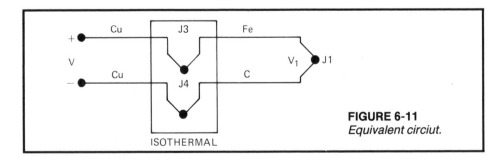

**FIGURE 6-11**
*Equivalent circiut.*

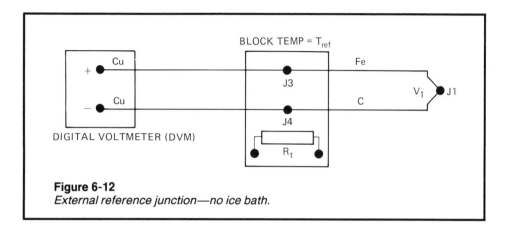

**Figure 6-12**
*External reference junction—no ice bath.*

A thermistor, whose resistance $R_t$ is a function of temperature, provides us with a way to measure the absolute temperature of the reference junction (see Figure 6-12). Junctions J3 and J4 and the thermistor are all assumed to be at the same temperature, due to the design of the isothermal block. Using a digital voltmeter under computer control, we simply:

1. Measure $R_t$ to find $T_{ref}$ and convert $T_{ref}$ to its equivalent reference junction voltage, $V_{ref}$.

2. Measure V and subtract $V_{ref}$ to find $V_1$, and convert $V_1$ to temperature $T_{J1}$.

This procedure is known as "software compensation" because it relies upon the software of a computer to compensate for the effect of the reference junction. The isothermal terminal block temperature sensor can be any device that has a characteristic proportional to absolute temperature: an RTD, a thermistor, or an integrated circuit sensor.

The logical question is, "If we already have a device that will measure absolute temperature (such as an RTD or thermistor), why do we even bother with a thermocouple that requires reference junction compensation?" The single most important answer to this question is that the thermistor, the RTD, and the integrated circuit transducer are useful only over a limited temperature range. Thermocouples, on the other hand, can be used over a wide range of temperatures and are much more rugged than thermistors, as evidenced by the fact that thermocouples are often welded to metal process equipment or clamped under a screw. They can be manufactured easily, either by soldering or welding. In short, thermocouples are the most versatile temperature transducers available. Furthermore, a computer-based temperature monitoring system can perform the entire task of reference compensation and software voltage-to-temperature conversion, so using a thermocouple in process control becomes as easy as connecting a pair of wires. The one disadvantage is that the computer requires a small amount of additional time to calculate the reference junction temperature, and this introduces *dead time* into a control loop.

## Resistance Temperature Detector (RTD)

**Introduction**   In principle, any material whose electrical resistance changes in a significant and repeatable manner when the surrounding temperature changes could be used to measure temperature. In practice, only certain metals and semiconductors are used in process control to measure temperature. In this section, we will discuss resistance thermometers with metallic sensing elements. These instruments are usually called resistance temperature detectors or RTDs. Resistance thermometers that use semiconductor elements are called thermistors and are discussed later.

**History of the RTD**   The same year that Seebeck made his discovery about thermoelectricity, Sir Humphrey Davy announced that the resistivity of metals showed a marked temperature dependence. Fifty years later, Sir William Siemens offered the use of platinum as the element in a resistance thermometer. His choice proved most correct, as platinum is used to this day as the primary element in all high-accuracy resistance thermometers. In fact, the platinum resistance temperature detector, or PRTD, is used today as an interpolation standard from the oxygen point (–182.96°C) to the antimony point (630.74°C).

Platinum is especially suited to this purpose because it can withstand high temperatures while maintaining excellent stability. As a noble metal, it shows limited susceptibility to contamination.

The classical resistance temperature detector (RTD) construction using platinum was proposed by C.H. Meyers in 1932. He wound a helical coil of platinum on a crossed mica web and mounted the assembly inside a glass tube as shown in Figure 6-13. This construction minimized strain on the wire while maximizing resistance. Although this construction produces a very stable element, the thermal contact between the platinum and the measured point is quite poor. This results in a slow thermal response time. The fragility of the structure limits its use today primarily to that of a laboratory standard.

In a more rugged construction technique, the platinum wire is wound on a glass or ceramic bobbin, as illustrated in Figure 6-14. The winding reduces the effective enclosed area of the coil to minimize a magnetic pickup and its related noise. Once the wire is wound onto the bobbin, the assembly is then sealed with a coating of molten glass. The sealing process assures that the RTD will maintain its integrity under extreme vibration, but it also limits the expansion of the platinum metal at high temperatures. Unless the coefficients of expansion of the platinum and the bobbin match perfectly, stress will be placed on the wire as the temperature changes, resulting in a strain-induced resistance change. This may result in a permanent change in the resistance of the wire.

**Metal Film RTDs**   In the newest construction technique, a platinum or metal-glass slurry film is deposited or screened onto a small flat ceramic substrate, etched with a laser-trimming system, and sealed (see Figure 6-15). The film RTD offers substantial reduction in assembly time and has the further advantage of increased resistance for a given size. Due to the manufacturing technology, the device size itself is small, which means it can respond quickly to step changes in

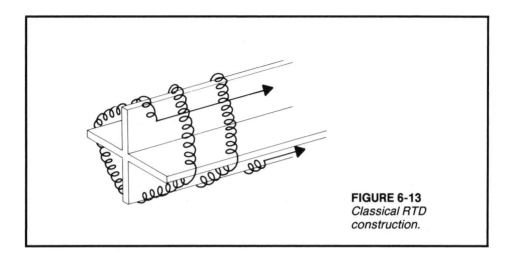

**FIGURE 6-13**
*Classical RTD
construction.*

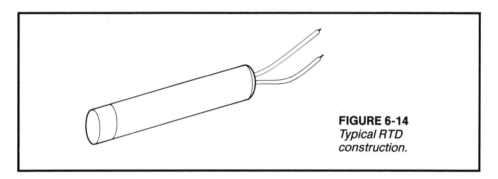

**FIGURE 6-14**
*Typical RTD
construction.*

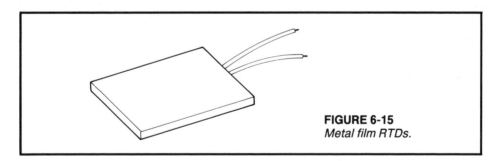

**FIGURE 6-15**
*Metal film RTDs.*

temperature. Film RTDs are presently less stable than their hand-made counter-parts, but they are becoming more popular because of their decided advantages in size and production cost.

**Resistance Measurement**    The common values of resistance for a platinum RTD range from 10 Ω for the bird-cage model to several thousand ohms for the film RTD. The single most common value is 100 Ω at 0°C, (see Figure 6-16). The standard temperature coefficient of platinum wire is $\alpha = 0.00385$ $\Omega/°C$. For a 100-ohm wire this corresponds to +0.385 $\Omega/°C$ at 0°C. This value for $\alpha$ is actually the average slope from 0°C to 100°C.

The more chemically pure platinum wire used in platinum resistance standards has an $\alpha$ of +0.392 ohms/°C.

Both the slope and the absolute value are small numbers, especially when we consider the fact that the measurement wires leading to the sensor may be several ohms or even tens of ohms. A small lead impedance can contribute a significant error to output temperature measurement.

A 10-$\Omega$ lead impedance implies $10/0.385 \cong 26°C$ error in our measurement. Even the temperature coefficient of the lead wire can contribute a measurable error. The standard method for avoiding this problem has been the use of a Wheatstone bridge circuit (see Figure 6-17). Refer to Chapter 3 for a detailed explanation of this circuit.

The bridge output voltage is an indirect indication of the RTD resistance. The bridge requires four connection wires, an external source, and three resistors that have a zero temperature coefficient. To avoid subjecting the three bridge resistors to the same temperature as the RTD, the RTD is separated from the bridge by a pair of extension wires as shown in Figure 6-18.

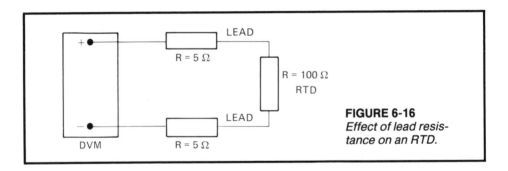

**FIGURE 6-16**
*Effect of lead resistance on an RTD.*

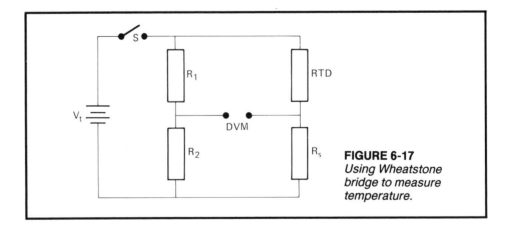

**FIGURE 6-17**
*Using Wheatstone bridge to measure temperature.*

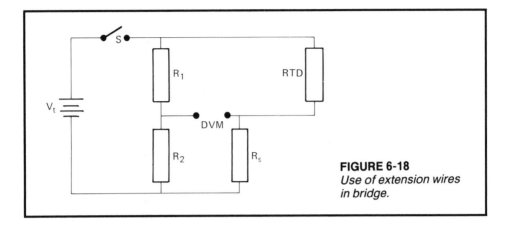

**FIGURE 6-18**
*Use of extension wires
in bridge.*

These extension wires recreate the problem that we had initially: the impedance of the extension wires affects the temperature reading. This effect can be minimized by using a "three-wire bridge" configuration as shown in Figure 6-19.

If wires A and B are perfectly matched in length, their impedance effects will cancel because each is in an opposite leg of the bridge. Third wire C acts as a sense lead and carries no current.

The Wheatstone bridge shown in Figure 6-19 creates a nonlinear relationship between resistance change and bridge output voltage change. This compounds the already nonlinear temperature resistance characteristic of the RTD by requiring an additional equation to convert bridge output voltage to equivalent RTD impedance.

**Four-Wire Resistance Measurement**   The technique of using a current source along with a remotely located digital voltmeter (DVM), as shown in Figure 6-20, corrects many problems associated with the bridge. The output voltage read by the DVM is directly proportional to RTD resistance, so only one conversion

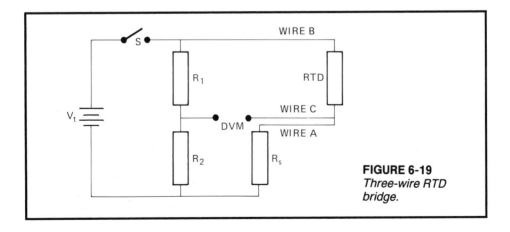

**FIGURE 6-19**
*Three-wire RTD
bridge.*

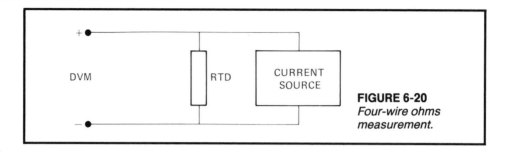

**FIGURE 6-20**
*Four-wire ohms measurement.*

equation is necessary. The three bridge resistors are replaced by one reference resistor. The digital voltmeter measures only the voltage dropped across the RTD and is insensitive to the length of the lead wires.

The one disadvantage of using a 4-wire system is that we need one more extension wire than the 3-wire bridge. This is a small price to pay if we are at all concerned with the accuracy of the temperature measurement.

**Resistance to Temperature Conversion**   The RTD is a more linear device than the thermocouple, but it still requires curve-fitting. The Callendar-Van Dusen equation has been used for years to approximate the plantium RTD curve:

$$R = R_0 + R_0\, \alpha \left[ T - \delta\, (\, \frac{T}{100} - 1)(\, \frac{T}{100}\, ) - \beta\, (\, \frac{T}{100} - 1)(\, \frac{T^3}{100}\, ) \right]$$

where:   $R$   =   resistance at temperature T
$R_0$   =   resistance at T = 0°C
$\alpha$   =   constant
$\delta$   =   constant
$\beta$   =   0 if T > 0 or B = 0.1 (typical) if T < 0

The exact values for coefficients $\alpha$, $\beta$, and $\delta$ are determined by testing the RTD at four temperatures and solving the resultant equations.

Typical values for platinum RTDs are:

$$\alpha = 0.00392$$
$$\delta = 1.49$$
$$\beta = 0 \text{ for } T > 0°C \text{ and } 0.1 \text{ for } T < 0°C$$

**EXAMPLE 6-4**

**Problem:** Calculate the resistance ratio for a platinum RTD with $\alpha$ = 0.00392 and $\delta$ = 1.49 when T = 100°C.

**Solution:** Since T is greater than 0°C, $\beta$ = 0, so that the Callendar-Van Dusen equation reduces to

$$R\; = R_0 + R_0\, \alpha \left[ T - \delta\, (\, \frac{T}{100} - 1)(\, \frac{T}{100}\, ) \right]$$

$$\frac{R}{R_0} = 1 + 0.00392 \left[ 100 - 1.49 \left( \frac{100}{100} - 1 \right) \left( \frac{100}{100} \right) \right]$$

$$\frac{R}{R_0} = 1.392$$

## The Thermistor

Like the RTD, the thermistor is also a temperature-sensitive resistor. While the thermocouple is the most versatile temperature transducer and the RTD is the most stable, the word that best describes the thermistor is "sensitive". Of the three major categories of sensors, the thermistor exhibits by far the largest parameter change with temperature.

Thermistors are generally composed of semiconductor materials. Although positive temperature coefficient units are available, most thermistors have a negative temperature coefficient (TC); that is, their resistance decreases with increasing temperature. The negative temperature coefficient can be as large as several percent per degree Celsius, allowing the thermistor circuit to detect minute changes in temperature that could not be observed with an RTD or thermocouple circuit.

The price we pay for this increased sensitivity is loss of linearity, as shown by curves in Figure 6-21. The thermistor is an extremely nonlinear device that is highly dependent upon process parameters. Consequently, manufacturers have not standardized thermistor curves to the extent that RTD and thermocouple curves have been standardized.

An individual thermistor curve can be very closely approximated using the Steinhart-Hart equation:

$$\frac{1}{T} = A + B \ln R + C(\ln R)^3$$

where:  $T$  = kelvins
  $R$  = resistance of the thermistor
  $A,B,C$  = curve-fitting constants

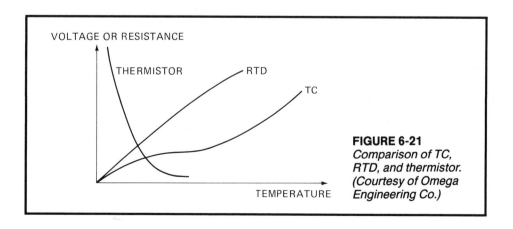

**FIGURE 6-21**
*Comparison of TC, RTD, and thermistor. (Courtesy of Omega Engineering Co.)*

A, B, and C are found by selecting three data points on the published data curve and solving the three simultaneous equations. When the data points are chosen to span no more than 100°C within the nominal center of the thermistor's temperature range, this equation approaches a rather remarkable +0.01°C curve fit.

### EXAMPLE 6-5

**Problem:** A typical thermistor has the following coefficients for the Steinhart and Hart equation:

$$A = 1.1252 \times 10^{-3}/K$$
$$B = 2.3478 \times 10^{-4}/K$$
$$C = 8.5262 \times 10^{-8}/K$$

Calculate the temperature when the resistance is 4000 Ω.

**Solution:**

$$\frac{1}{T} = A + B \ln R + C(\ln R)^3$$

$$\frac{1}{T} = 1.1252 \times 10^{-3} + 2.3478 \times 10^{-4} (\ln 4000) + 8.5262 \times 10^{-8} (\ln 4000)^3$$

$$\frac{1}{T} = 1.1252 \times 10^{-3} + 1.9471 \times 10^{-3} + 0.0486 \times 10^{-3}$$

$$\frac{1}{T} = 3.1209 \times 10^{-3}/K$$

$$T = 47.25°C$$

A great deal of effort has gone into the development of thermistors that approach a linear characteristic. These are typically 3- or 4-lead devices requiring external matching resistors to linearize the characteristic curve. The modern data acquisition system with built-in microcomputer has made this kind of hardware linearization unnecessary.

The high resistivity of the thermistor affords it a distinct measurement advantage. The four-wire resistance measurement is not required as it is with RTDs. For example: a common thermistor value is 5000 Ω at 25°C. With a typical temperature coefficient of 4%/°C, a measurement lead resistance of 10 Ω produces only a 0.05°C error. This is a factor of 500 times less than the equivalent RTD error.

Because they are semiconductors, thermistors are more susceptible to permanent decalibration at high temperatures than are RTDs or thermocouples. The use of thermistors is generally limited to a few hundred degrees Celsius, and manufacturers warn that extended exposures, even well below maximum operating limits, will cause the thermistor to drift out of its specified tolerance.

Thermistors can be made very small, which means they will respond quickly to temperature changes. It also means that their small thermal mass makes them

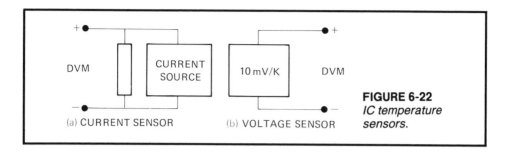

**FIGURE 6-22**
*IC temperature
sensors.*

(a) CURRENT SENSOR          (b) VOLTAGE SENSOR

especially susceptible to self-heating errors. Thermistors are a good deal more fragile than RTDs or thermocouples, and they must be carefully mounted to avoid crushing or bond separation.

## Integrated Circuit (IC) Temperature Sensor     A recent innovation in thermometry is the integrated circuit temperature transducer. These are available in both voltage and current-output configurations (see Figure 6-22). Both supply an output that is linearly proportional to absolute temperature. Typical values are 1 µA/K and 10 mV/K.

Except for the fact that they offer a very linear output with temperature, these devices share all the disadvantages of thermistors. They are semiconductor devices and, thus, have a limited temperature range. The same problems of self-heating and fragility are present, and they require an external power source.

IC temperature sensors are normally used in on/off or alarm point control applications. For example, they are used in electronic or electrical equipment cabinets to detect an over-temperature condition.

### EXERCISES

6.1  List the normal operating ranges of the following TC types: J, K, and S.

6.2  Given a temperature of 133°C, express this temperature in °F and kelvins.

6.3  Given a temperature of 400 °F, express this temperature in °C and kelvins.

6.4  Find the Seebeck voltage for a TC with $\alpha = 36$ µV/°C, if the junction temperatures are 25°C and 27°C.

6.5  Find the Seebeck voltage for a TC with $\alpha = 32$ µV/°C, if the junction temperatures are 20°C and 30°C.

6.6  A voltage of 10.10 mV is measured across a type K thermocouple at a °C reference. Find the temperature at the measurement junction.

6.7  A voltage of 19.50 mV is measured across a type J thermocouple at a °C reference. Find the temperature at the measurement junction.

6.8  Draw a graph of the type J TC with junction voltage in mV on the horizontal axis and temperature in °C on the vertical axis, using the temperature at every 50°C, starting at 0°C and ending at 700°C.

6.9  Draw a graph of the type K TC with junction voltage in mV on the horizontal axis and temperature in °C on the vertical axis, using the temperature at every 25°C, starting at 0°C and ending at 1000°C.

6.10  Explain the purpose and function of the isothermal blocks in a digital voltmeter temperature-measuring circuit.

6.11  Explain the Law of Intermediate Metals and demonstrate its use in temperature-monitoring circuits.

6.12  Calculate the resistance ratio for a platinum RTD with $\alpha = 0.00392$ and $\delta = 1.49$ when $T = 80°C$.

6.13  A typical thermistor has the following coefficients for the Steinhart and Hart equation:

$$A = 1.1252 \times 10^{-3}/K$$
$$B = 2.3478 \times 10^{-4}/K$$
$$C = 8.5262 \times 10^{-8}/K$$

Calculate the temperature when the resistance is 4000 $\Omega$.

# APPENDIX A

# Thermocouple Tables

The thermocouple tables below give the output voltage in millivolts (mV) over a range of temperatures in degrees centigrade (°C) for several different types of TCs. The first material listed is the positive terminal when the temperature measured is higher than the reference temperature.

**Type J: Iron-Constantan**

| C° | 0 | 5 | 10 | 15 | 20 | 25 | 30 | 35 | 40 | 45 |
|----|------|------|------|------|------|------|------|------|------|------|
| −150 | −6.50 | −6.66 | −6.82 | −6.97 | −7.12 | −7.27 | −7.40 | −7.54 | −7.66 | −7.78 |
| −100 | −4.63 | −4.83 | −5.03 | −5.23 | −5.42 | −5.61 | −5.80 | −5.98 | −6.16 | −6.33 |
| − 50 | −2.43 | −2.66 | −2.89 | −3.12 | −3.34 | −3.56 | −3.78 | −4.00 | −4.21 | −4.42 |
| − 0 | 0.00 | −0.25 | −0.50 | −0.75 | −1.00 | −1.24 | −1.48 | −1.72 | −1.96 | −2.20 |
| + 0 | 0.00 | 0.25 | 0.50 | 0.76 | 1.02 | 1.28 | 1.54 | 1.80 | 2.06 | 2.32 |
| 50 | 2.58 | 2.85 | 3.11 | 3.38 | 3.65 | 3.92 | 4.19 | 4.46 | 4.73 | 5.00 |
| 100 | 5.27 | 5.54 | 5.81 | 6.08 | 6.36 | 6.63 | 6.90 | 7.18 | 7.45 | 7.73 |
| 150 | 8.00 | 8.28 | 8.56 | 8.84 | 9.11 | 9.39 | 9.67 | 9.95 | 10.22 | 10.50 |
| 200 | 10.78 | 11.06 | 11.34 | 11.62 | 11.89 | 12.17 | 12.45 | 12.73 | 13.01 | 13.28 |
| 250 | 13.56 | 13.84 | 14.12 | 14.39 | 14.67 | 14.94 | 15.22 | 15.50 | 15.77 | 16.05 |
| 300 | 16.33 | 16.60 | 16.88 | 17.15 | 17.43 | 17.71 | 17.98 | 18.26 | 18.54 | 18.81 |
| 350 | 19.09 | 19.37 | 19.64 | 19.92 | 20.20 | 20.47 | 20.75 | 21.02 | 21.30 | 21.57 |
| 400 | 21.85 | 22.13 | 22.40 | 22.68 | 22.95 | 23.23 | 23.50 | 23.78 | 24.06 | 24.33 |
| 450 | 24.61 | 24.88 | 25.16 | 25.44 | 25.72 | 25.99 | 26.27 | 26.55 | 26.83 | 27.11 |
| 500 | 27.39 | 27.67 | 27.95 | 28.23 | 28.52 | 28.80 | 29.08 | 29.37 | 29.65 | 29.94 |
| 550 | 30.22 | 30.51 | 30.80 | 31.08 | 31.37 | 31.66 | 31.95 | 32.24 | 32.53 | 32.82 |
| 600 | 33.11 | 33.41 | 33.70 | 33.99 | 34.29 | 34.58 | 34.88 | 35.18 | 35.48 | 35.78 |
| 650 | 36.08 | 36.38 | 36.69 | 36.99 | 37.30 | 37.60 | 37.91 | 38.22 | 38.53 | 38.84 |
| 700 | 39.15 | 39.47 | 39.78 | 40.10 | 40.41 | 40.73 | 41.05 | 41.36 | 41.68 | 42.00 |

Thermocouple Tables from Reference 1.

**Type T: Copper-Constantan**

| C° | 0 | 5 | 10 | 15 | 20 | 25 | 30 | 35 | 40 | 45 |
|---|---|---|---|---|---|---|---|---|---|---|
| −150 | −4.60 | −4.71 | −4.82 | −4.92 | −5.02 | −5.11 | −5.21 | −5.29 | −5.38 | |
| −100 | −3.35 | −3.49 | −3.62 | −3.76 | −3.89 | −4.01 | −4.14 | −4.26 | −4.38 | −4.49 |
| − 50 | −1.80 | −1.97 | −2.14 | −2.30 | −2.46 | −2.61 | −2.76 | −2.91 | −3.06 | −3.21 |
| − 0 | 0.00 | −0.19 | −0.38 | −0.57 | −0.75 | −0.93 | −1.11 | −1.29 | −1.46 | −1.64 |
| + 0 | 0.000 | 0.193 | 0.389 | 0.587 | 0.787 | 0.990 | 1.194 | 1.401 | 1.610 | 1.821 |
| 50 | 2.035 | 2.250 | 2.467 | 2.687 | 2.908 | 3.132 | 3.357 | 3.584 | 3.813 | 4.044 |
| 100 | 4.277 | 4.512 | 4.749 | 4.987 | 5.227 | 5.469 | 5.712 | 5.957 | 6.204 | 6.453 |
| 150 | 6.703 | 6.954 | 7.208 | 7.462 | 7.719 | 7.987 | 8.236 | 8.497 | 8.759 | 9.023 |
| 200 | 9.288 | 9.555 | 9.823 | 10.09 | 10.36 | 10.64 | 10.91 | 11.18 | 11.46 | 11.74 |
| 250 | 12.02 | 12.29 | 12.58 | 12.86 | 13.14 | 13.43 | 13.71 | 14.00 | 14.29 | 14.57 |
| 300 | 14.86 | 15.16 | 15.45 | 15.74 | 16.04 | 16.33 | 16.63 | 16.93 | 17.22 | 17.52 |
| 395 | 17.82 | 18.12 | 18.43 | 18.73 | 19.03 | 19.34 | 19.64 | 19.95 | 20.26 | 20.57 |

**Type S: Platinum-Platinum/10% Rhodium**

| C° | 0 | 5 | 10 | 15 | 20 | 25 | 30 | 35 | 40 | 45 |
|---|---|---|---|---|---|---|---|---|---|---|
| + 0 | 0.000 | 0.028 | 0.056 | 0.084 | 0.113 | 0.143 | 0.173 | 0.204 | 0.235 | 0.266 |
| 50 | 0.299 | 0.331 | 0.364 | 0.397 | 0.431 | 0.466 | 0.500 | 0.535 | 0.571 | 0.607 |
| 100 | 0.643 | 0.680 | 0.717 | 0.754 | 0.792 | 0.830 | 0.869 | 0.907 | 0.946 | 0.986 |
| 150 | 1.025 | 1.065 | 1.166 | 1.146 | 1.187 | 1.228 | 1.269 | 1.311 | 1.352 | 1.394 |
| 200 | 1.436 | 1.479 | 1.521 | 1.564 | 1.607 | 1.650 | 1.693 | 1.736 | 1.780 | 1.824 |
| 250 | 1.868 | 1.912 | 1.956 | 2.001 | 2.045 | 2.090 | 2.135 | 2.180 | 2.225 | 2.271 |
| 300 | 2.316 | 2.362 | 2.408 | 2.453 | 2.499 | 2.546 | 2.592 | 2.638 | 2.685 | 2.731 |
| 350 | 2.778 | 2.825 | 2.872 | 2.919 | 2.966 | 3.014 | 3.061 | 3.108 | 3.156 | 3.203 |
| 400 | 3.251 | 3.299 | 3.347 | 3.394 | 3.442 | 3.490 | 3.539 | 3.587 | 3.635 | 3.683 |
| 450 | 3.732 | 3.780 | 3.829 | 3.878 | 3.926 | 3.975 | 4.024 | 4.073 | 4.122 | 4.171 |
| 500 | 4.221 | 4.270 | 4.319 | 4.369 | 4.419 | 4.468 | 4.518 | 4.568 | 4.618 | 4.668 |
| 550 | 4.718 | 4.768 | 4.818 | 4.869 | 4.919 | 4.970 | 5.020 | 5.071 | 5.122 | 5.173 |
| 600 | 5.224 | 5.275 | 5.326 | 5.377 | 5.429 | 5.480 | 5.532 | 5.583 | 5.635 | 5.686 |
| 650 | 5.738 | 5.790 | 5.842 | 5.894 | 5.946 | 5.998 | 6.050 | 6.102 | 6.155 | 6.207 |
| 700 | 6.260 | 6.312 | 6.365 | 6.418 | 6.471 | 6.524 | 6.577 | 6.630 | 6.683 | 6.737 |
| 750 | 6.790 | 6.844 | 6.897 | 6.951 | 7.005 | 7.058 | 7.112 | 7.166 | 7.220 | 7.275 |
| 800 | 7.329 | 7.383 | 7.438 | 7.492 | 7.547 | 7.602 | 7.656 | 7.711 | 7.766 | 7.821 |
| 850 | 7.876 | 7.932 | 7.987 | 8.042 | 8.098 | 8.153 | 8.209 | 8.265 | 8.320 | 8.376 |
| 900 | 8.432 | 8.488 | 8.545 | 8.601 | 8.657 | 8.714 | 8.770 | 8.827 | 8.883 | 8.940 |
| 950 | 8.997 | 9.054 | 9.111 | 9.168 | 9.225 | 9.282 | 9.340 | 9.397 | 9.455 | 9.512 |
| 1000 | 9.570 | 9.628 | 9.686 | 9.744 | 9.802 | 9.860 | 9.918 | 9.976 | 10.04 | 10.09 |
| 1050 | 10.15 | 10.21 | 10.27 | 10.33 | 10.39 | 10.45 | 10.51 | 10.56 | 10.62 | 10.68 |
| 1100 | 10.74 | 10.80 | 10.86 | 10.92 | 10.98 | 11.04 | 11.10 | 11.16 | 11.22 | 11.28 |
| 1150 | 11.34 | 11.40 | 11.46 | 11.52 | 11.58 | 11.64 | 11.70 | 11.76 | 11.82 | 11.88 |
| 1200 | 11.94 | 12.00 | 12.06 | 12.12 | 12.18 | 12.24 | 12.30 | 12.36 | 12.42 | 12.48 |
| 1250 | 12.54 | 12.60 | 12.66 | 12.72 | 12.78 | 12.84 | 12.90 | 12.96 | 13.02 | 13.08 |
| 1300 | 13.14 | 13.20 | 13.26 | 13.32 | 13.38 | 13.44 | 13.50 | 13.59 | 13.62 | 13.68 |
| 1350 | 13.74 | 13.80 | 13.86 | 13.92 | 13.98 | 14.04 | 14.10 | 14.16 | 14.22 | 14.28 |
| 1400 | 14.34 | 14.40 | 14.46 | 14.52 | 14.58 | 14.64 | 14.70 | 14.76 | 14.82 | 14.86 |
| 1450 | 14.94 | 15.00 | 15.05 | 15.11 | 15.17 | 15.23 | 15.92 | 15.35 | 15.41 | 15.47 |
| 1500 | 15.53 | 15.59 | 15.65 | 15.71 | 15.77 | 15.83 | 15.89 | 15.95 | 16.01 | 16.07 |
| 1550 | 16.12 | 16.18 | 16.24 | 16.30 | 16.36 | 16.42 | 16.48 | 16.54 | 16.60 | 16.66 |
| 1600 | 16.72 | 16.78 | 16.83 | 16.89 | 16.95 | 17.10 | 17.07 | 17.13 | 17.19 | 17.25 |
| 1650 | 17.31 | 17.36 | 17.42 | 17.48 | 17.54 | 17.60 | 17.66 | 17.72 | 17.77 | 17.83 |
| 1700 | 17.89 | 17.95 | 18.01 | 18.07 | 18.12 | 18.18 | 18.24 | 18.30 | 18.36 | 18.42 |

**Type K: Chromel-Alumel**

| C° | 0 | 5 | 10 | 15 | 20 | 25 | 30 | 35 | 40 | 45 |
|---|---|---|---|---|---|---|---|---|---|---|
| −150 | −4.81 | −4.92 | −5.03 | −5.14 | −5.24 | −5.34 | −5.43 | −5.52 | −5.60 | −5.68 |
| −100 | −3.49 | −3.64 | −3.78 | −3.92 | −4.06 | −4.19 | −4.32 | −4.45 | −4.58 | −4.70 |
| − 50 | −1.89 | −2.03 | −2.20 | −2.37 | −2.54 | −2.71 | −2.87 | −3.03 | −3.19 | −3.34 |
| − 0 | 0.00 | −0.19 | −0.39 | −0.58 | −0.77 | −0.95 | −1.14 | −1.32 | −1.50 | −1.68 |
| + 0 | 0.00 | 0.20 | 0.40 | 0.60 | 0.80 | 1.00 | 1.20 | 1.40 | 1.61 | 1.80 |
| 50 | 2.02 | 2.23 | 2.43 | 2.64 | 2.85 | 3.05 | 3.26 | 3.47 | 3.68 | 3.89 |
| 100 | 4.10 | 4.31 | 4.51 | 4.72 | 4.92 | 5.13 | 5.33 | 5.53 | 5.73 | 5.93 |
| 150 | 6.13 | 6.33 | 6.53 | 6.73 | 6.93 | 7.13 | 7.33 | 7.53 | 7.73 | 7.93 |
| 200 | 8.13 | 8.33 | 8.54 | 8.74 | 8.94 | 9.14 | 9.34 | 9.54 | 9.75 | 9.95 |
| 250 | 10.16 | 10.36 | 10.57 | 10.77 | 10.98 | 11.18 | 11.39 | 11.59 | 11.80 | 12.01 |
| 300 | 12.21 | 12.42 | 12.63 | 12.83 | 13.04 | 13.25 | 13.46 | 13.67 | 13.88 | 14.09 |
| 350 | 14.29 | 14.50 | 14.71 | 14.92 | 15.13 | 15.34 | 15.55 | 15.76 | 15.98 | 16.19 |
| 400 | 16.40 | 16.61 | 16.82 | 17.03 | 17.24 | 17.46 | 17.67 | 17.88 | 18.09 | 18.30 |
| 450 | 18.51 | 18.73 | 18.94 | 19.15 | 19.36 | 19.58 | 19.79 | 20.01 | 20.22 | 20.43 |
| 500 | 20.65 | 20.86 | 21.07 | 21.28 | 21.50 | 21.71 | 21.92 | 22.14 | 22.35 | 22.56 |
| 550 | 22.78 | 22.99 | 23.20 | 23.42 | 23.63 | 23.84 | 24.06 | 24.27 | 24.49 | 24.70 |
| 600 | 24.91 | 25.12 | 25.34 | 25.55 | 25.76 | 25.98 | 26.19 | 26.40 | 26.61 | 26.82 |
| 650 | 27.03 | 27.24 | 27.45 | 27.66 | 27.87 | 28.08 | 28.29 | 28.50 | 28.72 | 28.93 |
| 700 | 29.14 | 29.35 | 29.56 | 29.77 | 29.97 | 30.18 | 30.39 | 30.60 | 30.81 | 31.04 |
| 750 | 31.23 | 31.44 | 31.65 | 31.85 | 32.06 | 32.27 | 32.48 | 32.68 | 32.89 | 33.09 |
| 800 | 33.30 | 33.50 | 33.71 | 33.91 | 34.12 | 34.32 | 34.53 | 34.73 | 34.93 | 35.14 |
| 850 | 35.34 | 35.54 | 35.75 | 35.95 | 36.15 | 36.35 | 36.55 | 36.76 | 39.96 | 37.16 |
| 900 | 37.36 | 37.56 | 37.76 | 37.97 | 38.16 | 38.36 | 38.56 | 38.76 | 38.95 | 39.15 |
| 950 | 39.35 | 39.55 | 39.75 | 39.94 | 40.14 | 40.34 | 40.53 | 40.73 | 40.92 | 41.12 |
| 1000 | 41.31 | 41.51 | 41.70 | 41.90 | 42.09 | 42.29 | 42.48 | 42.67 | 42.87 | 43.06 |
| 1050 | 43.25 | 43.44 | 43.63 | 43.83 | 44.02 | 44.21 | 44.40 | 44.59 | 44.78 | 44.97 |
| 1100 | 45.16 | 45.35 | 45.54 | 45.73 | 45.92 | 46.11 | 46.29 | 46.48 | 46.67 | 46.85 |

## REFERENCES AND BIBLIOGRAPHY

1. "Thermocouple Reference Tables," NBS Monograph 125, National Bureau of Standards, Washington, D.C., 1979.

2. *Temperature Measurement Handbook 1986*, Omega Engineering, Stanford Connecticut, 1986.

3. Halliday, D. and Resnick, R., *Physics for Students of Science and Engineering*, John Wiley & Sons, Inc., 1963.

4. Johnson, C. D., *Process Control Instrumentation Technology*, John Wiley & Sons, Second Edition, 1982.

5. Liptak, B.G. and Venczel, K. (ed.), *Process Control—Instrument Engineers' Handbook*, Revised Edition, Chilton Book Company, 1982.

# 7

# Analytical Measurement

**Introduction**   This chapter will discuss the fundamental principles of chemical analytical measurements, with emphasis on the following major areas: (1) conductivity, (2) pH, (3) density and specific gravity, (4) humidity, and (5) gas analysis.

The purpose of analytical measurements is to provide data on the composition of the contents of a process stream. This data is then used to control or improve the chemical process.

**Conductivity Measurement**   The conductivity measurement, the determination of the solution's ability to conduct electric current, is referred to as specific conductance or, simply, "conductivity" and is expressed in mhos, which is the reciprocal of ohm (the unit used to express resistance).

Aqueous solutions of acids, bases, or salts are known as electrolytes and are conductors of electricity. Conductivity measurements are generally made to detect electrolytic contaminants around water and waste treatment areas. The degree of electrical conductivity of such solutions is affected by three factors: the nature of the electrolyte, the concentration, and the temperature. A measurement of the conductivity at a fixed temperature can be a measurement of the solution's concentration, which can be expressed in percent by weight, parts per million, or other applicable units.

If the conductivity value of various concentrations of an electrolyte are known, it is then possible to determine the concentration by passing current through a solution of known dimensions and measuring its electrical resistivity or conductivity.

The primary element in an electrical conductivity measurement system is the conductivity cell (see Figure 7-1).

These cells consist of a pair of electrodes whose areas and spacings are precisely fixed, a suitable insulating member to confine the conductive paths, and

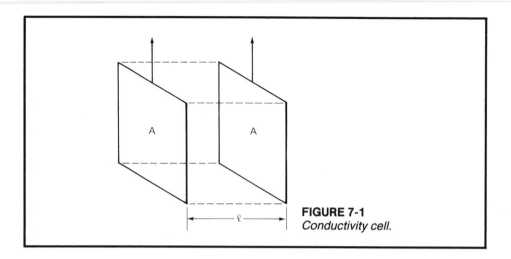

**FIGURE 7-1**
*Conductivity cell.*

suitable fittings for supporting and protecting the cell. The conductance between two electrodes varies as follows:

$$C \, \alpha \, \frac{A}{\ell} \qquad\qquad (7\text{-}1)$$

where:   C  = conductance, mhos
         A  = area of electrodes, cm²
         $\ell$  = distance between electrodes, cm

To establish a common basis when comparing conductivity of different solutions, a standard conductivity cell is considered where

$$A = 1\,cm^2$$
$$\ell = 1\,cm$$

and this volume of solution is completely insulated from its surroundings. Unless this insulated condition is met, no simple relationship exists between conductance and A/$\ell$, due to additional conducting paths available between electrodes. This conductance of the solution in a unit cell is called its specific conductivity k (sometimes called conductance) and has units of mhos per cm. In common practice, the specific conductance in mhos per cm is referred to as the solution's "conductivity" and is given in units of mhos only. For example, an electrolyte with a specific conductance of 0.03 mhos per cm is said to have a conductivity of 0.03 mhos. The two terms are synonymous in common usage.

Conductivity cells are constructed in a variety of configurations depending on the application requirements. However, the insertion-type cell is for installation in a process pipe or in the side of a tank (see Figure 7-2).

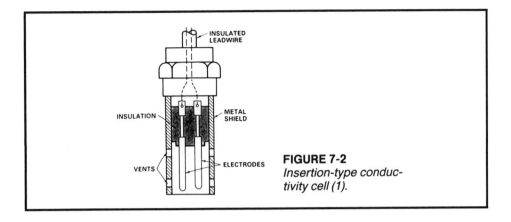

**FIGURE 7-2**
*Insertion-type conduc-
tivity cell (1).*

Conductivity instruments normally use an electronic circuit to measure resistance between the conductivity electrodes. The instrument may be calibrated for either resistance of conductance because

$$C = \frac{1}{R} \tag{7-2}$$

where:  C  = conductance, mhos
R  = resistance, ohms

By sending the output of a conductivity cell to an electronic instrument or an input module of a computer-based system, a readout of conductance or resistance can be obtained. These devices can be calibrated in either electrical units, such as ohms, mhos, and micromhos, or in terms of concentration of solution, such as percent concentration, grams per liter, and parts per million. The conductivity of most solutions increases as the temperature increases as shown in Figure 7-3.

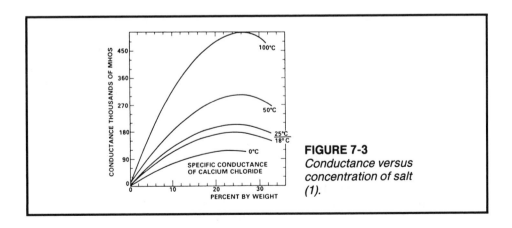

**FIGURE 7-3**
*Conductance versus
concentration of salt
(1).*

Therefore, if it is desirable to read the measurement in concentration units and the temperature of the solution cannot be kept constant, the effect of temperature on the conductivity of the solution can be compensated for either manually or automatically.

Manual compensation is normally accomplished by a manually operated adjustment in the circuit, calibrated in the actual temperature of the solution at the point of measurement.

Automatic temperature compensation is normally obtained by installing a resistance temperature element near the measuring cell, then using this temperature value in the measurement circuit. As the temperature of the solution changes, the resistance of the bulb changes. This resistance is incorporated into the measuring circuit to adjust the output span, rather than zero, since the effect of temperature on conductivity is a percentage change per degree temperature change.

## Hydrogen-Ion Concentration (pH) Measurement   The symbol pH represents the acidity or alkalinity of a solution. It is a measure of a key ingredient of aqueous solutions of all acids and bases—the hydrogen-ion concentration.

Earlier techniques for measuring the hydrogen ion concentration involved the use of paper indicators. When added to the sample, this indicator would produce a certain color change in relation to the value of the pH. The result could then be compared with a standard for an evaluation of the hydrogen-ion concentration.

Such a method does not lend itself well to automatic measurement, nor can it be used with liquids that are normally colored. For these reasons, a method of measurement was developed that was based on the potential created by a set of special electrodes in the solution. This method of measurement has actually become the standard pH measurement for indicating, recording, and/or control purposes. However, understanding this method requires a knowledge of what pH is and a familiarity with the fundamentals of a solution's properties.

**Basic Theory of pH**   Stable compounds are electrically neutral. When they are mixed with water, many of them break up into two or more charged particles. The charged particles formed in the dissociation are called *ions*. The amount of dissociation of a compound varies from one compound to another and with the temperature of the solution. At a specified temperature, a fixed relationship exists between the concentration of the charged particles and the neutral un-dissociated compound. This relationship is called the *dissociation constant* or *ionization constant*.

$$K = \frac{[M+][A-]}{[MA]} \tag{7.3}$$

where:   K      = dissociation constant
          [M+]   = concentration of positive ions
          [A-]   = concentration of negative ions
          [MA]   = concentration of undissociated ions

For an acid like hydrochloric (HCl), which breaks up completely into positively charged hydrogen ions and negatively charged chlorine ions (HCl $\rightarrow$ H$^+$+ Cl$^-$), the dissociation constant is practically infinity. For this reason it is called a "strong" acid. On the other hand, when an acid like acetic (HC$_2$H$_3$O$_2$) breaks up (CH$_3$COOH $\longleftrightarrow$ H$^+$ + CH$_3$COO$^-$), very few hydrogen ions show up in the solution, less than one in every 100 undissociated molecules. Therefore, it has a low dissociation constant and is called a "weak" acid. It can then be seen that the strength of an acid solution depends on the number of hydrogen ions available, which, in turn, depends on the weight of the compound and, in water, the dissociation constant of the particular compound.

When the free hydroxyl ions (OH$^-$) predominate, the solution is alkaline or basic. For example, sodium hydroxide in water completely dissociates as follows, NaOH $\rightarrow$ Na$^+$ + OH$^-$, and, therefore, is a strong base. On the other hand, ammonium hydroxide (NH$_4$OH) weakly dissociates into NH$_4^+$ ions and OH$^-$ ions and is a weak base.

Pure water dissociates into H$^+$ and OH$^-$ ions (HOH $\longleftrightarrow$ H$^+$ + OH$^-$), but is considered extremely "weak" because very little of the HOH breaks up into H$^+$ and OH$^-$ ions. The number of water molecules dissociated is so small in comparison to those undissociated that the value of (HOH) can be considered equal to one (1) or 100%. The ionization constant of water has been determined to have a value of $10^{-14}$ at 25°C. The product of the activites (H$^+$)(OH$^-$) is then $10^{-14}$.

If the concentration of hydrogen ions and hydroxyl ions is the same, they must be $10^{-7}$ and $10^{-7}$, respectively. No matter what other compounds are dissolved in the water, the product of the concentrations of H$^+$ ions and OH$^-$ ions is always $10^{-14}$.

Therefore, if a strong acid is added to water, many hydrogen ions are added and will reduce the hydroxyl ions accordingly. For example, if HCL at 25°C is added until the H$^+$ concentration becomes $10^{-2}$, the OH$^-$ concentration must become $10^{-12}$.

Because it is awkward to work in terms of small fractional concentrations like $1/10^7$, $1/10^{12}$, $1/10^2$, Sorenson in 1909 proposed for convenience that the expression pH be adopted for hydrogen-ion concentration to represent degree of acidity or activity of hydrogen ions. This term was derived from the phrase "the power of hydrogen." Sorenson defined pH as the negative of the logarithm of the hydrogen-ion concentration (pH = $-$log [H$^+$]), or as the log of the reciprocal of the hydrogen-ion concentration (pH = log 1/[H$^+$]). If the hydrogen-ion concentration is $1/10^x$, then the pH is said to be x. In pure water, where the concentration of the hydrogen-ion is $1/10^7$, the pH is, therefore, 7.

If acid solution always has more hydrogen ions than hydroxyl ions, the pH and the concentration of the hydrogen ions will be greater than $1/10^7$ (i.e., $1/10^6$, $1/10^5$, $1/10^4$) and the pH will be lower than 7 (i.e., 6, 5, 4).

The pH number itself is an exponential number; a change of a pH unit means a tenfold change in acid strength, as shown in Table 7.1.

**pH Electrode Systems**   Industrial electrode systems for pH determinations consist of two separate electrodes: (1) the active or measuring electrode, which produces a voltage proportional to the hydrogen-ion concentration; and (2) a ref-

**TABLE 7-1**
**Change in pH**

| Hydrogen Ion, Moles/Liter | Hydroxyl Ion, Moles/Liter | pH | |
|---|---|---|---|
| 1.0 | 0.00000000000001 | 0 | |
| 0.1 | 0.0000000000001 | 1 | |
| 0.01 | 0.000000000001 | 2 | |
| 0.001 | 0.00000000001 | 3 | Acidic |
| 0.0001 | 0.0000000001 | 4 | |
| 0.00001 | 0.000000001 | 5 | |
| 0.000001 | 0.00000001 | 6 | |
| 0.0000001 | 0.0000001 | 7 | Neutral |
| 0.00000001 | 0.000001 | 8 | |
| 0.000000001 | 0.00001 | 9 | |
| 0.0000000001 | 0.0001 | 10 | |
| 0.00000000001 | 0.001 | 11 | Basic |
| 0.000000000001 | 0.01 | 12 | |
| 0.0000000000001 | 0.1 | 13 | |
| 0.00000000000001 | 1 | 14 | |

erence electrode, which serves as a source of constant voltage against which the output of the measuring electrode is compared (see Figure 7-4).

A number of measuring electrodes have been developed for pH applications, but the glass electrode has evolved as the only universally used for industrial process purposes. Typically, it consists of an envelope of special glass designed to be sensitive only to hydrogen ions. It contains a neutral solution of constant pH (called buffer solution) and a conductor, immersed in the internal solution, which makes contact with the electrode lead. Figure 7-4 shows a diagram of the measur-

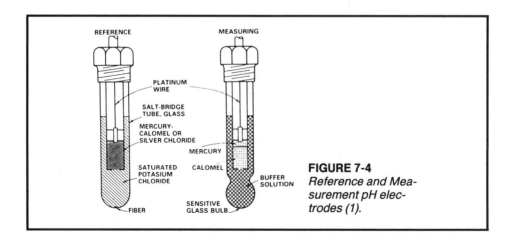

**FIGURE 7-4**
*Reference and Measurement pH electrodes (1).*

ing electrode in which this special glass is used. A thin layer of the special glass is at the tip of the electrode.

The electrode operates on the principle that a potential is observed between two solutions of different hydrogen-ion concentration when they are separated by a thin glass wall. The solution within the electrode has a constant concentration of hydrogen ions. Therefore, whenever the hydrogen-ion concentration of the solution being measured is different from that of the neutral solution within the electrode, a potential difference (or voltage) is developed across the electrode. If the solution being measured has a pH of 7.0, the potential difference is 0. When the pH of the measured solution is greater than 7.0, a positive potential exists across the glass tip; when the pH is less than 7.0, a negative potential exists.

The glass electrode responds in a predictable fashion in the 0 to 14 pH range, developing 59.2 mV per pH unit at 25°C, consistent with the Nernst equation:

$$E = \frac{RT}{F} \ln \frac{[H^+] \text{ outside}}{[H^+] \text{ inside}} \qquad (7\text{-}4)$$

where:  $E$ = potential, volts
$R$ = the Gas Law constant
$F$ = Faraday's number, a constant
$T$ = temperature kelvins
$[H^+]$ = hydrogen-ion concentration

Many types of glass electrodes are available, and the selection of a particular electrode is usually based on the temperature range and physical characteristics of the process.

The reference electrode is used to complete the circuit so that the potential across the glass electrode can be measured.

Due to the temperature coefficient of the glass electrode, the system must be compensated for temperature if it is to continue to read pH correctly. This is done manually where temperatures do not vary widely. Otherwise, it is done automatically by means of a temperature element located in the vicinity of the electrodes and connected into the circuit. Therefore, the industrial pH assembly can consist of as many as three units: the glass measurement electrode, the reference electrode, and a temperature element mounted in various holders of different designs.

**pH Measurement Applications**   Applications for pH measurement and control can be found in waste treatment facilities, in pulp and paper plants, in petroleum refining, synthetic rubber manufacturing, power generation plants, and a broad spectrum of the chemical industry. In other words, continuous pH analyzers can be found in almost every industry that uses water within its processes.

An example of pH control is shown in Figure 7-5. The figure is a process and instrument diagram (P&ID) showing the manufacturing of disodium phosphate using flow and pH control. The automatic control system shown produces a high purity salt and prevents unnecessary waste of both reagents (i.e., soda ash and phosphoric acid).

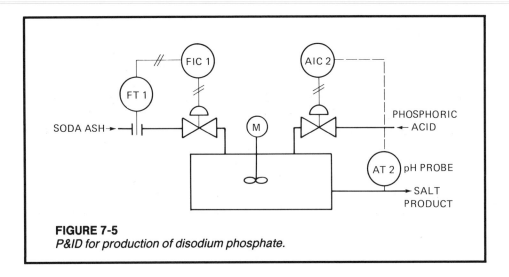

**FIGURE 7-5**
*P&ID for production of disodium phosphate.*

## Density and Specific Gravity Measurement    Although control
of the more common variables, such as flow, temperature, and pressure, is the
basic criterion for process control, there are cases where measurement of density
or specific gravity is the best method for determining and controlling the concentration of a process solution.

For a fluid, density is defined as the mass per unit volume and is usually expressed in units of grams per cubic centimeter, pounds per cubic foot, or pounds
per gallon. The specific gravity of a fluid is the ratio of the density of the fluid to the
density of water at 60°F.

**Hydrometer**    The simple hand hydrometer, consisting of a weighted float with a
small diameter stem proportioned so that more or less of the scale is submerged according to the specific gravity, is widely used for making "spot" or off-line intermit-
tent specific gravity measurements of process liquids.

A typical example of the use of a hydrometer is checking the state of discharge for a lead-acid cell by measuring the specific gravity (SG) of the electrolyte.
Concentrated sulfuric acid is 1.835 times as heavy as water for the same volume.
Therefore, its specific gravity equals 1.835. The specific gravity of water is 1, since
it is the reference.

In a fully charged automotive cell, the mixture of sulfuric acid and water results in a specific gravity of 1.280 at a room temperature of 70°F. As the cell discharges, more water is formed, lowering the specific gravity. When it is down to
about 1.150, the cell is completely discharged. Specific gravity readings are taken
with a battery hydrometer as shown in Figure 7-6. Note that the calibrated float
with the SG marks will rest higher in an electrolyte of higher specific gravity.

The importance of the specific gravity can be seen from the fact that the
open-circuit voltage of the lead-acid cell is given approximately by the following:

$$V = SG + 0.84 \tag{7-5}$$

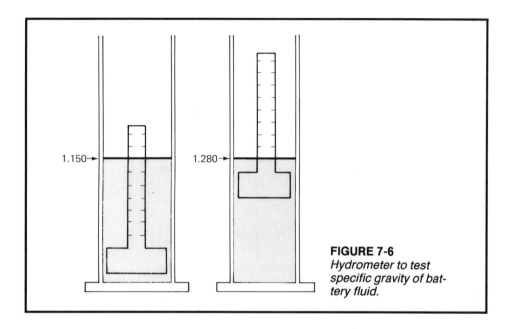

**FIGURE 7-6**
*Hydrometer to test specific gravity of battery fluid.*

For SG = 1.280, the voltage is 1.280 + 0.84 = 2.12 V. This value is for a fully charged battery.

The problem with the simple hydrometer is that it cannot perform the continuous measurement needed for process control. However, the photoelectric hydrometer shown in Figure 7-7 can be used to obtain a continuous specific gravity value. In this instrument, a glass hydrometer is placed in a continuous-flow vessel. Since the instrument stem is not opaque, it affects the amount of light passing through a slit to the photocell as the stem rises and falls. This instrument can be used in any specific gravity application not harmful to the glass and is normally accurate to two or three decimal places.

**Fixed Volume Method**    A common continuous density-measuring device utilizing the fixed-volume density principle is the so-called displacement meter, schematically illustrated in Figure 7-8. Liquid flows continuously through the displacer chamber with the buoyant body, or displacer, completely immersed. A buoyant force, which is dependent upon the weight of the displaced liquid and, in turn, is a function of the volume and specific gravity, is exerted on the displacer. If the volume is constant, the force will vary directly with the specific gravity. An increase in specific gravity will produce a greater upward force on the displacer and on the left end of the rigid beam. Since the beam moves about a fulcrum located between the displacer and the balancing bellows, this causes the right-hand end of the beam to move closer to the nozzle, creating an increase in the pressure at the nozzle that is sensed by the balancing bellows, which will expand. As the bellows expands, the right-hand end of the beam moves away from the nozzle, moving the baffle away from the nozzle tip, causing a reduction in pressure in the pneumatic system. The bellows will move just enough

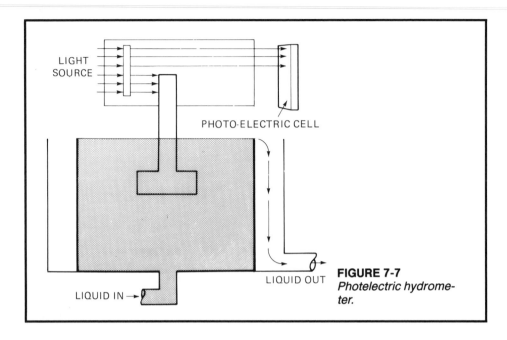

LIGHT
SOURCE

PHOTO-ELECTRIC CELL

LIQUID OUT

LIQUID IN →

**FIGURE 7-7**
*Photelectric hydrome-
ter.*

to re-establish a new position or torque balance with somewhat different pressure, which is read on a pressure instrument calibrated in density or specific gravity units.

**Differential Pressure Method**   One of the simplest and most widely used methods of continuous density measurement is based on pressure variation produced by a fixed height of liquid.

As shown in Figure 7-9, the difference in pressure between any two elevations below the surface is equal to differences in liquid pressure (head) between these elevations, regardless of variation in level above the higher elevation.

This difference in elevations is represented by dimension h, which must be multiplied by the specific gravity (SG) of liquid to obtain the difference in head in inches of water, the standard unit for measurement calibration. To measure the change in head resulting from a change in specific gravity from minimum ($SG_{min}$) to maximum ($SG_{max}$), the difference between $hSG_{min}$ and $hSG_{max}$ must be calculated.

$$\Delta P = h(SG_{max} - SG_{min}) \tag{7-5}$$

where:   $\Delta P$   = differential pressure in inches of water
          $h$    = difference in elevations (inches)
          $SG_{min}$ = minimum specific gravity
          $SG_{max}$ = maximum specific gravity

It is common practice to measure only the span of actual density changes by elevating the instrument "zero" to the minimum pressure head to be en-

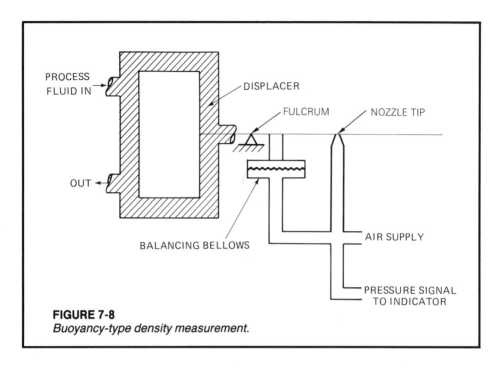

**FIGURE 7-8**
*Buoyancy-type density measurement.*

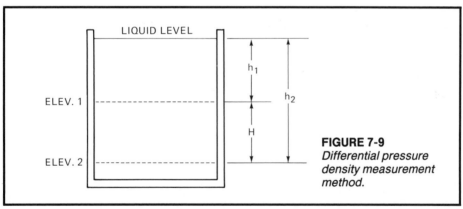

**FIGURE 7-9**
*Differential pressure density measurement method.*

countered, allowing the entire instrument working range to be devoted to the differential caused by density changes. For example, if SG = 1.0 and h = 100 inches, the range of the measuring instrument must be elevated h × SG, or 100 inches of water. For a SG = 0.6 and h = 100 inches, the elevation would be 60 inches of water. The two principal relationships to be considered in this type of measuring device are then:

$$\text{Span} = \text{h}(\text{SG}_{\text{max}} - \text{SG}_{\text{min}}) \tag{7-6}$$

$$\text{Elevation} = \text{h} \times \text{SG} \tag{7-7}$$

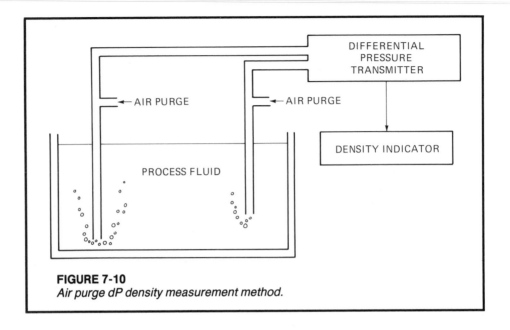

**FIGURE 7-10**
*Air purge dP density measurement method.*

An open tank installation of this type utilizing air purges consists of two bubbler tubes installed in the fluid, so that the end of one tube is lower than the end of the other (Figure 7-10). The pressure required to bubble air into the fluid is equal to the pressure of the fluid at the ends of the bubble tubes.

Since the outlet of one is lower than that of the other, the difference in pressure will be the same as the weight of a constant-height column of liquid. Therefore, the differential pressure measurement is equivalent to the weight of a constant volume of the liquid and can be represented directly as density.

**Boiling Point Rise Method**   Water boils at a definite temperature for any given set of conditions. Under the same conditions, a solution boils at a higher temperature depending on the amount of material dissolved in it; therefore, the difference between these temperatures is called boiling point rise, which is directly proportional to the density of the liquid and can be calibrated in specific gravity units. This principle is commonly used to measure density, as shown in Figure 7-11.

To determine boiling point rise, the temperature of the boiling solution is usually measured by a resistance-type temperature element (TE) and compared to a reference temperature, measured in the same manner. The reference temperature is essentially that of pure water boiling at the same pressure as that of the solution being measured. A simple and convenient method for providing a reference temperature measurement is to install the resistance bulb in a chamber located in such a manner that vapors rising from the boiling solution will condense in it. The vapors, being free of materials in the solution, will condense and form a liquid also free of dissolved material and at a temperature representing its boiling point.

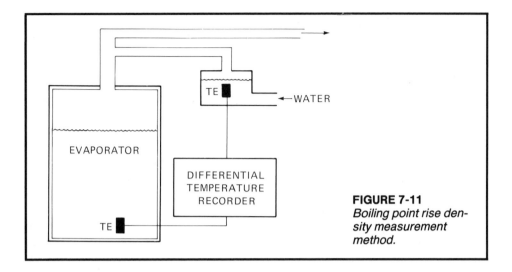

**FIGURE 7-11**
*Boiling point rise density measurement method.*

**Nuclear Method**  Nuclear devices can also be used to measure density. Their operation is based on the principle that absorption of gamma radiation increases with the mass of the material measured. A representative radiation-type density measuring element is depicted in Figure 7-12. It consists of a constant gamma ray radiation source, which can be of radium, cesium, or cobalt, mounted on the wall of the pipe and a radiation detector mounted on the opposite side. Gamma rays are emitted from the source, through the pipe, and into the detector. Materials flowing through the pipeline and between the source and detector absorb radioactive energy in proportion to their densities. The remainder of the radioactive energy is received by the radiation detector. The amount varies inversely with the density of the process stream. The radiation detector unit converts this energy into an electrical signal, which is transmitted to an electronics module.

**Vibration Method**  The most widely used method to determine process fluid density is based on the fact that the natural oscillating frequency of a fluid changes

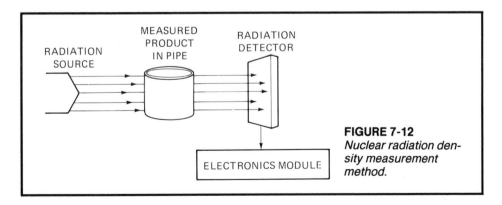

**FIGURE 7-12**
*Nuclear radiation density measurement method.*

with changes in density. The common transducers that use this principle are (1) the vibrating U-tube, (2) the vibrating cylinder, (3) the vibrating vane, (4) the vibrating single-tube, and (5) the vibrating twin-tube.

In the *vibrating U-tube* transducer, when the density of the process fluid in the fixed-volume tube changes, the amplitude of the vibration changes. This change can be measured with the proper mechanical and electronic equipment and calibrated to read in density units.

The *vibrating cylinder* transducer consists of a thin-walled cylinder located concentrically inside the sensor housing. The process fluid flows in the thin cylinder, and the entire mass is excited into circumferential resonance electrically. The vibrating frequency changes as the mass of the fluid changes. The instrument can be used for both gases and liquids. Its main advantage is that it can measure the density of both gas or gas-liquid combinations.

The *vibrating vane* sensor oscillates at its natural frequency when inserted into the process fluid, and the density of the fluid requires additional energy to maintain the natural frequency of the sensor. More energy is required if the density of the fluid increases and less if the density decreases.

The *vibrating single-tube* transducer is shown in Figure 7-13. This sensor has two cantilevered masses, quite similar to end-to-end tuning forks. The active part of the device consists of a flow-through tube for the process fluid, with the cantilevered masses mounted on the same structure under the flow tube. This structure is driven into oscillation at a frequency determined by the combined mass of the device and the process fluid at any given instant.

A change in the density of the flowing fluid will change the frequency of the device, and this change is an indirect measure of the density or specific gravity of the fluid.

In the *vibrating twin-tube* sensor there are two parallel flow tubes, and the process fluid flows through the tubes and converges into a single flow at each end. This device is similar to a tuning fork, since the tubes are driven at their mean nat-

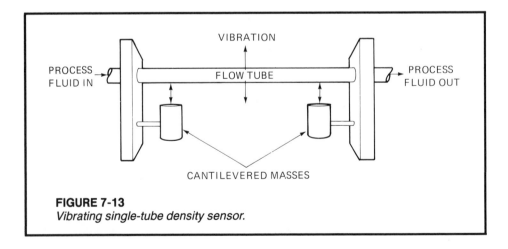

**FIGURE 7-13**
*Vibrating single-tube density sensor.*

ural frequency. This oscillation varies inversely with changes in fluid density. Two drive coils and their associated electronic circuits maintain the tubes in resonance.

## Humidity Measurements
Humidity is an expression of the amount of moisture in a gas or gases, whether isolated or as a part of the atmosphere. There are two basic quantitative measures of humidity: absolute and relative. Absolute humidity is the amount of water vapor present in each cubic foot or other unit volume, expressed in various units such as dew point, grains of water per pound of air, or pounds of water per million standard cubic feet. Relative humidity describes the ability of air to moisten or dry materials and compares the actual amount of water vapor present with the maximum amount of water vapor the air could hold at that temperature. For example, air that is considered saturated at 50°F (100 percent relative humidity) would be considered quite dry if heated to 100°F (19 percent relative humidity). The graph in Figure 7-14 shows the maximum amount of moisture that can be held by air at various temperatures.

Humidity can be calculated by assuming that the atmosphere to be measured is an ideal gas. The ideal gas law states that the partial pressure of one of the constituents of a mixture is the pressure that would exist if that constituent alone occupied the volume of the mixture at the same temperature. This is expressed mathematically by:

$$W_v = \frac{P_v V}{R_v T}$$

and

$$W_g = \frac{P_g V}{R_g T}$$

where:   $W$ = weight of constituent (v = vapor and g = gas)
$P$ = absolute partial pressure of constituent
$V$ = volume
$T$ = absolute temperature
$R$ = gas constant for a given gas

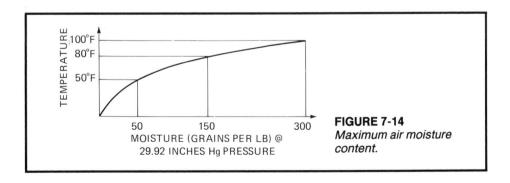

**FIGURE 7-14**
*Maximum air moisture content.*

The absolute humidity ($H_a$) (weight of vapor per unit weight of dry gas) is, therefore:

$$H_a = \frac{W_v}{W_g} = \frac{R_g(P_v)}{R_v(P_g)}$$

The density of the water vapor ($D_v$) (weight of vapor per unit volume, which is the same as the weight of the water vapor per unit volume of dry gas) is sometimes referred to as absolute humidity and is expressed as:

$$D_v = \frac{P_v}{R_v T}$$

The relative humidity ($H_r$), which is the ratio of actual partial pressure of the vapor ($P_v$) in the gas to the saturation partial pressure ($P_{sat}$) is then:

$$H_r = \frac{P_v}{P_{sat}} \cong \frac{D_v}{P_{sat}}$$

The value of saturation pressure can be found in steam tables in engineering handbooks.

Dew point is defined as the temperature at which the air or a gas becomes saturated. If the mixture is cooled at constant pressure to the dew point, condensation of vapor will begin.

Dry bulb and wet bulb temperatures are also used to determine humidity of a gas or air mixture. The dry bulb temperature of a gas mixture is measured by an ordinary thermal measuring element. The wet bulb temperature is measured by a thermal element covered by a wick fully wetted by water vapor. The difference between dry bulb temperatures and wet bulb temperatures is sometimes called the wet bulb depression. This is due to the cooling effect on the bulb from evaporation of the water on the wick.

Humidity affects many materials in diverse ways, and the measurement of water present, dew point and other variables is accomplished by a wide variety of instruments employing quite different methods and principles. Humidity measurements are considered to be inferred because they depend on differences between two thermometers, expansion or contraction of different materials, temperature at which the water vapor will condense, or the temperature at which certain salt solutions are in equilibrium.

These measurement methods are classified according to the physical effects on which they are based: psychrometric, hygrometric, dew point, heat of absorption, electrolytic, moisture absorption, vapor equilibrium, and infrared.

**Psychrometric Method**   A well-established empirical method of measuring relative humidity is based on psychrometry and involves the reading of two thermometers, one bulb directly exposed to the atmosphere and the other covered by a continuously wet wick. Actually, the second bulb measures the thermodynamic equilibrium temperature reached between the cooling effected by evaporation of water and the heating by convection. The device used for making this measurement is called a psychrometer.

This device consists of two mercury-in-glass thermometers mounted on a suitable frame and arranged with a chain handle at one end so that the assembly can be swung rapidly to give proper air velocity. In use, one bulb (the wet bulb) is covered with a wetted wick within a few degrees of room temperature. It is then whirled in a regular circular path for 15 to 20 seconds and readings are quickly made, the wet bulb first before temperature begins to rise. This is repeated until two consecutive wet bulb readings agree. The sling psychrometer is a common checking device for other humidity instruments. Once wet-bulb and dry-bulb temperatures are known, relative humidity can be determined by tables, special slide rules, or psychrometric charts.

Wet- and dry-bulb psychrometers for continuous industrial measurement of humidity are available in a wide variety of configurations. A typical system is schematically shown in Figure 7-15. It consists of temperature recorder connected to two temperature bulbs, a "wet" and a "dry" bulb. The dry bulb is located in the open while a wick or a porous, ceramic-covered wet bulb is located in the moving air stream. A reservoir of supply water maintains the proper wetness of the wick.

The wet-bulb/dry-bulb temperature readings are converted to suitable relative humidity values by use of proper scales or charts in the temperature recorder.

**Hygrometric Method**    This method of measurement depends on the change in dimensions of hygroscopic materials, such as hair, wood, animal membrane, or paper, as the relative humidity in the surrounding atmosphere changes. The hygrometer is calibrated to read directly in terms of relative humidity.

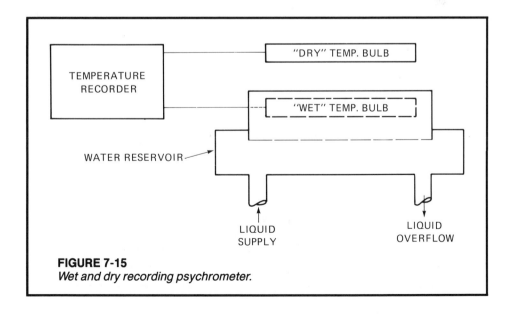

**FIGURE 7-15**
*Wet and dry recording psychrometer.*

Human hair is one of the most common hygroscopic materials used (see Figure 7-16). The hair absorbs moisture from the ambient atmosphere in an amount that is a function of the temperature of the hair and of the partial pressure of water vapor in the atmosphere. As the water content of the hair increases, it lengthens with relation to relative humidity. Expansion and contraction of the hair are used to move a pointer or a pen to provide a continuous reading of relative humidity.

**Dew Point Method**   As previously stated, dew point is the temperature at which a mixture of air and water vapor is saturated. The classical method of determining dew point consists of slowly cooling a polished surface until condensation takes place. The temperature of the surface when the first droplet appears is considered the dew point. This method can be used to determine absolute humidity of partial pressure of the vapor.

A widely used approach to continuous measurement of dew point is based on the temperature of vapor equilibrium. The temperature at which a saturated solution of a hygroscopic salt (lithium chloride) is in vapor equilibrium with the atmosphere is measured. The temperature of the salt solution, being much higher than the temperature of pure water, is reached by electric heating.

Structurally (see Figure 7-17), a tube containing a temperature-measuring element is wrapped with a glass fiber wetted with a saturated lithium chloride salt solution. Two conductors are wrapped around the assembly in contact with the wick and supplied with low-voltage (25 volt) alternating current. Current flow through the salt solution generates heat, raising the temperature. When temperature of vapor equilibrium is reached, water evaporates, reducing current flow and heat input. The temperature cannot go any higher because all the water would evaporate and heat input would cease. It cannot fall because all the salt would then go into solution and too much heat would be generated. Therefore, equilibrium is reached with a portion of the lithium chloride in solution and conductive and the remainder of lithium chloride dry and nonconductive; thus, heat input is balanced with heat loss. The thermometer bulb, when placed inside the metal tube, will measure cell temperature or dew point. This is also a measurement of absolute hu-

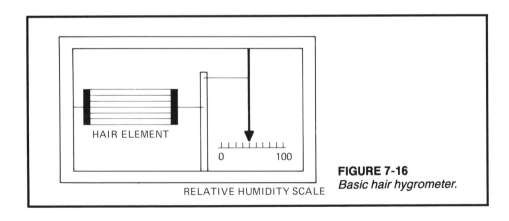

**FIGURE 7-16**
*Basic hair hygrometer.*

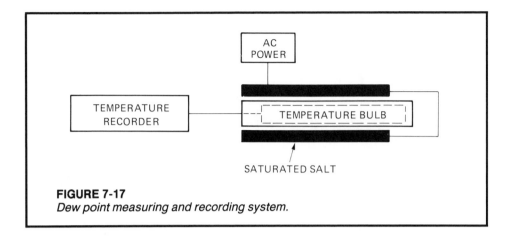

**FIGURE 7-17**
*Dew point measuring and recording system.*

midity and can be expressed in grains of moisture per pound of dry air, percent water vapor by volume, and other units.

Since there is no provision for cooling with this method, its operation is limited to conditions where equilibrium temperature of lithium chloride is above ambient temperature. This corresponds to a minimum of approximately 12 to 15 percent relative humidity over ordinary temperature ranges and is usable up to saturation, or 100 percent relative humidity. Ambient temperatures may vary from 200°F to –30°F. Dew points at higher temperatures must be measured on a cooled sample.

# Gas Analysis    Continuous measurements for determining the concentration of one or more components in a certain gas stream are widely made in the process industry. The following sections describe several common analyzers used for this application.

**Particulates**    Particle emissions are usually monitored using light transmission techniques. The normal objective is to indicate particle density, but some applications may also call for measurements of size.

Opacimeters are most common for particulate measurements. These instruments transmit measurement beams across process plant stacks as shown in Figure 7-18.

Opacimeter light sources and detectors are sometimes housed together with passive reflectors across the stack. Distances to 50 feet can be accommodated in these double-pass instruments, but alignment is difficult. The sources and detectors may also be mounted at opposite ends of assembled pipes to simplify installation.

**Oxygen Analyzers**    Electrochemical zirconium oxide cells are popular for oxygen measurements. Cell output voltages respond to changes in partial pressures of oxygen. The cell output voltages are linearized to produce standardized concentra-

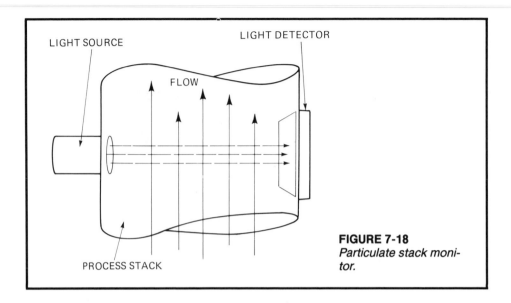

LIGHT SOURCE

LIGHT DETECTOR

FLOW

**FIGURE 7-18**
*Particulate stack moni-tor.*

PROCESS STACK

tion signals. Ranges are typically between 0 to 10% and 0 to 30%. Air is used as a reference, and oxygen standards are used for calibration.

Some oxygen analyzers exhibit thermal sensitivity and are usually operated at elevated temperatures for stability. Sample extraction versions are advantageous when stack temperatures are low because the cells can be installed in ovens outside the stacks.

Paramagnetic gas sensors were among the earliest oxygen detectors. Analyzers can be specified for ranges between 0 to 1% and 0 to 100%. The instruments respond to the magnetic susceptibility of the sample. The susceptibility of oxygen is two orders of magnitude greater than that of most other stack constituents, so accuracy is high.

**Carbon Monoxide Analyzers**   Carbon monoxide concentrations are commonly measured with infrared spectrometers. Measurements are typically made in ranges between 0 to 100 and 0 to 5000 ppm.

Polarographic sensors can detect carbon monoxide concentrations in limited ranges, typically between 0 to 50 ppm. Ultraviolet analyzers have also been used for this determination.

**Combustibles**   Combustible gases and vapors are detected by measuring the thermal properties of samples. Catalytic bead devices are most common, with active and inactive filaments arranged in bridge circuits. As gas contacts the catalytically treated filaments, combustible materials diffuse into the surfaces and are oxidized. The heat of reaction raises the temperature, inducing resistance differences. Flammable gases or vapors can also be detected by mixing samples with hydrogen and burning the product. Concentration of combustibles in the sample is inferred from flame temperature.

Combustibles are usually monitored for explosion hazards, so outputs are calibrated to read in percent of lower explosive limit (LEL).

**Hydrocarbon Analyzers**  Flame ionization detectors (FIDs) are often employed for measuring hydrocarbon concentrations in ranges between 0 to 1 ppm and 0 to 12,000 ppm. The samples are mixed with hydrogen and burned. Carbon ions released during the combustion are sensed with electrodes around the flames. FIDs typically have response times under 10 seconds. Sensitivity is also good with concentrations as low as 0.01 ppm.

Infrared analyzers may be used for selected hydrocarbons but cannot measure total hydrocarbon concentrations.

**Carbon Dioxide Analyzers**  Many instruments are available for sensing carbon dioxide. One uses an approach based on thermal conductivity that provides measurements between 0 to 20% and 0 to 100%.

**Sulfur Dioxide Analyzers**  Several types of general-purpose analyzers are available for sulfur dioxide measurements. Most utilize some form of spectrophotometry.

Ultraviolet spectrophotometers are often used for measurement. This approach provides high accuracies and sensitivities. Ranges as narrow as 0 to 100 ppm are encountered, but instruments can also detect concentrations up to 100% by volume. Ultraviolet analyzers are capable of fast response, i.e., 1 second or less.

Infrared analyzers can be used for sulfur dioxide. The instruments lack the sensitivity and response of ultraviolet devices but are more versatile and less costly.

Fluorescence analyzers are also used for sulfur dioxide monitoring in ranges between 0 to 0.25 ppm and 0 to 5,000 ppm. This gas emits light when exposed to ultraviolet radiation, with intensity depending on concentration.

**Nitrogen Oxide Analyzers**  Nitrogen oxides are measured with spectral or electrochemical analyzers. Instrument selection often depends on whether the desired data are to show nitric oxide, nitrogen dioxide, or total oxides of nitrogen.

Chemiluminescence instruments are accurate and sensitive. These analyzers respond directly to nitric oxide; nitrogen dioxide must be reduced for detection.

Chemiluminescence occurs when the samples react with ozone. Intensities, measured with photomultipliers, are correlated with nitric oxide concentration. Detection ranges vary between 0 to 0.1 ppm and 0 to 10,000 ppm. Instruments can be specified for concentrations as low as 0.5 ppm.

Ultraviolet analyzers are capable of oxide as well as dioxide monitoring. Lower detection limits are only 10 ppm for nitric oxide, however; sensitivity is, therefore, usually raised by converting the nitric oxide to the dioxide. Measurements are taken before and after the oxidation to compensate for initial nitrogen dioxide concentrations.

Infrared analyzers are sensitive to nitric oxide, but not to dioxide. Units are available for measurements between 0 to 1,000 ppm and 0 to 10,000 ppm. Ranges can also be specified before 0 to 1% and 0 to 10%.

**Hydrogen Sulfide Analyzers**   Hydrogen sulfide is difficult to monitor accurately and often requires chemical conditioning. Some HS analyzers expose sample gases to chemically treated paper tape. Hydrogen sulfide reacts with the tape, and the resulting color change is used to infer hydrogen sulfide concentration.

Conventional fluorescence analyzers are used, but the hydrogen sulfide is first converted to sulfur dioxide. Automatic titrators are also employed to determine hydrogen sulfide concentrations.

Ultraviolet analyzers respond to hydrogen sulfide, but sensitivities are low. Polarographic instruments can also be used but require filters to remove unsaturated hydrocarbons.

## Analyzer Measurement Application   We will close the discussion
of analyzers with a measurement system application using a gas analyzer. A typical $SO_2$ stack analyzer instrument loop is shown in Figure 7-19. The system consists of an $SO_2$ analyzer, a temperature element, and a flow measurement system. The temperature and flow signals are used in this system to obtain the amount of $SO_2$ in pounds per hour. The computation is made in the control unit (AIT). Note that there is electrical heat tracing of the analyzer sample line. The heat tracing is needed to keep the sulfur dioxide in the gaseous state.

Analyzer operation is based on the absorption of light by the sample gas. By rigid definition, light is only that narrow band of electromagnetic radiation visible to the naked eye. However, in this discussion the term "light" is used to refer to electromagnetic radiation over specific wavelengths covered by the analyzer.

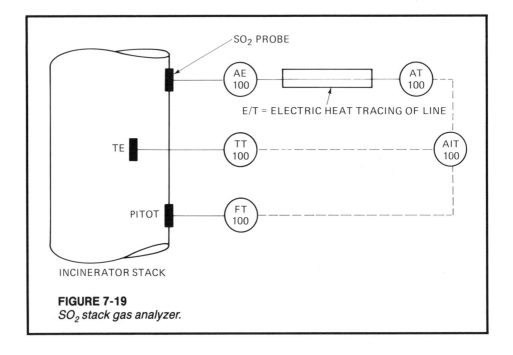

**FIGURE 7-19**
*SO$_2$ stack gas analyzer.*

Wavelengths used for $SO_2$ analysis are in the 280 to 313-nm range for the measuring and 578 nm for the reference channel (see Figure 7-20).

A block diagram of a typical $SO_2$ analyzer is given in Figure 7-21.

The optical system operates as follows: Radiation from the light source (A) passes through the sample (B) flowing through a sample cell. Some light of the measuring wavelength is adsorbed by $SO_2$ in the sample. Light transmitted through the sample is divided by a semitransparent mirror (C) into two beams (D) and (H). Each beam then passes through its own optical filter (E) or (I). Each filter permits only a particular wavelength to reach its associated photo tube (G) or (K).

Optical filters in one beam permit only radiation at the measuring wavelength (J) to pass through. The measuring wavelength is chosen so light intensity reaching the measuring photo tube (K) varies greatly with a change in $SO_2$ concentration.

The optical filter in the second beam permits only light at the reference wavelength (F) to pass through. The reference wavelength is chosen so light intensity reaching the reference photo tube (G) varies little or none with a change in $SO_2$ concentration. Each photo tube sends a current to its logarithmic amplifier (log amp) proportional to the intensity of the light striking the photo tube. The signal output of the analyzer circuit is the voltage difference produced by the log amps.

If $SO_2$ concentration increases, light arriving at the measuring photo tube decreases and so does the measuring photo tube current. The reference circuit is not affected. Since voltage generated in the measuring circuit increases with the decreases in photo tube current, the output voltage (measuring voltage minus reference voltage) increases with a concentration increase.

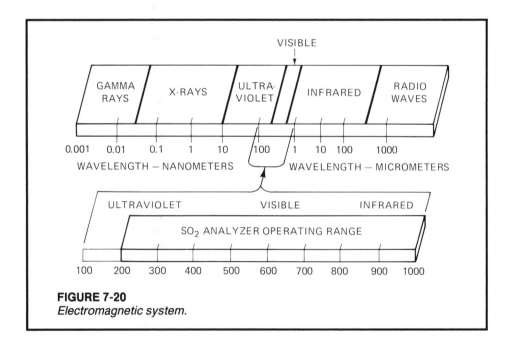

**FIGURE 7-20**
*Electromagnetic system.*

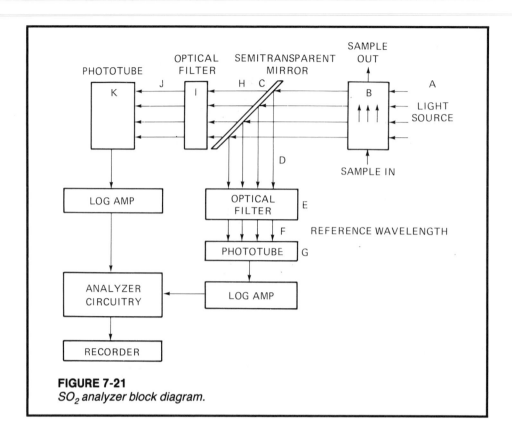

**FIGURE 7-21**
*SO$_2$ analyzer block diagram.*

This analyzer design also provides inherent compensation for changes in overall light intensity. Factors such as light source variations or dirt on the cell windows, which equally affect intensities of both the measuring and reference wavelengths, will equally change the output voltages. Therefore, these variations have minimal net effect on the difference or the final output voltage.

## EXERCISES

7.1 Given the following hydrogen-ion concentrations in liquid: (a) 0.0001 g/l, (b) 0.00001 g/l, and (c) 0.00000001 g/l, calculate the pH value. Identify the solutions that are bases or acids.

7.2 Given the following resistance values for a given solution, calculate the conductance: (a) 50,000 $\Omega$, (b) 100,000 $\Omega$, (c) 1,000,000 $\Omega$.

7.3 Calculate the span in inches of a differential pressure density instrument, if the minimum specific gravity is 1.0, the maximum specific gravity is 1.25, and the difference in liquid elevation is 50 inches.

7.4 If the air temperature is 80°F and the atmospheric pressure is 29.92 inches, what is the maximum moisture content of the air?

7.5 The specific gravity of a lead-acid cell in a 12-V (6-cell) battery is 1.24. Calculate the no load voltage of the battery.

7.6 Explain the measurement of density using the boiling point rise method.

7.7 Discuss in detail the operation and function of the wet and dry recording psychrometer.

7.8 Discuss the different types of gas analyzers used to measure sulfur dioxide.

7.9 What is the main reason for measuring flow and temperature as well as $SO_2$ in the $SO_2$ stack gas analyzer?

## REFERENCES AND BIBLIOGRAPHY

1. Moore R.L., *Basic Instrumentation Lecture Notes and Study Guide Volume 2, Process Analyzers and Recorders*, Third Edition, Instrument Society of America, 1982.

2. Considine, D.M. (ed.), *Handbook of Applied Instrumentation*, McGraw-Hill Company, 1964.

3. Kirk, F.W., and Rimboi, N.R., *Instrumentation*, Third Edition American Technical Publishers, Inc., 1975.

4. *Fundamentals of Ion-Selective Measurements*, Technical Information, The Foxboro Company, 1972.

5. *pH Electrodes and Holders*, Technical Information, The Foxboro company, 1979.

6. *Ion-Selective Measuring Electrodes*, Technical Information, The Forboxo Company.

7. *Theory and Application of Electrolytic Conductivity Measurement*, Technical Information, The Foxboro Company, 1982.

8. *Conductivity Cells*, Technical Information, The Foxboro Company, 1962.

9. Considine, D.M. (ed.), *Process Instruments and Controls Handbook*, Third Edition, McGraw-Hill Book Company, 1985.

**Introduction**   This chapter will first discuss the basic principles of flow and then cover the most common types of flow-measuring instruments, such as orifice plates, Venturi tubes, flow nozzles, Pitot tubes, rotameters, magnetic flowmeters, turbine flowmeters, and ultrasonic flowmeters.

**Flow Principles**   Since all flow involves some form of energy change, we need to review the concept of energy or work. Work (energy) can be expressed in many different forms, including thermal, chemical, and electrical energy. However, in flow measurement we encounter two types of energy: potential and kinetic.

$$\text{Work} = \text{Potential Energy} = \text{Force} \times \text{Distance} = F \times d$$

and    $$\text{Work} = \text{Kinetic Energy} = 1/2\,(\text{Mass})(\text{Velocity})^2 = 1/2\,mv^2$$

Let's examine the concepts of potential and kinetic energy in more detail.

**Potential Energy**   The term "potential energy" probably came from the idea that we give an object the potential to do work when we raise it against gravity. The "potential energy" of water at the top of a water fall is converted into a "kinetic energy" of motion at the bottom of the fall.

Potential energy is usually applied to the work required to raise a mass against gravity. Since force is defined as mass (m) times acceleration (g),

$$F = mg$$

The work required to raise a mass through a height h is

$$Fh = mgh$$

The term mgh is called potential energy because this energy can be recovered by allowing the object to drop through the height h, at which point the potential energy of position is converted into the kinetic energy of motion.

**Kinetic Energy**  Any object that falls through a height (h) under the influence of gravity is said to gain kinetic energy at the expense of its potential energy. Let's assume that a mass (m) falls through the distance (h), converting all its potential energy (mgh) into kinetic energy. Since energy must be conserved, the kinetic energy must equal the potential energy. Therefore, all we need to do to find this kinetic energy is to find the velocity of fall and express the object's energy (mgh or Fh) in terms of this velocity, as follows:

$$\text{Velocity (v)} \quad = \text{Acceleration} \times \text{Time}$$
$$= \int g\,dt = gt$$

$$\text{Distance} = h = (\text{Velocity})(\text{Time})$$
$$= \int v\,dt$$
$$= \int (gt)\,dt$$

$$\text{So that} \quad h = gt^2/2$$
$$= (gt)^2/2g$$

$$\text{But,} \quad v = gt$$

$$\text{therefore,} \quad h = v^2/2g$$

$$\text{or} \quad v^2 = 2gh$$

which is the velocity of a falling mass. If we multiply $h = v^2/2g$ by mg, we obtain

$$mgh = mv^2/2$$

However, we saw earlier that potential energy equals mgh. Therefore, the term $mv^2/2$ is the velocity form of the energy or the kinetic energy.

We can note:

$$\text{Energy in terms of height} = mgh$$
$$\text{Energy in terms of velocity} = mv^2/2$$

**Flow in a Uniform Pipe**  A typical example of flow in a process plant would be flow in a pipe of uniform and constant cross section (A) as shown in Figure 8-1. The differential pressure ($\Delta P$) between the inlet and the outlet causes the fluid to flow in the pipe.

The flow of fluid is maintained by the energy difference between the inlet and outlet. Let us find the fluid velocity (v) in terms of the inlet pressure $P_1$ and the outlet pressure $P_2$ assuming no energy loss in the pipe.

Since the pipe has a uniform area A, the pressure at the inlet is $P_1$ and the pressure at the outlet is $P_2$, the total force at the input is $F_1 = P_1A$ and the total force at the output is $F_2 = P_2A$.

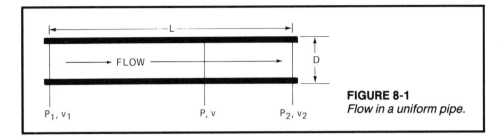

**FIGURE 8-1**
*Flow in a uniform pipe.*

The energy (work) involved in moving the fluid through the distance L is force times distance:

$$(F_1 - F_2)\,L \;=\; P_1\,AL - P_2 AL$$
$$=\; (P_1 - P_2)AL$$

Since AL is the volume of the pipe, the work is given by:

$$\text{Work} = \text{Energy} \;=\; (P_1 - P_2)(\text{Volume})$$
$$=\; \Delta P \times \text{Volume}$$

The complete energy equation for a flow system must include all possible energy terms, including "internal energy" changes (the energy stored in each molecule of the fluid). This energy includes molecular kinetic energy, molecular rotational energy, potential energy binding forces between molecules, and so on. This internal energy is only significant in laminar flow, where high frictional forces can raise the temperature of the fluid. However, we normally encounter turbulent flow in process control, so we can neglect internal energy in most cases.

Assuming the flow in Figure 8-1 is turbulent, let us find the energy relationship for flow in a uniform pipe.

We have just shown that the work (energy) done in moving a fluid through a section of pipe is

$$\text{Energy} = \Delta P \times \text{Volume}$$

This energy is spent giving the fluid a velocity of v, and we can express this energy of the moving fluid in terms of its kinetic energy, as follows:

$$\text{Energy} = mv^2/2$$

Since the two energies are the same, we have

$$\Delta P \times \text{Volume} = mv^2/2$$

However, by definition mass (m) = volume $\times$ density = (vol.)($\rho$)

$$\Delta P \times \text{Volume} \;=\; \text{Volume}(\rho)v^2/2$$

so
$$v^2 = 2\Delta P/\rho$$

or
$$v = \sqrt{\frac{2\Delta P}{\rho}} \qquad (8\text{-}1)$$

This gives the velocity of flowing fluid in terms of the pressure differential and density of the fluid.

This flow equation is also expressed in some books in terms of head instead of differential pressure ($\Delta P$). Where head is the height (z) of a column of liquid. It can be easily shown that head (z) and $\Delta P$ are related as follows:

$$z = \Delta P/\rho g$$
$$\text{or} \quad \Delta P = \rho z g$$

The flow velocity v can be expressed in terms of head z as follows:

$$v^2 = 2\Delta P/\rho = 2(\rho z g)/\rho = 2gz$$
$$v = \sqrt{2gz} \qquad (8\text{-}2)$$

We can define another term Q as the volumetric flow rate where

$$Q = Av \qquad (8\text{-}3)$$

and A is the cross-sectional area of the flow carrier (i.e., pipe, etc.)

We can also define a weight flow rate (W) as the weight flowing per unit time. Typical units are lb/hr. This is related to the volumetric flow rate by

$$W = \rho Q \qquad (8\text{-}4)$$

where: W = weight flow rate
ρ = weight density
Q = volumetric flow rate

### EXAMPLE 8-1

**Problem:** Water is pumped through a 1-inch diameter pipe with a flow velocity of 2.0 ft per second. Find the volumetric flow rate and the weight flow rate. The weight density (ρ) of water is 62.4 lb/ft³.

**Solution:** The flow velocity is given as 2.0 ft/sec, so the volumetric flow rate can be found from Equation 8-3:

$$Q = Av$$

The area is given by $\quad A = \pi d^2/4$
so that $\qquad\qquad\quad A = \pi(1\text{ in.} \times 1\text{ ft}/12\text{ in.})^2/4$
$\qquad\qquad\qquad\quad A = 0.0055\text{ ft}^2$

Then, the volume flow rate is

$$Q = Av$$
$$Q = (0.0055 \text{ ft}^2)(2 \text{ ft/sec})(60 \text{ sec/min})$$
$$Q = 0.654 \text{ ft}^3/\text{min}$$

The weight flow rate is found using Equation 8-4:

$$W = \rho Q$$
$$W = (62.4 \text{ lb/ft}^3)(0.654 \text{ ft}^3/\text{min})$$
$$W = 40.8 \text{ lb/min}$$

## EXAMPLE 8-2

**Problem:** An incompressible fluid is flowing in a 12-inch pipe under a pressure head of 16 inches. Calculate the fluid velocity and volumetric flow rate.

**Solution:** The fluid velocity is given by Equation 8-2:

$$v = \sqrt{2gz}$$

where $g = 32.2 \text{ ft/sec}^2$ and $z = (16 \text{ in.})(1 \text{ ft}/12 \text{ in.}) = 1.33 \text{ ft}$

So
$$v = \sqrt{2(32.2 \text{ ft/sec})(1.33 \text{ ft})}$$
$$v = 9.3 \text{ ft/sec}$$

The volumetric flow rate is obtained using Equation 8-3:

$$Q = Av$$
$$Q = \pi [(1 \text{ ft})^2/4] (9.3 \text{ ft/sec})$$
$$Q = 7.3 \text{ ft}^3/\text{sec}$$

**Differential Pressure Flow Equation**    In the last section we derived the basic equation for steady flow through a pipe with a constant cross section. The differential pressure ($\Delta P$) required to maintain the flow through such a pipe is very small, so it is difficult to measure. However, if the cross-sectional area of the pipe is reduced, we find that the velocity increases through the reduced area and the pressure is also reduced at that point. Thus, if an artificial restriction as shown in Figure 8-2 is placed in the pipe, we are able to measure this pressure drop and obtain a measurement of the flow in the pipe. Many $\Delta P$ flowmeters (orifice, Venturi, etc.) that we will discuss in this chapter use this method of placing a restriction in the process line.

We need to develop the equation for the velocity $v_2$ at the restriction (i.e., orifice) in a circular pipe. The area of the pipe is $A_1 = \pi D^2/4$ and the area of the orifice is $A_0 = \pi d^2/4$.

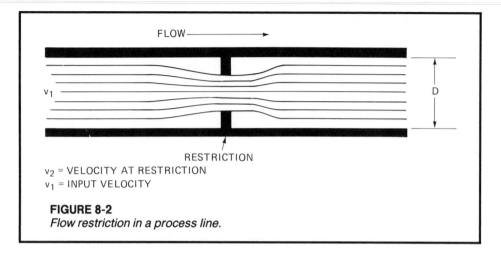

RESTRICTION
$v_2$ = VELOCITY AT RESTRICTION
$v_1$ = INPUT VELOCITY

**FIGURE 8-2**
*Flow restriction in a process line.*

Since the same quantity (Q = volume/time) of material must flow through any cross section of pipe, and since (area)(velocity) = volume/time:

$$A_1 v_1 = A_0 v_2$$

$$v_1 = v_2 \; \frac{A_0}{A_1}$$

$$v_1 = v_2 \; \frac{4\pi d^2}{4\pi D^2}$$

$$v_1 = v_2 \; \frac{d^2}{D^2}$$

Let us now relate the two energy terms, one due to the differential drop across the orifice ($\Delta P$), and the other being the kinetic energy of the moving fluid. The differential pressure is the result of the change in velocity across the restriction and *vice versa*. Thus, the energy due to $\Delta P$ must be exactly the same energy that causes the change in velocity. We know that the energy due to the change in velocity is given by

$$\Delta(\text{Kinetic Energy}) = \frac{mv_1^{\,2}}{2} - \frac{mv_2^{\,2}}{2}$$

The energy (force × distance) due to the differencial pressure acting through a given length of pipe (L) is

$$\text{Energy} = (\Delta P)AL = (\Delta P) \times \text{volume}$$

Since these two energies are equal, we have

$$\frac{mv_1^{\,2}}{2} - \frac{mv_2^{\,2}}{2} = (\Delta P) \times \text{volume}$$

But the mass of the fluid (m) is related to the volume as follows:

$$m = (\text{volume})(\text{density}) = (\text{volume})(\rho)$$

$$m \left[ \frac{v_1^2 - v_2^2}{2} \right] = (\Delta P) \times \text{volume}$$

$$(\text{volume})(\rho) \left[ \frac{v_1^2 - v_2^2}{2} \right] = (\Delta P) \times (\text{volume})$$

Canceling the volume from the equation, we have

$$\Delta P = \rho \left[ \frac{v_1^2 - v_2^2}{2} \right]$$

$$v_1^2 - v_2^2 = 2\Delta P/\rho \tag{8-5}$$

We had previously shown that

$$v_1 = v_2 \ \frac{d^2}{D^2}$$

If we square this equation, we obtain

$$v_1^2 = v_2^2 \ \frac{d^4}{D^4}$$

Substituting for $v_1^2$ in Equation 8-5 above:

$$v_2^2 - v_2^2 \left( \frac{d^4}{D^4} \right) = 2\Delta P/\rho$$

$$v_2^2 \left[ 1 - \left( \frac{d^4}{D^4} \right) \right] = 2\Delta P/\rho$$

$v_2$ is the velocity we measure at the orifice, so letting $v_2 = v$ and solving for v, we obtain

$$v = \sqrt{\frac{2\Delta P}{\rho \ [1 - (d/D)^4]}} \tag{8-6}$$

The ratio d/D is so important, it is called *beta* ($\beta$) and is defined as:

$$\beta = \frac{d}{D} \qquad (\text{beta ratio})$$

Substituting $\beta$ into Equation 8-3, we obtain the flow equation when the internal energy (pipe losses, molecular-energy losses, etc.) is assumed to be zero.

$$v = \sqrt{\frac{2\Delta P}{\rho\,[1 - \beta^4]}}$$

$$(8\text{-}7)$$

**Bernoulli Theorem**   We can also use the principle of conservation of energy to obtain the Bernoulli Theorem for fluid flow in a pipe. Figure 8-3 shows a typical energy flow diagram.

The energy possessed by a flowing fluid consists of internal energy and energies due to pressure, velocity, and position. In the direction of flow, the conservation of energy principle can be summarized by the following energy equation:

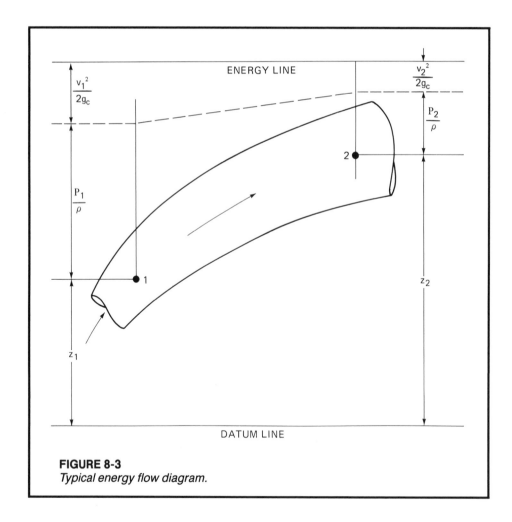

**FIGURE 8-3**
*Typical energy flow diagram.*

$$\text{Energy In } (E_1) + \text{Energy Added } (E_A) - \text{Energy Lost } (E_L) = \text{Energy Out}(E_2)$$

This equation, for steady flow of incompressible fluid in which the change in internal energy is negligible, is called the Bernoulli Theorem and simplifies to the following form:

$$\frac{P_1}{\rho} + \frac{v_1^2}{2g_c} + \frac{g_l}{g_c} z_1 = \frac{P_2}{\rho} + \frac{v_2^2}{2g_c} + \frac{g_l}{g_c} z_2 \qquad (8\text{-}8)$$

where:  $z$  = elevation above a datum of pipe centerline, ft (m)
$P$  = static pressure, absolute, lb/ft³ (Pa)
$\rho$  = fluid density, lb/ft³ (kg/m³)
$v$  = average fluid velocity, ft/sec (m/sec)
$g_c$  = conversion constant, 32.2 ft/sec (1 kg m/N sec²)
$g_l$  = local acceleration due to gravity, ft/sec² (m/sec²)
1, 2 = upstream and downstream measurement points

In Figure 8-3, these factors are identified for upstream (subscript 1) and downstream (subscript 2). Normally in most engineering applications $g_c = g_l$, so we can use a simpler version of Equation 8-8 as follows:

$$\frac{P_1}{\rho} + \frac{V_1^2}{2g_c} + z_1 = \frac{P_2}{\rho} + \frac{v_2^2}{2g_c} + z_2 \qquad (8\text{-}9)$$

Most problems dealing with the flow of liquids use the Bernoulli Theorem as the basis of a solution. Flow of gases, in most instances, involves the principles of thermodynamics and heat transfer so that this basic flow equation cannot be used. An example problem will help to demonstrate the utility of *Bernoulli's Theorem* for a typical liquid flow problem.

### EXAMPLE 8-3

**Problem:** In the figure shown, water flows from point 1 to point 2 at the volumetric flow rate (Q) of 10.0 cfs and the pressure head at point 1 is 20 ft. If there is no energy loss from point 1 to 2, find the pressure head at point 2. If $z_1 = 10$ ft, and $z_2 = 25$ ft (assume $g_c = g_l = 32.2$ ft/sec²).

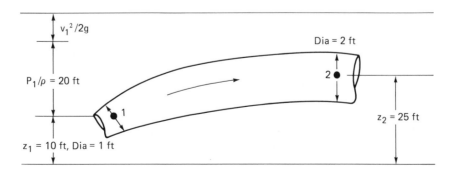

**Solution:** First we need to find the fluid velocities at points 1 and 2.

$$V_1 = Q/A_1 = 10 \text{ cfs}/ \left(\frac{1}{4} \pi \ 1 \text{ ft}^2\right) = 12.7 \text{ ft/sec}$$

$$V_2 = Q/A_2 = 10 \text{ cfs}/ \left(\frac{1}{4} \pi \ (2 \text{ ft})^2\right) = 3.2 \text{ ft/sec}$$

Then, using Equation 8-9,

$$\frac{P_1}{\rho} + \frac{V_1^2}{2g_c} + z_1 = \frac{P_2}{\rho} + \frac{v_2^2}{2g_c} + z_2$$

and substituting,

$$\left(20 + \frac{(12.7)^2}{2(32.2)} + 10\right) = \left(\frac{P_2}{\rho} + \frac{(3.2)^2}{2(32.2)} + 25\right)$$

so that    $\dfrac{P_2}{\rho} = 7.34 \text{ ft}$

**Reynolds Number**   The basic equations of flow assume that the velocity of flow is uniform across a given cross section. In practice, flow velocity at any cross section approaches zero in the boundary layer adjacent to the pipe wall and varies across the diameter. This flow velocity profile has a significant effect on the relationship between flow velocity and pressure difference developed in a flowmeter. In 1883, Sir Osborne Reynolds, an English scientist, presented a paper before the Royal Society that proposed a single dimensionless ratio, now known as Reynolds number, as a criterion to describe this phenomenon. This number $R_e$, is expressed as:

$$R_e = \frac{vD\rho}{\mu}$$

where:    v   = velocity
D   = diameter
$\rho$   = density
$\mu$   = absolute viscosity

Reynolds number expresses the ratio of inertial forces to viscous forces. At a very low Reynolds number, viscous forces predominate and inertial forces give little effect. Pressure difference approaches direct proportionality to average flow velocity and to viscosity.

At high Reynolds numbers, inertial forces predominate, and viscous drag effects become negligible. At low Reynolds numbers, flow is laminar and may be regarded as a group of concentric shells; and each shell reacts in a viscous shear manner on adjacent shells; the velocity profile across a diameter is substantially parabolic. At high Reynolds numbers flow is turbulent, with eddies forming between the boundary layer and the body of the flowing fluid and propagating through the stream pattern. A very complex, random pattern of velocities develops in all directions. This turbulent, mixing action tends to produce a uniform average axial velocity across the stream. Change from the laminar flow pattern to the turbulent flow pattern is gradual with no distinct transition point. For Reynolds numbers above 10,000, flow is definitely turbulent.

## The Orifice Plate

The orifice plate is the most common $\Delta$P-type flow-measuring device. An orifice plate is inserted in the line, and the differential pressure across it is measured.

The orifice plate has important advantages, including low cost, manufactured to very close tolerances, and ease of installation and replacement. Orifice measurement of liquids, gases, and vapors under a wide range of conditions enjoys a high degree of confidence based on a great deal of accurate test work.

The standard orifice plate is a circular disc, usually stainless steel, from 1/8 in. to 1/2 in. thick, depending on size and flow velocity, with a hole (orifice) in the middle and a tab, which is used as a data plate, projecting out (Figure 8-4).

The orifice plate, when inserted in the line, causes an increase in flow velocity and a corresponding decrease in pressure. The flow pattern shows an effective decrease in cross section beyond the orifice plate, with a maximum velocity and minimum pressure at the vena contracta (Figure 8-5).

This flow pattern and the sharp leading edge of the orifice plate (Figure 8-4) that produces it are very important. The sharp edge results in an almost pure line contact between the plate and the effective flow, with negligible fluid-to-metal friction drag at this boundary. Any nicks, burrs, or rounding of the sharp edge can result in surprisingly large errors in measurement.

When the normal practice of measuring the differential pressure at a location close to the orifice plate is followed, friction effects between fluid and pipe wall upstream and downstream from the orifice are minimized so that pipe roughness has little effect. Fluid viscosity, as reflected in Reynolds number, does have a considerable influence, particularly at low Reynolds numbers. Since the formation of

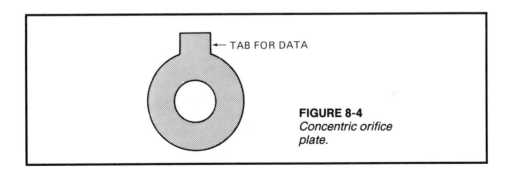

← TAB FOR DATA

**FIGURE 8-4**
*Concentric orifice plate.*

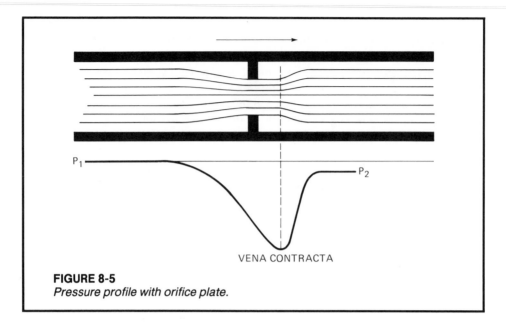

**FIGURE 8-5**
*Pressure profile with orifice plate.*

the vena contracta is an inertial effect, a decrease in the ratio of inertial to frictional forces (decrease in Reynolds number) and the corresponding change in the flow profile results in less constriction of flow at the vena contracta and an increase of the coefficient.

So far, we have mentioned only the concentric orifice plate (see Figure 8-4). However, there are several other important types of orifice plates such as the eccentric and the segmental.

**Eccentric and Segmental Orifice Plates**    The eccentric orifice plate is exactly like the concentric orifice plate except the hole is bored off center, as shown in Figure 8-6.

The segmental orifice has a hole that is a segment of a circle, also shown in Figure 8-6. It must be installed so that the circular section is concentric with the

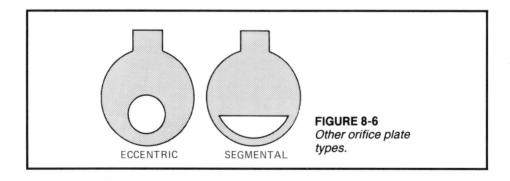

**FIGURE 8-6**
*Other orifice plate types.*

pipe and so that no portion of the flange or gasket covers the hole. The same pre-cautions regarding the sharp upstream edge of the plate apply as with circular orifices.

Eccentric and segmental orifices are preferable to concentric orifices for measurement of slurries or dirty liquids as well as for measurement of gas or vapor where liquids may be present, especially large slugs of liquid. Where the stream contains particulate matter, the segmental orifice, which provides an open path at the bottom of the pipe, may be preferable. However, for conditions within the capa-bility of the eccentric orifice, the latter is preferred because of greater ease of man-ufacture to precise tolerances and generally more accurate and repeatable performance.

**Orifice Plate Flow Equation** The basic flow equation (8-3) was developed based on the assumption that internal energy (pipe losses, molecular-energy losses, etc.) was zero. Since these losses are not zero and there is no direct way of measuring them, empirical correction factors, based on flow experiments with var-ious pipes sizes, are tabulated in the literature. These factors are called flow coeffi-cients or discharge coefficients.

Following is a list of correction factors required to obtain accurate flow read-ing from orifice plates:

Specific gravity ($F_g$)
Base pressure ($F_{pb}$)
Flowing temperature ($F_{tf}$)
Base temperature ($F_{tb}$)
Supercompressibility $F_{pv}$ (for gases only)
Expansion factor Y (for gases only)
Reynold's number ($F_r$)
Basic orifice flow factor ($F_b$)

By combining all the correction factors into a single factor called the orifice flow constant (C), we obtain a practical method for computing flow through an ori-fice plate:

$$v = C \sqrt{\frac{\Delta P}{\rho}} \qquad (8\text{-}10)$$

or
$$v = C \sqrt{2gz} \qquad (8\text{-}11)$$

where $C = F_g \times F_{tf} \times F_{tb} \times F_{pb} \times F_{pv} \times Y \times F_r \times F_b$

**EXAMPLE 8-4**

**Problem:** An incompressible fluid is flowing through an orifice plate with a flow coefficient of 0.6 causing a pressure drop of 16 inches. Calculate the fluid velocity.

**Solution:** The fluid velocity measured by an orifice is given by Equation 8-11:

$$v = C \sqrt{2gz}$$

Since $g = 32.2 \text{ ft/sec}^2$, $z = (16 \text{ in.})(1 \text{ ft}/12 \text{ in.}) = 1.33 \text{ ft}$, and $C = 0.6$, we obtain

$$v = 0.6 \sqrt{2(32.2 \text{ ft/sec})(1.33 \text{ ft})}$$

$$v = 5.55 \text{ ft/sec}$$

## The Venturi Tube

The Venturi tube (Figure 8-7) consists of a converging conical inlet section in which the cross section of the stream decreases and the velocity increases with consequent increase of velocity head and decrease of pressure head; a cylindrical throat that provides for a point of measurement of this decreased pressure in an area where flow rate is neither increasing nor decreasing; and a diverging recovery cone in which velocity decreases and the decreased velocity head is recovered as pressure. Pressure taps are taken at one half diameter upstream of the inlet cone and at the middle of the throat.

The Venturi tube has no sudden changes in contour, no sharp corners, and no projections into the fluid stream. Because of this, it can be used for measurement of slurries and dirty fluids, which tend to build up on or clog orifice plates. The major disadvantages of the Venturi tube is cost, both for the tube itself and the frequency of installation changes in the larger sizes. A Venturi tube is much more difficult to inspect in place than an orifice. For several reasons, the accuracy of measurement with a Venturi tube may be less than with a sharp-edged orifice plate unless the Venturi tube is flow calibrated in place.

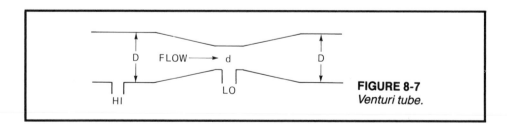

**FIGURE 8-7**
*Venturi tube.*

**Flow Nozzles**    The flow nozzle (Figure 8-8) consists of a restriction with an elliptical, or near elliptical, contour approach section that terminates in tangency with a cylindrical throat section.

Flow nozzles are commonly used for measurement of stream flow and other high velocity fluid flows where erosion may be a problem. Since the exact contour is not particularly critical, the flow nozzle can be expected to retain precise calibration for a long time under hostile conditions.

Flow nozzles, because of their streamlined contour, tend to sweep solids through the throat. They are not recommended for measurement of fluids with a large percentage of solids. When appreciable solids are present, flow nozzles should be mounted in a vertical pipe with flow in the downward direction.

**The Pitot Tube**    The Pitot tube, although one of the early developments in flow measurement, has limited industrial application. Its primary use is measurement of low velocity air flow.

A common industrial type of Pitot tube (see Figure 8-9) consists of a cylindrical probe inserted into the air stream. Fluid flow velocity at the upstream face of the probe is reduced substantially to zero. Velocity head is converted to impact

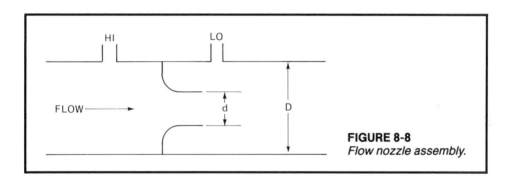

**FIGURE 8-8**
*Flow nozzle assembly.*

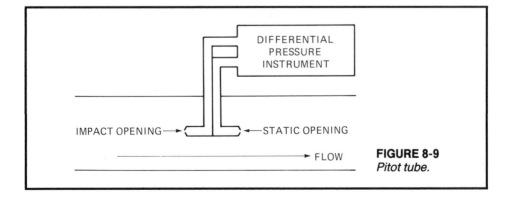

**FIGURE 8-9**
*Pitot tube.*

pressure, which is sensed through a small hole in the upstream face of the probe. A corresponding small hole in the side of the probe senses static pressure without the addition of impact pressure. An instrument measures the differential pressure, which is proportional to the square of the stream velocity in the vicinity of the impact pressure-sensing hole. The velocity equation for the Pitot is given by

$$v = C_P \sqrt{2gz} \qquad (8\text{-}12)$$

where $C_P$ is the Pitot tube coefficient.

**EXAMPLE 8-5**

**Problem:** A Pitot tube having a coefficient of 0.98 is used to measure the velocity of water in a pipe. The differential pressure head is 3 ft. What is the velocity?

**Solution:** Applying Equation 8-12 yields

$$v = C_P \sqrt{2gz}$$

$$v = 0.98 \sqrt{2(32.2 \text{ ft/sec}^2)(3 \text{ ft})}$$

$$v = 13.6 \text{ ft/sec}$$

The Pitot tube causes practically no pressure loss in the flow stream. It is normally installed through a nipple in the side of the pipe. It is frequently installed through an isolation valve, so that it can be moved back and forth across the stream to establish the profile of flow velocity.

Certain characteristics of Pitot tube flow measurement have limited its industrial application. For true measurement of flow, it is essential to establish an average value of flow velocity. To obtain this with a Pitot tube, it is necessary to move the tube back and forth across the stream to establish velocity at all points and then to take an average.

For high velocity flow streams, care in design is required to provide necessary stiffness and strength. A tube inserted in a high velocity stream has a tendency to vibrate, and mechanical damage is probable. As a result, Pitot tubes are generally used only in low to medium flow gas applications where high accuracy is not required.

To obtain a better average value of flow, Pitot tubes with several impact pressure openings distributed across the stream are available. These are proprietary products designated as Annubar™ tubes. Characteristics are available from the manufacturer.

## Rotameters
The rotameter is a variable area-type flowmeter consisting of a tapered metering tube and a float that is free to move up and down within the tube. The metering tube is mounted vertically with the small end at the bottom.

The fluid to be measured enters at the bottom of the tube, passes upward around the float, and out at the top. Figure 8-10 is a representation of a typical rotameter.

When there is no flow through the rotameter, the float rests at the bottom of the metering tube where the maximum diameter of the float is approximately the same as the bore of the tube. When fluid enters the metering tube, the buoyant effect of the fluid lightens the float, but it has a greater density than the fluid and the buoyant effect is not sufficient to raise it. There is a small annular opening between the float and the tube. The pressure drop across the float increases and raises the float to increase the area between the float and tube until the upward hydraulic forces acting on it are balanced by its weight less the buoyant force. The float moves up and down in the tube in proportion to the fluid flow rate and the annular area between the float and the tube. It reaches a stable position in the tube when the forces are in equilibrium. With upward movement of the float toward the larger end of the tapered tube, the annular opening between the tube and the float increases. As the area increases, the pressure differential across the float decreases. The float will assume a position in dynamic equilibrium when the pressure differential across the float plus the buoyancy effect balances the weight of the float. Every float position corresponds to one particular flow rate and no other for a fluid of a given density and viscosity. To obtain a flow reading, it is necessary to provide a calibrated scale on the tube.

Glass rotameters are used in a large number of applications, but metal rotameters are used in applications where glass is not satisfactory. In this case, the float position must be indirectly determined by either magnetic or electrical techniques. The use of indirect float position sensors also provides functions other than direct visual indication. Some rotameters output pneumatic, electronic, or pulse signals.

Bernoulli's Theorem can be used to derive the following basic equation for liquid flow through a rotameter:

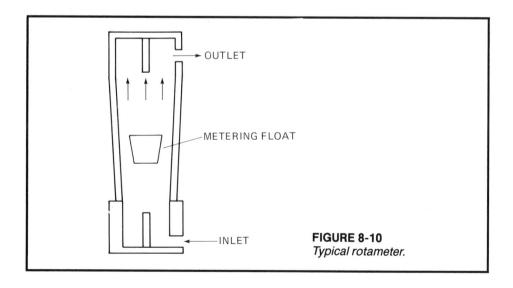

**FIGURE 8-10**
*Typical rotameter.*

$$Q = CA_a \sqrt{\frac{\rho_F - \rho_f}{\rho_f}}$$

(8-13)

where:  $Q$  = volumetric flow rate
          $C$  = meter flow constant
          $A_a$ = annular area between tube and float
          $\rho_F$ = density of float
          $\rho_f$ = density of fluid

The rotameter is an inexpensive flowmeter for gas flow measurement. The pressure drop across the meter is essentially constant over the full 10:1 operating range. Pressure drop is low, generally less than 1 psi.

The position of the float in the metering tube varies in a linear relationship with flow rate. This is true over ranges up to 10:1. Rotameters can directly measure flows as high as 4000 gpm. Higher flow rates can be economically handled using the bypass-type rotameter. The capacity of the rotameter can be changed by changing the float. By using the same housing, but changing both the metering tube and the float, a gross change in capacity is possible. These changes can account for both a change in flow rate and a change in fluid density.

The rotameter tends to be self-cleaning. The velocity of the flow past the float and the freedom of the float to move vertically enables the meter to clean itself of some buildup of foreign material. Liquids with fibrous materials are an exception and should not be metered with rotameters. Generally, the size of a particle, the type of particle (whether fibrous or particulate), and the abrasiveness of the particle determine the suitability of the rotameter for a given application. Also, the percent of solids by weight or by volume and the density of the solids influence the selection of the rotameter for flow measurement.

## Magnetic Flowmeters

Magnetic flowmeters use Faraday's Law of Induction for making a flow measurement. This law states that relative motion at right angles between a conductor and a magnetic field will develop a voltage in the conductor. The induced voltage is proportional to the relative velocity of the conductor and the magnetic field. This is the principle used in direct current and alternating current generators. The most common magnetic flowmeters are a modified form of alternating current generators. In the magnetic flowmeter, the fluid itself must have some minimum conductivity and acts as the conductor.

Fluid is the conductor (see Figure 8-11) and has a length equivalent to the inside diameter of the flowmeter (D). The fluid conductor moves with an average velocity ($\bar{v}$) through a magnetic field (B). The voltage (E) induced in the conductor is proportional to the volumetric flow rate (Q). The mathematical relationship for the magnetic flowmeter is $E = BDQ/C$ or $Q = CE/BD$, where C is a meter constant, and the magnetic field (B) and the diameter (D) of the flowmeter are constants.

The magnetic field generated is in a plane that is mutually perpendicular to the axis of the instrument and the plane of the electrodes. The velocity of the fluid is along the longitudinal axis of the detector body; therefore, the voltage induced

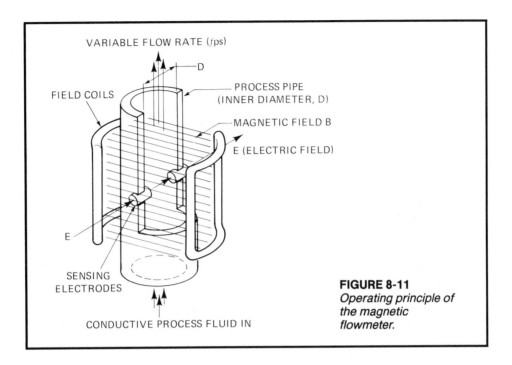

VARIABLE FLOW RATE (fps)

D

FIELD COILS

PROCESS PIPE
(INNER DIAMETER, D)

MAGNETIC FIELD B

E (ELECTRIC FIELD)

E

SENSING
ELECTRODES

**FIGURE 8-11**
*Operating principle of
the magnetic
flowmeter.*

CONDUCTIVE PROCESS FLUID IN

within the fluid is mutually perpendicular to both the velocity of the fluid and the magnetic field, and the voltage is generated along the axis of the meter electrodes. The fluid can be considered as a series of fluid conductors moving through the magnetic field. An increase in flow rate will result in a greater relative velocity between the conductor and the magnetic field, and a greater instantaneous value of voltage will be generated.

The instantaneous voltage generated at the electrodes represents the average fluid velocity of the flow profile. The output signal of the meter is equal to the continuous average volumetric flow rate regardless of flow profile. Therefore, magnetic flowmeters are independent of viscosity changes. It is always absolutely essential that the meter be full since the meter senses velocity as analogous to volumetric flow rate.

The magnetic flowmeter is constructed of a nonmagnetic tube that carries the flowing liquid, which must have a minimum level of conductivity. Surrounding the metering tube are magnetic coils and cores, which, when electric current is applied, provide a magnetic field across the full width of the metering tube. The fluid flowing through the tube is the conductor, and, as the conductor moves through the magnetic field, a voltage is generated proportional to the volumetric flow rate. The voltage generated is mutually perpendicular to the magnetic field and the direction of the flowing liquid.

Some mass flowmetering systems use magnetic flowmeters in association with density instruments. A typical system is shown in Figure 8-12. The signal developed by the magnetic flowmeter relates to volumetric flow and the output signal

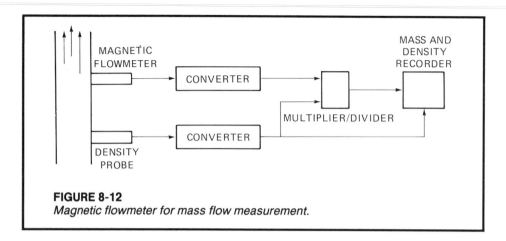

**FIGURE 8-12**
*Magnetic flowmeter for mass flow measurement.*

from the density probe is proportional to density. The two signals are multiplied and an output signal proportional to mass flow rate is obtained.

## Turbine Flowmeters

The turbine flowmeter provides a frequency output signal that varies linearly with volumetric flow rate over specified flow ranges. The entire fluid to be measured enters the flowmeter, then passes through a rotor. The fluid passing the rotor causes it to turn with an angular velocity that is proportional to the fluid linear velocity; therefore, the volumetric flow rate is linear within given limits of flow rate.

The pick-off probe converts the rotor velocity to an equivalent frequency signal. Variable reluctance-type pick-off assemblies are the most commonly used. In this system, the meter housing must be nonmagnetic, usually stainless steel. The rotor must also be stainless steel.

The pick-off probe consists of a small, powerful permanent magnet and a coil winding. The field of the magnet is influenced by the moving blades of the rotor, which are of permeable material. As a rotor blade passes through the field of the magnet, it provides an easier path for the field, and the field distorts, thus moving across the coil winding. The relative motion between the magnetic field and the coil winding generates an ac voltage, the frequency of which is proportional to flow rate. This can be stated as:

$$K = \frac{\text{Cycles per time}}{\text{Volume per time}} = \frac{\text{Cycles}}{\text{Volume}} = \text{Meter coefficient}$$

A characteristic of turbine flowmeters (the meter coefficient) is to develop a precisely known number of pulses for a given volume measured.

The output signal from a turbine flowmeter is a frequency proportional to volumetric flow rate: therefore, each pulse generated by the turbine flowmeter is equivalent to a measured volume of liquid. Generally, flow rates are converted to flow totals by totalizer-type instruments. For the totalization to be valid, the value of each pulse must be essentially constant; therefore, the turbine flowmeter must be linear. The turbine flowmeter is generally used over its linear range, which is $\pm 0.5\%$ of rate. Totalization is also used for turbine flowmeters that are linear over only a part of the operating range. In such cases, flow monitoring is used to be certain that the flowmeter is used only over the linear portion of its operating range.

Totalizers are available in two general configurations. One form simply either totalizes pulse or does necessary scaling (factoring of the frequency information so that each pulse is equal to a unit volume or decimal part of a volume) in direct-reading units. A second configuration not only totalizes but also predetermines the number of counts or unit volumes proportional to a given batch size; it then provides a signal, generally a contact closure, to control the process. Batching totalizers with a ramping function provide an analog output to (1) open a control valve to a given position, (2) control volumetric flow rate, and (3) at a predetermined point in the batch, program shutdown of the valve to some reduced flow rate, which is then maintained until the process is terminated.

Flow rate indication can be made digitally or in analog form. Digital counters with adjustable time base provide flow rate indication as frequency or in direct-reading units (such as gallons per minute) depending on the established time base. Analog indicators require an analog signal proportional to frequency.

## Ultrasonic Flowmeters

Ultrasonic flowmeters operate on the principle of measuring the velocity of sound as it passes through the fluid flowing in a pipe. The most common approach to this application is described below and is shown in Figure 8-13.

Piezoelectric crystals (barium titanate or lead zirconate-titanate) are used as transmitters to send acoustic signals through the fluid flowing through the pipe to receivers that are also piezoelectric crystals. The fluid flows through the pipe at a velocity, v. The distance between each transmitter-receiver pair is X. The velocity of the sound through the fluid is $v_s$. The path of the sound is at an angle $\alpha$ from the pipe wall. The velocity of sound from transmitter A to receiver B (increased by the fluid velocity) is $v_s + v \cos \alpha$, and its frequency is

$$f_A = \frac{v_s + v \cos \alpha}{X}$$

The velocity of sound from transmitter B to receiver A (reduced by fluid velocity ) is given by $v_s - v \cos \alpha$ and its frequency is

$$f_B = \frac{v_s - v \cos \alpha}{X}$$

The beat or difference frequency $\Delta f$ is

$$f_A - f_B \text{ or } \Delta f = \frac{2 v \cos \alpha}{X} \tag{8-14}$$

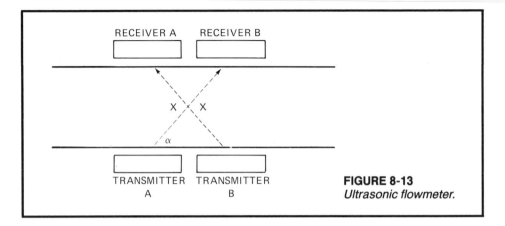

RECEIVER A     RECEIVER B

X   X

α

TRANSMITTER   TRANSMITTER
     A             B

**FIGURE 8-13**
*Ultrasonic flowmeter.*

Since α and X are constant, the flow velocity can be obtained by measuring this beat frequency. Flow rate is then derived by multiplying the flow velocity by the pipe cross-sectional area.

The beat frequency is measured by the use of an electronic mixer. The purpose of the mixer is to translate the high frequencies to a lower frequency level where more efficient amplification and selectivity are possible. In general, the design of a mixer is similar to that of an rf amplifier with the addition of the injection of an oscillator frequency into the amplifier. The combination of two oscillators and mixer is referred to as a beat frequency oscillator (bfo).

### EXAMPLE 8-6

**Problem:** Given a beat frequency ($\Delta f$) of 1000 cps for an ultrasonic flow-meter, the angle ($\alpha$) between the transmitters and receivers is 45° and the sound path (X) is 12 inches. Calculate the fluid velocity in feet per second.

**Solution:** Rearranging the beat frequency equation:

$$\Delta f \quad = \quad \frac{2\,v\,\cos\alpha}{X}$$

$$v \quad = \quad \frac{\Delta f X}{2\cos\alpha}$$

$$v \quad = \quad 1000\,\text{sec}^{-1}\,(1\,\text{ft})/2\cos 45°$$

$$v \quad = \quad 649.4\ \text{ft/sec}$$

Ultrasonic flowmeters are normally installed on the outside of liquid-filled pipes, so the measuring element is nonintrusive and will not induce a pressure drop or disturbance in the process stream. They generally cost more than standard flow-measuring devices, such as orifice plates or Venturi tubes. However, the instrument can be readily attached to the outside of existing pipes without shutdown, special pipe sections, or isolations valves, so their overall costs, compared to conventional flowmeters, is generally less in the larger pipe sizes.

## EXERCISES

8.1 Show that if the height of a liquid in a U-tube manometer is z, the head (z) is related to differential pressure ($\Delta P$) by the equation: $z = \Delta P/\rho g$, where $\rho$ is the density of the liquid.

8.2. Water is pumped through a 6-inch diameter pipe with a flow velocity of 12 ft per second. Find the volume flow rate and the weight flow rate. The weight density of water is 62.4 lb/ft$^3$.

8.3. An incompressible fluid is flowing in a 4-inch pipe under a pressure head of 20 inches. Calculate the fluid velocity and volume flow rate.

8.4. In the figure shown, water flows from point 1 to point 2 at the rate of 15.0 cfs and the pressure head at point 1 is 5 ft. If there is no internal energy loss from point 1 to 2, find the pressure head at point 2.

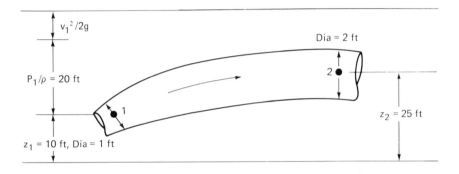

8.5. An incompressible fluid is flowing through an orifice plate with a flow coefficient of 0.5, causing a pressure drop of 20 inches. Calculate the fluid velocity.

8.6. A Pitot tube having a coefficient of 0.95 is used to measure the velocity of water in a pipe. The differential pressure head is 12 inches. What is the velocity of the water in the pipe?

8.7. In an ultrasonic flowmeter the beat frequency ($\Delta f$) is 850 cps, the angle ($\alpha$) between the transmitters and receivers is 45°, and the sound path (X) is 5 inches. Calculate the fluid velocity in feet per second.

## BIBLIOGRAPHY

1. Liptak, B.G., and Venczel, K., (ed.) *Process Control—Instrument Engineers' Handbook*, Chilton Book Company, 1982.

2. Johnson, C.D., *Process Control Instrumentation Technology*, Second Edition, John Wiley & Sons, 1982.

3. *Flow Measurement - A Professional Course*, Measurement & Data Corp., 1986.

4. Giles, R.V., *Theory and Problems of Fluid Mechanics and Hydraulics, Schaum's Outline Series*, Second Edition, McGraw-Hill Book Co., 1962.

5. Spitzer, David W., *Industrial Flow Measurement*, Instrument Society of America, 1984.

# 9

# Final
# Control Elements

**Introduction**   In the first chapter, we introduced the concept and defined the three elements of process control: measurement, evaluation, and final control. The final control element is probably the most important because it exerts a direct influence on the process. Final control elements contain the necessary pieces of equipment to convert the control signal (generated by a process controller) into the action needed to correctly control the process.

In this chapter, the fundamentals of the final control elements (such as control valves, motors, and pumps) are discussed. Since control valves are the single most common type of final control element in process control, they will be discussed first and in the greatest detail.

**Control Valve Basics**   This section will discuss the basic principles of control valves and control valve sizing for liquid service.

A control valve is simply a variable orifice used to regulate the flow of a process fluid in accordance with the process requirements. A typical control valve assembly is shown in Figure 9-1. The two main components of a control valve are the *actuator* and the *valve body*. The diaphragm actuator shown in Figure 9-1 uses a supplied fluid pressure from a controller to move the valve stem and in turn the valve plug to the desired control position. The valve body is mounted in the process line and is used to control the flow of fluid in the process.

Other important components of the control valve shown in Figure 7-1 are the actuator spring, the valve stem, the valve cage. The actuator spring enclosed in the yoke is used to move the valve stem in a direction opposite to that created by the diaphragm. The valve stem is a rod connected between the diaphragm plate and the valve plug. The valve cage is a hollow cylindrical trim element that is used as a guide to align the movement of the valve plug.

There are two main features of control valves: valve capacity and valve characteristics.

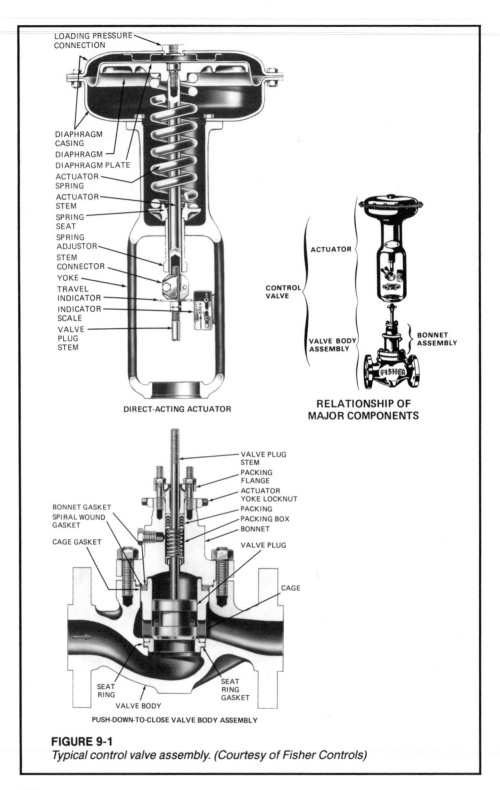

**FIGURE 9-1**

*Typical control valve assembly. (Courtesy of Fisher Controls)*

**Control Valve Characteristics**   The valve characteristic is the relationship of the change in valve opening to the change in flow through the valve. The most frequently used characteristics are equal percentage, linear, and quick opening (see Figure 9-2).

The quick opening valve is used predominantly for ON/OFF control applications. The valve characteristic of Figure 9-2 shows that a relatively small motion of the valve stem results in maximum possible flow rate through the valve. Such a valve, for example, may allow 85% of maximum flow rate with only 25% stem travel.

The linear valve, as shown in Figure 9-2, has a flow rate that varies linearly with the position of the stem. This relationship can be expressed as follows:

$$\frac{Q}{Q_{max}} = \frac{X}{X_{max}}$$

where:   $Q$ = flow rate
$Q_{max}$ = maximum flow rate
$X$ = stem position
$X_{max}$ = maximum stem position

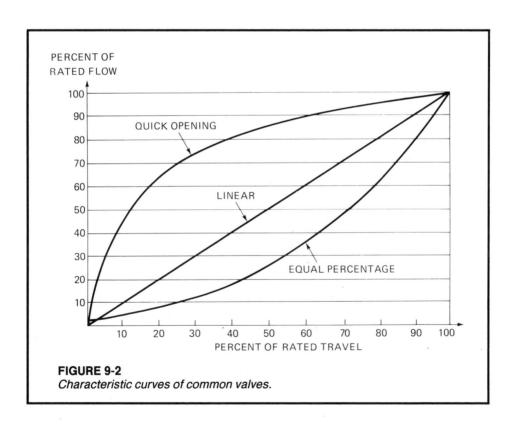

**FIGURE 9-2**
*Characteristic curves of common valves.*

The equal percentage valve is manufactured so that a given percentage change in stem position produces an equal percentage change in flow. Generally, this type of valve does not shut off the flow completely in its limit of travel. We can define a term called *rangeability* (R) as the ratio of maximum flow ($Q_{max}$) to minimum flow ($Q_{min}$):

$$R = \frac{Q_{max}}{Q_{min}}$$

**EXAMPLE 9-1**

**Problem:** An equal percentage valve has a maximum flow of 100 gpm and a minimum flow of 2 gpm. Find its rangeability (R).

**Solution:** The rangeability is

$$R = \frac{Q_{max}}{Q_{min}}$$

$$R = \frac{100 \text{ gpm}}{2 \text{ gpm}} = 50$$

**Valve Sizing for Liquids**  Improper valve sizing is a mistake, both technically and economically. A valve that is too small will not pass the required flow, and the process will be starved. A valve that is oversize will be unnecessarily expensive, and it can lead to instability and other problems.

Selecting the correct size valve for a given application requires a knowledge of process conditions that the valve will actually see in service. The technique for using this information to size the valve is based upon a combination of theory and experimentation.

Daniel Bernoulli was one of the first to take a scientific interest in the flow of liquids. Using the principle of conservation of energy, he discovered that as a liquid flows through an orifice, the square of the fluid velocity is directly proportional to the pressure differential across the orifice and inversely proportional to the specific gravity of the fluid. In other words, the greater the pressure differential, the higher the velocity. The greater the fluid density, the lower the velocity. In addition, as indicated in Chapter 8, the volumetric flow of liquid can be calculated by multiplying the fluid velocity by the flow area, or Q = Av.

Equation 9-1 combines these two concepts into a single expression relating flow in gallons per minute (Q) to the pressure differential ($\Delta P$) in psi, specific gravity (G), and the flow area (A) in square inches. The constant (C) is all of the combined proportionality constants and accounts for the proper units of flow measurement.

$$v = C \ \sqrt{\Delta P/G}$$
$$Q = Av$$

$$Q = CA \sqrt{\Delta P/G} \qquad\qquad (9\text{-}1)$$

Although this equation has a strong theoretical base, it does not take into account energy losses due to turbulence and friction as the fluid passes through the orifice. This is compensated for by adding a discharge coefficient ($C_d$) that is different for each type of flow orifice. Since the flow area is also a unique function of each type of flow orifice, all three of these terms can be combined into a single coefficient. When applied to valves, this coefficient is called the valve sizing coefficient ($C_v$).

$$Q = C_d CA \sqrt{\Delta P/G}$$

$$Q = C_v \sqrt{\Delta P/G} \qquad\qquad (9\text{-}2)$$

$C_v$ is experimentally determined for each different size and style of valve using water in a test line under carefully controlled standard conditions. Figure 9-3 shows the standard test piping arrangement established by the Fluid Controls Institute (FCI) to provide uniform measurement of $C_v$ data.

A careful look at this basic liquid flow equation will help to develop a feel for what $C_v$ really means. Consider the case of water at 60°F flowing through a valve. Here the specific gravity (G) is equal to one. Let's also assume that a 1-psi pressure differential is maintained across the valve. Under these conditions, the entire square root factor becomes one. This specific example shows that $C_v$ is numerically equal to the number of U.S. gallons of water that will flow through the valve in one minute when the water temperature is 60°F and the pressure differential across the valve is 1 psi. Thus, $C_v$ provides an index for comparing the liquid flow capacities of different types of valves under a standard set of conditions.

$C_v$ varies with both the size and style of valve. Published $C_v$ data, combined with the basic liquid sizing equation and the actual service conditions, allows the user to accurately select the right valve size for any given application. Typical values of $C_v$ for different size valves are shown in Table 9-1.

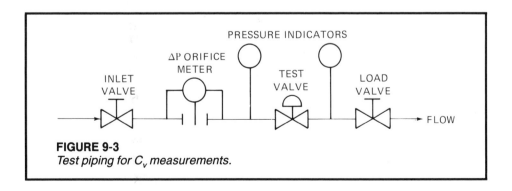

**FIGURE 9-3**
*Test piping for $C_v$ measurements.*

**TABLE 9-1**
**Typical Valve Flow Coefficients**

| Valve Size (inches) | $C_v$ |
|---|---|
| 1/4 | 0.3 |
| 1/2 | 3 |
| 1 | 15 |
| 1-1/2 | 35 |
| 2 | 55 |
| 3 | 110 |
| 4 | 175 |
| 6 | 400 |
| 8 | 750 |

## EXAMPLE 9-2

**Problem:** Water is pumped through a pipe with an inside diameter of 6 inches at a flow rate of 10 inches per second. Find the volume flow rate.

**Solution:**

$$A = \frac{\pi D^2}{4} = \frac{(\pi)(6 \text{ in.})^2}{4}$$

$$A = 28.26 \text{ in.}^2$$

Thus, the flow rate is

$$Q = Av = 28.26 \text{ in.}^2 (10 \text{ in./sec})$$
$$Q = 282.6 \text{ in.}^3/\text{sec}$$

## EXAMPLE 9-3

**Problem:** Calculate the $C_v$ and select the required valve size from Table 9-1 for a valve that must regulate 300 gpm of ethyl alcohol with a specific gravity of 0.8 at a pressure drop of 100 psi.

**Solution:** We find the correct valve sizing factor from

$$Q = C_v \sqrt{\Delta P/G} \qquad (9\text{-}2)$$

$$C_v = Q \sqrt{G/\Delta P}$$

$$C_v = 300 \text{ gpm } \sqrt{0.8/100 \text{ psi}}$$

$$C_v = 26.8$$

Based on the calculated $C_v$ a 1-1/2 in. valve would be selected.

**Flashing and Cavitation**   To simplify the discussion of flashing and cavitation, a control valve can be represented by a simple restriction in the line. As the flow passes through the physical restriction, there is a necking down, or contraction, of the flow stream. The minimum cross-sectional area of the flow stream occurs at a point called the vena contracta, which is just a short distance downstream of the physical restriction (see Figure 9-4).

In order to understand flashing and cavitation, it is first necessary to understand the interchange between the kinetic energy and the potential energy of a fluid that is flowing through a valve or other restriction. To maintain a steady flow of liquid through the valve, the velocity must be greatest at the vena contracta where the cross-sectional area is the least. This increase in velocity, or kinetic energy, comes about at the expense of the pressure, or potential energy.

The pressure profile along the valve shows a sharp decrease in the pressure as the velocity increases. The lowest pressure, of course, will occur at the vena contracta where the velocity is the greatest. Then, further downstream as the fluid stream expands into a larger area, there is a decrease in the velocity and a corresponding increase in the pressure. The pressure downstream of the valve never recovers completely to the pressure that existed upstream.

The pressure differential that exists across the valve is called the $\Delta P$ (delta P) of the valve. This $\Delta P$ is a measure of the amount of energy that was dissipated in the valve. Useful energy is lost in the valve because of turbulence and friction. The more energy dissipated in a valve, the greater the $\Delta P$ for a given area and flow.

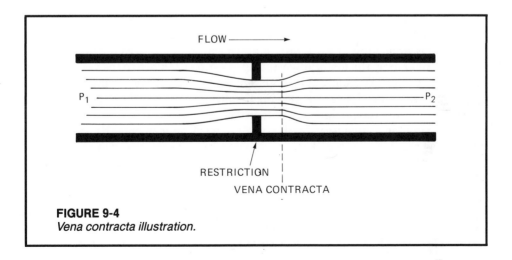

**FIGURE 9-4**
*Vena contracta illustration.*

If two valves have the same flow area, the same upstream pressure, and are passing the same flow, then it follows that they must have the same velocities at the vena contracta. This, in turn, means that the pressure drop from the inlet to the vena contracta must also be the same. On the other hand, if one valve dissipates less energy due to turbulence and friction, there will be more energy left over for recovery in the form of downstream pressure. Such a valve would be relatively streamlined and would be classified as a high recovery valve. In contrast, a low recovery valve dissipates more energy and, consequently, has a greater $\Delta P$ for the same flow.

Regardless of the recovery characteristics of the valve, the amount of liquid flow is determined by both the flow area and the flow velocity. If the flow area is constant, such as when the valve is wide open, then any increase in flow must come from an increase in the fluid velocity. An increase in velocity results in a lower pressure at the vena contracta. This logic leads to the conclusion that the pressure differential between the inlet and the vena contracta is directly related to the flow rate. The greater the flow, the larger this pressure differential.

If the flow through the valve increases, the velocity at the vena contracta must increase, and the pressure at that point will decrease accordingly. If the pressure at the vena contracta should drop below the vapor pressure for the liquid, bubbles will form in the fluid stream. The rate at which bubbles are formed will increase greatly as the pressure is lowered further below the vapor pressure. At this stage of development, there is no difference between flashing and cavitation. It is what happens downstream of the vena contracta that makes the difference.

If the pressure at the outlet of the valve is still below the vapor pressure of the liquid, the bubbles will remain in the downstream system and result in what is known as flashing. If the downstream pressure recovery is sufficient to raise the outlet pressure above the liquid vapor pressure, the bubbles will collapse, or implode, producing cavitation. It is easy to visualize that high recovery valves tend to be more subject to cavitation, since the downstream pressure is more likely to rise above the vapor pressure.

The implosion of the vapor bubbles during cavitation releases energy that shows up in the form of noise as well as physical damage to the valve. Millions of tiny bubbles imploding in close proximity to the solid surfaces in the valve can gradually wear away the material, resulting in serious damage to the valve body or its internal parts. It is usually quite apparent when a valve is cavitating since it will produce a noise much like gravel flowing through the valve. The area damaged by cavitation appears rough, dull, and cinderlike.

Flashing can also cause valve damage, but it will appear smooth and polished, rather than rough and pitted like that of cavitation, since flashing damage is essentially that of erosion. The greatest flashing damage tends to occur at the point of highest velocity.

**Choked Flow**   Noise and physical damage to the valve are important considerations, but even more important from a valve sizing standpoint is the fact that both flashing and cavitation limit the flow through the valve. During both flashing and cavitation, bubbles begin to form in the flow stream when the pressure drops below the vapor pressure of the liquid.

The formation of these vapor bubbles causes a crowding condition at the vena contracta, which tends to restrict the amount of liquid mass that can be forced through the valve. Eventually, a condition is reached where the flow is saturated, or choked, and can no longer be increased.

Equation 9-2 implies that there is no limit to the flow that can be obtained as long as the $\Delta P$ across the valve increases. This is not a true representation because flashing or cavitation can occur. Assuming that the upstream pressure is constant, there is a limit to the flow that can be achieved by decreasing the downstream pressure.

The flow curve deviates from the relationship predicted by the basic liquid sizing equation (Equation 9-2) because of the vapor bubbles that appear in the flow stream during flashing or cavitation. If the valve pressure drop is increased slightly beyond the point where bubbles begin to form, a choked flow condition is reached. Assuming constant upstream pressure, a further increase in $\Delta P$ will not increase the flow. This limiting pressure differential is called $\Delta P$ allowable. Figure 9-5 shows how $\Delta P$ allowable is related to the basic liquid sizing equation and the choked flow. Equation 9-2 plots as a straight line with a slope equal to the valve sizing coefficient ($C_v$).

If the actual service $\Delta P$ is used in the basic liquid sizing equation, when $\Delta P >$ $\Delta P_{allow}$, a much larger flow will be predicted than will actually exist in the service.

The choked flow is the flow that will actually exist in service when the $\Delta P$ is greater than $\Delta P$ allowable. These two conditions are illustrated in Figure 9-5. The predicted flow, using the actual $\Delta P$, is indicated on the dashed portion of the curve plotted for the liquid sizing equation; only the choked flow would actually exist in service. This example clearly shows why the smaller of the two $\Delta P$'s must be used in Equation 9-2 for accurate results.

$\Delta P$ allowable, the pressure drop at which choked flow occurs due to flashing or cavitation, is a function of the flow geometry of the valve. Although it can vary widely from one style of valve to the next, it is quite predictable for any given valve

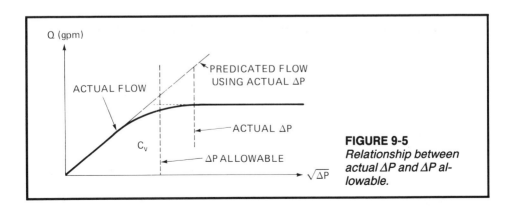

**FIGURE 9-5**
*Relationship between actual ΔP and ΔP allowable.*

and is easily determined by test. The experimental coefficient used to define the point of choked flow for any valve is called $K_m$.

For a given flow, the pressure drop across the valve is a measure of the valve recovery characteristics. At the point of choked flow, the pressure drop is $\Delta P$ allowable. It was also shown earlier that the pressure differential from the inlet to the vena contracta is a measure of the amount of flow being forced through the valve. The ratio of these two pressure differentials, when the valve has just reached choked flow, is defined as the valve recovery coefficient ($K_m$).

$$K_m = \Delta P \text{ allowable}/(P_1 - P_{vc}) \qquad (9\text{-}3)$$

where:   $P_1$  = inlet pressure (pisa)
$\phantom{where:}$   $P_{vc}$  = vena contracta pressure at the point of choked flow (psia)

With constant upstream pressure, $\Delta P$ allowable is the maximum pressure drop across the valve that will be effective in increasing the flow. From this definition, it can be noted that $K_m$ relates the pressure recovery characteristics of the valve to the amount of flow passing through the valve.

Consider two valves that are passing the same choked flow but have different recovery characteristics. One is a high recovery valve and the other is low recovery. The pressure profiles for two such valves are shown in Figure 9-6. Since both valves have just reached the same choked flow, the pressure differential from the inlet to the vena contracta is the same for both valves. On the other hand, the pressure recovery characteristics, and consequently the $\Delta P$ allowable values, are quite different. Relating this to the definition of $K_m$, it is easy to see that the high recovery valve will have a much smaller $K_m$ value than the low recovery valve.

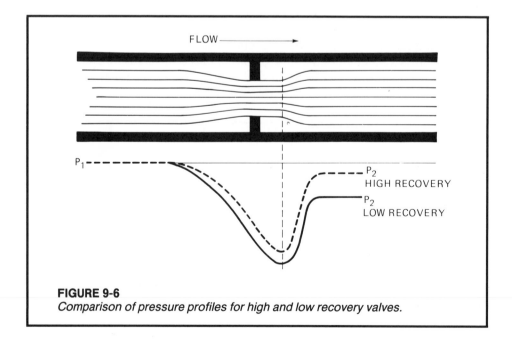

**FIGURE 9-6**
*Comparison of pressure profiles for high and low recovery valves.*

In effect, $K_m$ describes the relative pressure recovery characteristics of a valve. High recovery valves will tend to have low $K_m$ values, and low recovery valves will tend to have higher $K_m$ values. A typical range of $K_m$ values is from about 0.3 to 0.9. Valves with intermediate recovery characteristics will have values somewhere within this range.

$$\Delta P \text{ allowable} = K_m (P_1 - P_{vc}) \qquad (9\text{-}4)$$

Equation 9-4 shows the $K_m$ expression rearranged into a more useful form. $P_1$ is a known service condition and $K_m$ is obtainable from the sizing data catalog. If the vena contracta pressure is known, it is possible to calculate the limiting pressure drop for choked flow. We can define a term called the critical pressure ratio ($r_c$).

$$r_c = P_{vc}/P_v \qquad (9\text{-}5)$$

$r_c$ is the ratio of the vena contracta pressure $P_{vc}$ at choked flow to the vapor pressure $P_v$ of the flowing liquid. This expression is easily rearranged into a form that can be used to replace $P_{vc}$ in Equation 9-4. The result is as follows:

$$\Delta P \text{ allowable} = K_m (P_1 - r_c P_v) \qquad (9\text{-}6)$$

For any type of liquid, it is possible to determine the value of $r_c$ as a function of the vapor pressure and critical pressure of the liquid. Curves, such as those shown in Figures 9-7 and 9-8, are available in manufacturers' literature. Figure 9-7 is used for water. Enter on the abscissa at the water vapor pressure at the inlet to the control valve, then proceed vertically to intersect the curve, and finally move horizontally to the left to read the critical pressure ratio, $r_c$, on the ordinate. Use

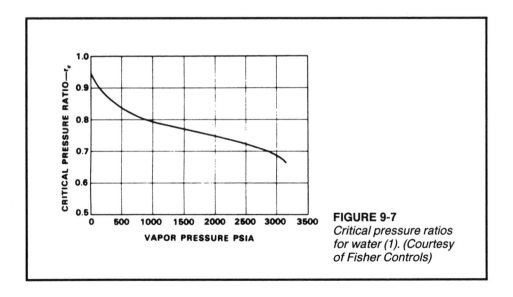

**FIGURE 9-7**
*Critical pressure ratios for water (1). (Courtesy of Fisher Controls)*

Figure 9-8 for liquids other than water. First, determine the vapor pressure/critical pressure ratio by dividing the liquid vapor pressure ($P_v$) at the control valve inlet by the critical pressure ($P_c$) of the liquid. Then enter on the abscissa at the ratio just calculated and proceed vertically to intersect the curve and, finally, move horizontally to the left and read the critical pressure ratio, $r_c$, on the ordinate.

Using Equation 9-6, the limiting pressure drop for choked flow is easily calculated. Inlet pressure and vapor pressure are part of the known service conditions for the application. The equation determines the flow-limiting pressure drop for either flashing or cavitation. The chief difference in these two conditions is in the relationship of the downstream pressure to the liquid vapor pressure. With flashing, the downstream pressure remains at the vapor pressure; whereas, with cavitation, the downstream pressure is above the vapor pressure.

Equation 9-6 indicates that the limiting pressure drop depends on the valve design ($K_m$), on the liquid properties ($r_c$ and $P_v$), and on the upstream pressure ($P_1$). It is obvious from the equation that a higher $\Delta P$ allowable can be achieved by increasing $P_1$. Therefore, if a flashing or cavitation condition is limiting flow, a required flow increase might be achieved by increasing the upstream pressure.

### EXAMPLE 9-4

**Problem:** A six-inch control valve is operated under the following conditions:

Fluid: Water
Flow rate: 1000 gpm
Temperature: 90°F
$P_v$: 0.70
$P_1$: 40 psia
$P_2$: 15 psia
$r_c$: .95
$K_m$: 0.5

Calculate the valve $C_v$ and determine if the valve will cavitate under these service conditions.

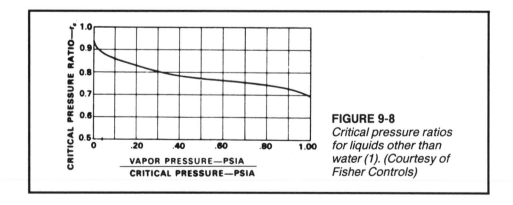

**FIGURE 9-8**
*Critical pressure ratios for liquids other than water (1). (Courtesy of Fisher Controls)*

**Solution:** The required $C_v$ can be calculated as follows:

$$C_v = Q \sqrt{G/\Delta P}$$

$$C_v = 1000 \text{ gpm} \sqrt{1.0/25 \text{ psi}} = 200$$

The allowable $\Delta P$ is given by Equation 9-6:

$$
\begin{aligned}
\Delta P \text{ allowable} &= K_m(P_1 - r_c P_v) \\
&= 0.5[40 - (0.95)(0.7)]\text{psi} \\
&= 19.7 \text{ psi}
\end{aligned}
$$

Since the allowable $\Delta P$ is lower then the actual $\Delta P = 25$ psi, the valve will cavitate.

# AC and DC Motors

An electric motor is a device that converts electrical energy to mechanical energy. In many chemical processes, rotary or linear motion is imparted to a mechanical load by an electric motor. For example, motor-driven stirrers are used to mix chemicals. Electric motors find wide use in automatic process control systems since their operation can be accurately and continuously controlled over a wide range of speeds and mechanical loads.

Electric motors are available with power ratings from fractional horsepower to thousands of horsepower. A wide variety of designs are available to meet specific process applications. Generally, motors are classified in terms of operation from either dc or ac voltage.

**DC Motors**   The dc motor is used extensively in low- and high-power control system applications. The motor consists of a field magnet and an armature. The motor operates on the principle that a force is exerted on a current-carrying conductor in a magnetic field. In a dc motor the conductors are in the form of loops (armature) and the force acts as a torque that tends to rotate the armature. The direction of the torque is dependent upon the relative direction of the magnetic flux and the armature current. To provide an unidirectional torque when the armature is rotating, the direction of the current must be reversed at appropriate points. This reversal is accomplished using a commutator on the moving part and brushes connected to the dc power. In the motor, the armature is wound with a large number of loops to provide a more uniform torque and smoother rotation; therefore, the commutator must have segments cut corresponding to the number of loops in the armature winding.

The torque developed by a dc motor is proportional to both the magnetic flux and the armature current. The magnetic flux may be produced by permanent magnets in smaller motors or electromagnetically from windings on the field magnet. The current that produces the magnetic field is called the field current.

In the typical control system application, the armature and field are powered from separate sources and either the armature or the field can be controlled to vary the speed and torque of the motor. The most common method is shown in Figure 9-9. In this case, a constant field current, $I_f$, is provided and a variable control voltage, $V_a$, is applied to the armature. In this method, the control source must supply the full power requirements of the motor.

An alternative arrangement is shown in Figure 9-10. In this application, a constant armature current $(I_a)$ is provided and the field current $(I_f)$ is varied. The advantage of this method is that the control source must supply only a relatively small field current, and the torque is closely proportional to the control current. The disadvantage in this setup is that the speed of response of the motor to a changing input is generally slower than with armature control, and it proves more difficult and inefficient to provide a constant current to the armature. Therefore, control of the field is generally limited to low-power dc motors of up to several horsepower.

DC motors used in servo applications are based on the same principles as conventional motors, but with several special design features. They are designed for high torque and low inertia. A high torque inertia ratio is produced by reducing the armature diameter and increasing its length compared to a standard motor. The main requirement in most servo control system applications is that the motor operate smoothly without jumping or clogging action and the set point is reached smoothly and quickly.

A disadvantage in using electric motors is that their shaft speeds are normally much higher than the desired speed in moving the load. Some method of speed reduction must be used, such as the gear train, to obtain efficient control. A

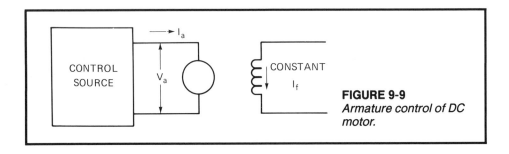

**FIGURE 9-9**
*Armature control of DC motor.*

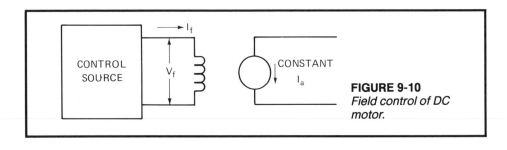

**FIGURE 9-10**
*Field control of DC motor.*

type of dc motor that can operate correctly at low speeds and be directly attached to the load is the direct-drive dc torque motor. The motor has a wound armature and a permanent magnet that convert electric current directly into torque. In general, torque motors are used in high-torque positioning systems and in slower-speed control systems.

Most of the design performance information can be obtained from the torque and speed specifications of the motor. If the field is kept constant, the torque produced by the motor is closely proportional to the armature current, as shown in Figure 9-11. The intercept of the line and the horizontal axis is the value of current required to overcome the static-friction torque of the motor. The slope of the line is defined as the torque constant of the dc motor.

$$K_i = \frac{\Delta T}{\Delta I_a} \tag{9-7}$$

where:   $K_i$ = torque constant in oz-in./A
$\quad\quad\quad$ T = torque in oz-in.
$\quad\quad\quad$ $I_a$ = armature current in amps (A)

When the armature is rotating, a voltage proportional to the speed is generated in the winding given by

$$V_g = K\varphi\omega$$

where:   $V_g$ = voltage generated
$\quad\quad\quad$ $\varphi$ = magnetic flux
$\quad\quad\quad$ $\omega$ = armature speed
$\quad\quad\quad$ K = constant

This voltage is called a back electromotive force (emf) because it opposes the voltage applied to the armature and limits the armature current. The motor speed will be such that the back emf is just enough smaller than the applied voltage to allow an armature current to drive the load. If the load on the motor is increased,

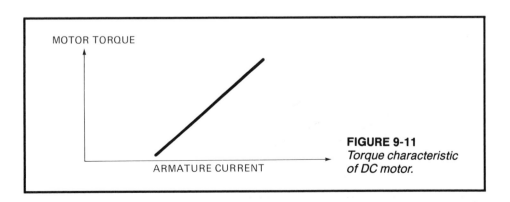

MOTOR TORQUE

ARMATURE CURRENT

**FIGURE 9-11**
*Torque characteristic
of DC motor.*

the armature slows down. As the motor slows, the back emf is reduced and a higher current flows. This larger current causes the motor to drive the increased load but at a lower speed. If the original speed is required, the applied voltage can be automatically increased by the control system. This motor characteristic is shown by the family of curves in Figure 9-12.

These curves, known as speed-torque curves, give motor torque as a function of speed for constant values of armature voltage. The zero torque points on the curve represent the no-load speed of the motor. At this speed no torque can be obtained from the motor.

Although motor torque for armature-controlled motors is proportional to armature current, it is more convenient to define a torque constant in terms of armature voltage. At zero speed, or stall condition, no back emf is generated, and the armature current is determined solely by the armature resistance. Therefore, under stall conditions

$$K_t = \frac{\Delta T_s}{\Delta V_a}$$

(9-8)

where:    $K_t$ = torque constant in oz-in./V
          $T_s$ = torque in oz-in.
          $V_a$ = armature voltage in V

The decrease in motor speed with increasing torque is characterized by a damping constant that is the slope of the speed-torque curves:

$$D_m = \frac{\Delta T_s}{\Delta S}$$

(9-9)

where:    $D_m$ = damping constant in oz-in./(rad/sec)
          $T_s$ = torque in oz-in.
          $S$ = speed in rad/sec

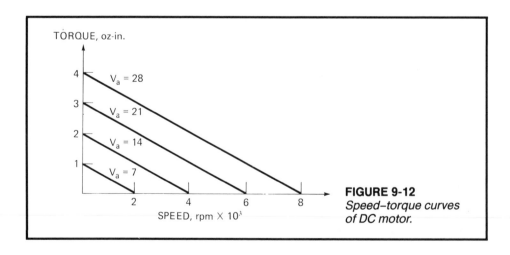

**FIGURE 9-12**
*Speed–torque curves
of DC motor.*

If the speed-torque curves are linear, as shown in Figure 9-12, the damping constant is given by

$$D_m = \frac{T_s}{S_{nl}} \tag{9-10}$$

where:  $T_s$ = stall torque at rated voltage in oz-in.
$S_{nl}$ = no-load speed at rated voltage in rad/sec

**EXAMPLE 9-5**

**Problem:** Determine the torque and damping constants for the armature-controlled dc motor whose speed-torque curves are shown in Figure 9-12. The armature voltage is 21 V.

**Solution:** Using Equation 9-8

$$K_t = \frac{\Delta T_s}{\Delta V_a}$$

$$K_t = \frac{3}{21} = 0.143 \text{ oz-in./V}$$

Using Equation 9-10

$$D_m = \frac{T_s}{S_{nl}}$$

Since armature voltage is 21 V, we obtain $T_s$ = 3 oz-in. and $S_{nl}$ = 6000 rpm from Figure 9-12, so that

$$D_m = \frac{3}{6000 \times 2\pi/60} = 4.8 \times 10^{-3} \text{ oz-in./(rad/sec)}$$

With field control of a dc motor, the armature current is supposed to be held constant, and the armature torque and current are unaffected by the back emf. Therefore, the torque should be independent of speed as shown by the horizontal lines in Figure 9-13, which shows torque versus speed for various values of field current.

In practice, the armature current is not always obtained from a true constant current source and, therefore, will be somewhat affected by the back emf. Furthermore, mechanical friction increases with speed, further reducing the available torque. Thus, the torque-speed curves for field-controlled dc motors exhibit a slight drop with increasing speed. This decrease in torque is generally advantageous in closed-loop control systems since this damping feature reduces the tendency toward overshoot and instability.

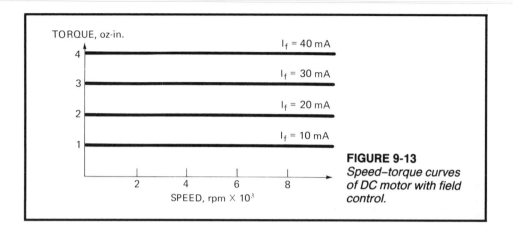

**FIGURE 9-13**
*Speed–torque curves of DC motor with field control.*

## EXAMPLE 9-6

**Problem:** Determine the torque and damping constants for the field-controlled dc motor whose speed-torque curves are shown in Figure 9-13.

**Solution:** By definition,

$$K_i = \frac{T}{I_f} = \frac{4}{0.04} = 100 \text{ oz-in./A}$$

Using Equation 9-8

$$D_m = \frac{4 - 3.8}{8000 \times 2\pi/60}$$

$$= 2.4 \times 10^{-4} \text{ oz-in./(rad/sec)}$$

**AC Motors**  The properties that make an ac motor the choice for most constant speed industrial drives are not necessarily those needed for control system applications. Instead, a motor that can operate over a wide range of speeds with high starting torque is needed in most control loops. The main advantage of the ac motor over the dc motor is its compatibility with the ac signals of synchros and other ac transducers without the need for demodulation.

However, one type of ac motor that finds extensive use in low-power control system applications is the two-phase induction motor shown in Figure 9-14.

This motor has two stator windings physically located at 90° with respect to each other. The rotor consists of a slotted cylinder of iron laminate mounted on the motor shaft. Solid copper or aluminum bars are set lengthwise in the slots of the rotor and are connected together at both ends by rings. An elongated, small diameter rotor is normally used to minimize inertia to produce faster motor response.

The principle of operation of the induction motor is shown in Figure 9-15. Stator winding B, the reference winding, is operated from a sinusoidal source of

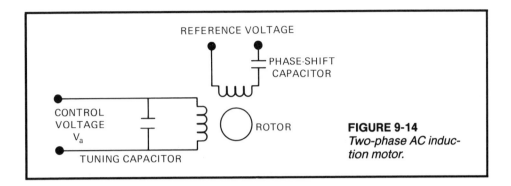

FIGURE 9-14
*Two-phase AC induction motor.*

fixed voltage and frequency. This is generally the 60-Hz ac power. The second winding A, the control winding, is powered from the same voltage source of the same frequency, but shifted by 90° in electrical phase. The currents through the two stator windings produce lines of magnetic flux that pass through the rotor. These magnetic flux lines combine, and at any instant the effect of all the lines can be represented by a single vector having some angular position relative to the axis of the rotor. As the amount of the currents change at successive instants, the vector angle changes. The result is a magnetic field that rotates at the frequency of the applied voltage. This is indicated in Figure 9-15 at four successive times; $t_1$, $t_2$, $t_3$, and $t_4$. As the lines of flux rotate, they cut across the rotor bars, which induce currents in the bars. These electric currents, in turn, produce a magnetic field that re-

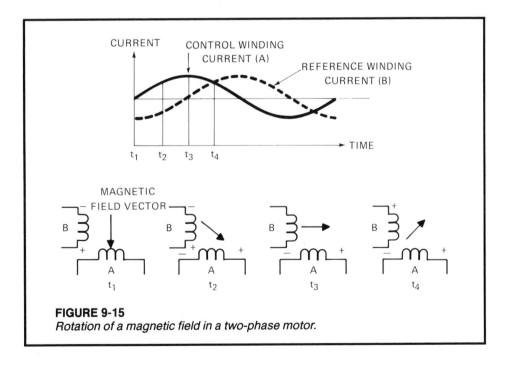

FIGURE 9-15
*Rotation of a magnetic field in a two-phase motor.*

acts with the stator magnetic field and causes the rotor to turn in a smooth and continuous manner.

The method used in control system applications is to make the control winding voltage variable. The resultant motor characteristics are shown in the speed-torque curves of Figure 9-16. In these curves, we note that the stall torque is proportional to the control voltage.

The effect of load torque is to reduce the speed of the motor, causing a greater speed difference between the rotating magnetic field and the motor. The induced magnetic field will increase with this difference, creating additional torque to pull the load but at a lower speed.

Although the internal effects of rotor slowdown are somewhat more complex in the induction motor than in the dc motor, the external effects are about the same.

In this discussion, we will consider the speed-torque characteristics of the ac motor to be linear, as shown in Figure 9-16. Using this assumption, ac motor constants can be derived that are similar to those of the armature-controlled dc motor.

**EXAMPLE 9-7**

**Problem:** Determine the torque and damping constants for the ac motor whose speed-torque curves are shown in Figure 9-16, assuming linear operation at a control voltage of 25 V.

**Solution:**

$$K_t = \frac{T}{V_a} = \frac{2.0}{25} = 0.08 \text{ oz-in./V}$$

$$D_m = \frac{2.0 \text{ oz-in.}}{2500 \times 2\pi/60 \text{ rad/sec}}$$

$$= 7.64 \times 10^{-3} \text{ oz-in./(rad/sec)}$$

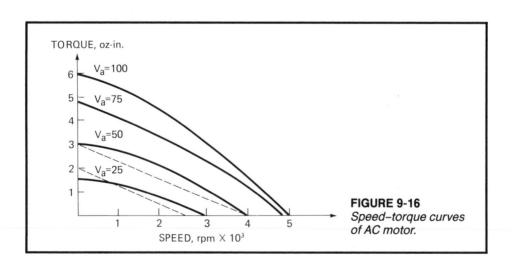

TORQUE, oz-in.

$V_a = 100$

$V_a = 75$

$V_a = 50$

$V_a = 25$

SPEED, rpm $\times 10^3$

**FIGURE 9-16**
*Speed–torque curves of AC motor.*

To help match the output impedance of the control circuit to the input of the motor, a tuning capacitor is added in parallel with the control winding, as shown in Figure 9-14. The capacitor is normally chosen to produce a unity power factor, so that the parallel resonant circuit will have a maximum input impedance (i.e., minimum power drain on the control circuit). The equation for determining the input tuning capacitor needed to obtain a unity power factor is

$$C = \frac{X_L}{2\pi f Z^2}$$  (9-11)

where:    C   = capacitance in farads
          $X_L$  = inductive reactance of control winding in $\Omega$
          Z    = impedance of control winding in $\Omega$
          f    = frequency of excitation in Hz

The normal method used to obtain the 90° phase shift required between the two motor currents is to use a phase-shifting capacitor in series with the reference winding, as shown in Figure 9-14. The correct value for this capacitor is normally given in the motor engineering specifications.

Another factor to be considered in ac and dc motor applications is the static friction associated with the armature. This requires that a minimum control voltage be applied to produce rotation of the armature. Static friction represents a form of dead time error in the control system, which degrades system performance. It causes system insensitivity since the controller must develop enough output voltage to overcome the static friction. The static can be expressed as a torque and is generally between 1 and 10% of the rated torque of the motor.

## Pumps    Pumps find extensive use in liquid flow control system applications because they are simple to operate, energy efficient, and can provide both flow and pressure control in a single piece of equipment. The most common types of pumps used in process control systems are centrifugal, positive displacement, and reciprocating.

**Centrifugal Pumps**    The centrifugal pump is the most widely used process fluid-handling device. It is generally operated at a fixed speed in the recirculation or transfer of process fluids. If controlled fluid flow is required, a control valve is generally installed in the discharge line. However, a control valve is an energy-consuming device, and in some applications this energy loss cannot be tolerated, so a variable speed drive is used to control the pump.

A centrifugal pump imparts velocity to a process fluid. This velocity energy is then transformed mainly into pressure energy as the fluid leaves the pump. The pressure (head) developed is approximately equal to the velocity at the discharge of the pump. This relationship was expressed earlier in the discussion of fluid flow in Chapter 8 and is given by

$$H = \frac{V^2}{2g}$$  (9-12)

where:   H  = pressure (head) in feet
         V  = velocity in feet per sec
         g  = 32.2 ft/sec

We can obtain the approximate head of any centrifugal pump by calculating the peripheral velocity of the impeller and substituting this velocity into Equation 9-12. The formula for peripheral velocity is

$$V = \pi d\omega \qquad\qquad (9\text{-}13)$$

where:   d  = diameter in meters or inches
         ω  = angular speed in radians/sec or rev/min (rpm)

In English units, velocity is normally expressed in ft/sec and angular velocity in rpm, so Equation 9-13 can be simplified as follows:

$$V = \frac{(3.14)(\text{rpm})(d)}{(12 \text{ in./ft})(60 \text{ sec/min})}$$

$$V = \frac{\text{rpm} \times d}{229} \qquad\qquad (9\text{-}14)$$

where d = impeller diameter in inches.

**EXAMPLE 9-8**

**Problem:** Determine the total head developed in feet by a centrifugal pump with a 12-inch impeller and rotating at 1000 revolutions per minute (rpm).

**Solution:**
Using Equation 9-14 to find the fluid velocity:

$$V = \frac{\text{rpm} \times d}{229} = \frac{(1000)(12)}{229} = 52.4 \text{ ft/sec}$$

Using Equation 9-12 to find the total head developed:

$$H = \frac{V^2}{2g} = \frac{(52.4 \text{ f}/\text{sec})^2}{2(32.2 \text{ ft/sec}^2)} = 42.64 \text{ ft}$$

**Positive Displacement Pumps**   Positive displacement pumps can be divided into two main types: rotary and reciprocating.

**Rotary Pumps**
Rotary pumps function by continuously producing reduced pressure cavities on the suction side, which fills with fluid. The fluid is moved to the discharge side of the pump where it is compressed and then discharged from the pump. In most cases, flow is directly proportional to pump speed. Therefore, the control system

needs only to control the pump speed to control the process fluid flow. This type of pump provides accurate, uniform flow and a minimized power requirement.

To help maintain a constant $\Delta P$ across the pump, pressure on the suction side can be held constant by using a small storage tank with a level controller, as shown in Figure 9-17.

The discharge pressure can be held constant by pumping fluid to the top of the delivery tank. A low-slip pump delivers nearly all its internal displacement in each pump revolution and meters fluid accurately.

The types of rotary pumps used for flow control are: (1) gear pumps, (2) circumferential piston pumps, and (3) progressing cavity pumps.

Gear pumps are used to pump high viscosity fluids or to generate moderately high differential pressures. Because these pumps have close gear-to-gear contact, they are used for clean, nonabrasive lubricating fluids.

Circumferential piston pumps are widely used in sanitary and food applications. This type of pump has two noncontacting fluid rotors. Because the length of the sealing area is relatively long, slip is just about eliminated at viscosities above 200 cp. Flow control applications include pumping dairy and bakery products, plastics and resins, and pharmaceuticals. They cannot be used to pump large solids or extremely abrasive fluids or in high back-pressure applications.

In the progressing cavity pump, a single helical rotor turns eccentrically in a stationary stator. As the rotor turns, cavities are produced, which are filled at the inlet by the process fluid and move through the stator to the discharge side of the pump. Normally, elastomer stators are used because they resist abrasion, provide a tight seal, and can be changed easily. If long pumping sections are used in the construction of the pump, relatively high pressure can be obtained from the pump.

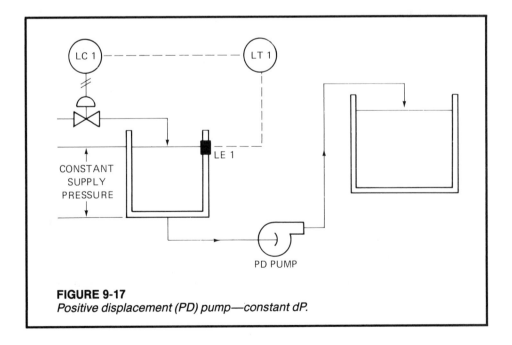

**FIGURE 9-17**
*Positive displacement (PD) pump—constant dP.*

### Reciprocating Pumps

Reciprocating pumps use a linear reciprocal stroke in combination with check valves to pump fluid. Reciprocating pumps are commonly used to control the rate at which a volume of fluid is injected into a process stream or vessel. These pumps are also called metering pumps in some applications, because they are highly accurate and consistent in the volume of fluid discharged per cycle. Large reciprocating pumps generally have variable speed drives. Small, controlled volume reciprocating pumps used for precise chemical injection normally use a variable stroke controller. Two basic types of reciprocating pumps normally used in metering applications are plunger pumps and diaphragm pumps.

In the plunger pump, a packed plunger draws in and then expels fluid through a one-way check valve. A diaphragm reciprocating pump can be mechanically driven, directly coupled to a plunger, or hydraulically actuated. Like the plunger pump, it draws in a precise amount of fluid and discharges it cyclically.

### EXERCISES

9.1  An equal percentage valve has a maximum flow of 65 gpm and a minimum flow of 5 gpm. Find its rangeability.

9.2  A liquid is pumped through a pipe with an inside diameter of 18 inches at a flow rate of 10 ft per second. Find the volume flow rate.

9.3  Calculate the $C_v$ and select the required valve size from Table 9-1 for a valve with the following service conditions:

Fluid: ethyl alcohol (G = 0.8)

Flow rate: 200 gpm

$P_1$: 100 psi
$P_2$: 90 psi

9.4  An eight-inch control valve is operated under the following conditions:

Fluid: water

Flow rate: 800 gpm

Temperature: 70°F

$P_v$: 0.36

$P_1$: 100 psia

$P_2$: 90 psia

$r_c$: 0.95

$K_m$: 0.6

Calculate the valve $C_v$ and determine if the valve will cavitate under these service conditions.

9.5  Determine the torque and damping constants for the armature-controlled dc motor whose speed-torque curves are shown in Figure 9-12. The armature voltage is 28 V.

9.6 Determine the torque and damping constants for the field-controlled dc motor whose speed-torque curves are shown.

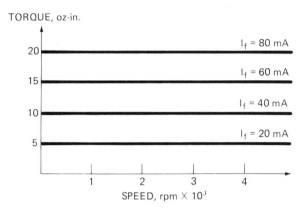

9.7 A 60-Hz two-phase induction motor has a control field winding resistance of 250 $\Omega$ and an inductive reactance of 200 $\Omega$. Find the value of parallel capacitance required to make the winding appear purely resistive.

## REFERENCES AND BIBLIOGRAPHY

1. *Control Valve Handbook*, Second Edition, Fisher Controls Company, 1977.
2. Driskell, L., *Control-Valve Selection and Sizing*, Instrument Society of America, 1983.
3. Murrill, P.W., *Fundamentals of Process Control Theory*, Instrument Society of America, 1981.
4. Weyrick, R.C., *Fundamentals of Automatic Control*, McGraw-Hill Book Company, 1975.
5. Fischer, K.A., and Leigh, D.J., "Using pumps for flow control," *Instrument & Control Systems*, March 1983.

# 10

# Digital Computers in Process Control

**Introduction**    This chapter will discuss the design and application of digital computer-based control systems for use in process industries. The topics to be covered are history of process control computers, the basics of computers for process control, and microcomputer basics.

## History of Process Control Computers    Before the introduction of computers for industrial process control applications, the standard industrial control system consisted of a large number of single-loop analog controllers, either pneumatic or electronic, as discussed in Chapters 1 and 2. This method provided, and still provides, excellent control of industrial processes. The main disadvantages of stand-alone controllers is that they are not easily reconfigurated and they cannot easily communicate with other plant computers.

Although computer designers had been predicting the use of digital computers for process control applications from the inception of the first computers, the first practical digital computer-based control system was one designed for the U.S. Air Force by Hughes Aircraft Company using a computer called the DIGITAC™. This system controlled an airplane in flight by computed set point changes to an analog-based automatic pilot. This system was flown successfully in 1954.

The losing company in the competition for the Air Force contract was Ramo-Wooldridge with their computer, the RW-30™. Ramo-Wooldridge decided to market their computer as a process control computer, so they repackaged it as the RW-300™. This was a very important entry in the early history of process computers. It is interesting to note that computer control developed not as a process and manufacturing industries initiative but through the efforts of computer and electronics vendors to expand their markets outside of military applications.

The first industrial installation of a computer system was made by the Daystrom Company at the Louisiana Power and Light plant in Sterlington, Louisiana. It was not a closed-loop control system, but a supervisory data monitoring system as shown in Figure 10-1.

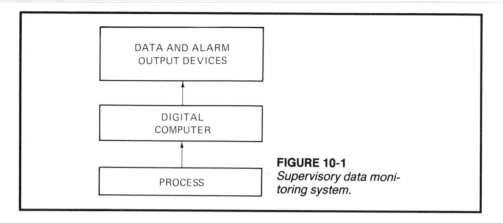

**FIGURE 10-1**
*Supervisory data monitoring system.*

The first industrial closed-loop computer system was at the Texaco Company, Port Arthur, Texas, refinery, using an RW-300 in March of 1959. The first chemical plant control computer was at the Monsanto Chemical Company ammonia plant in Luling, Louisiana, in April 1960. It also used an RW-300 to achieve closed-loop control.

**Direct Digital Control (DDC)**    The goal of the control system engineer in the early days of computer control was to bypass the process controllers as shown in Figure 10-2 and have the computer directly control the process as shown in Figure 10-3. This was the start of direct digital control (DDC).

Direct digital control was achieved independently by Imperial Chemicals Industries, Ltd., in England, using an ARGUS 100™ computer built by the Ferranti Company and installed in a soda ash plant at Fleetwood in Lancastershire, En-

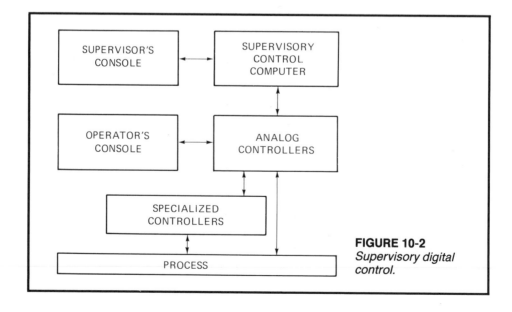

**FIGURE 10-2**
*Supervisory digital control.*

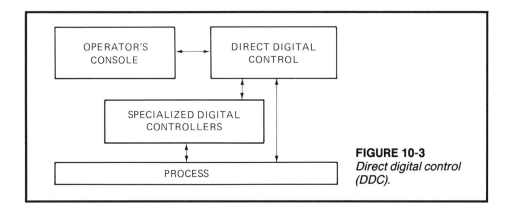

**FIGURE 10-3**
*Direct digital control
(DDC).*

gland, and by the Monsanto Company with an RW-300 computer in their ethylene plant at Texas City, Texas. The latter installation was under closed-loop control in March 1962, controlling two distillation columns. The former was installed in the summer of that same year.

The success of these early DDC installations generated a great deal of interest in the user and vendor communities alike and resulted directly in the establishment of the DDC Users Workshop by the Instrument Society of America in 1963. This organization is important because *Guidelines and General Information on User Requirements Concerning Direct Digital Control* is generally credited with having been a major impact on the development of the minicomputer for process control.

Although the direct digital control system has always had the potential for unlimited variety and complexity of the automatic control functions in each and every control loop, the vast majority of them were implemented as digital approximations to the conventional three-mode analog controller.

**The Centralized Computer Concept**    The early digital computers had many disadvantages, among which were the following:

1. The computers were very slow. A common addition time for such machines was four milliseconds.

2. The memories were also very small, commonly 4-8000 words of 8-16 bits each.

3. All programming had to be done in machine language, since assembly language or higher level languages had not been designed or written in the early stages of process computers.

4. Neither instrument vendor nor user personnel had any experience in computer applications. Thus, it was very difficult to properly size the project within computer capabilities and most had to be reduced in size to fit the available machines.

5. Many of the early computer systems were very unreliable, particularly if they used germanium rather than silicon transistors as many did because it was so

temperature-sensitive; also these computers depended on unreliable mechanical devices, air conditioners, for their successful operation.

The response of the computer manufacturers to this situation was to design a much larger computer system with arithmetic functions designed in and magnetic core memory. These changes made the computers much faster, but, because of the high cost of core memories and of the additional electronic circuitry, they were much more expensive. In addition, to help justify this cost the vendors promoted the incorporation of all types of computer functions, including both supervisory control and DDC, in one computer mainframe at a central control room location, as shown in Figure 10-4.

While these computers greatly alleviated the speed and memory size problems of the earlier systems, their use led to still further problems.

1.  Most computer systems were sold and installed before their designs were thoroughly proven or their programming aids (compilers, higher-level languages, etc.) were fully developed. Thus, they were the cause of many frustrating delays on the part of the user who tried to install them.

2.  Because of the centralized computer location, the vast plant communication system required to bring the plant signals to them and return control signals to the field was very expensive and, unless carefully designed and installed, was prone to electrical noise problems.

3.  Because all of the control functions were located in one computer, fear of failure of that one computer resulted in demands for a complete analog backup system paralleling the DDC. The resulting system is shown in Figure 10-5.

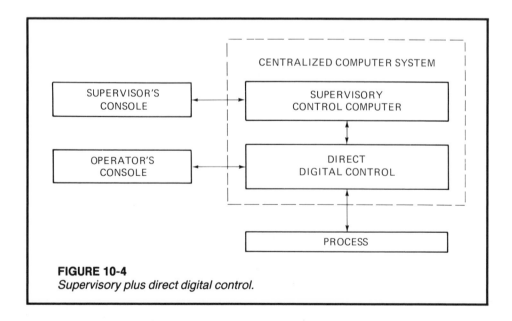

**FIGURE 10-4**
*Supervisory plus direct digital control.*

4. To compensate for these high costs, user and vendor alike tried to squeeze as large a project as possible into the computer system, drastically complicating its programming and installation.

The result of these problems and failures was a sharp negative management reaction in many companies against computer control and a slowdown in computer system installations until about the middle of the 1970s.

**Distributed Control Systems**   Because of the reliability problems and high cost of the control process computer systems of the 1960s, the number of new process computer projects in the early 1970s was small. The few projects that were started in this period were based on the medium-priced minicomputers that had been developed. These control systems were small in size and followed the block diagram of Figure 10-4.

At the same time, there were two developments in the electronic field that would make a profound change on the application of digital computers to process control. The first was the development of integrated circuits and microprocessors. The second advancement was the design of the distributed computer system by Honeywell in 1969. The basis of this new design concept was to widely distribute the control to computer modules containing one or more microprocessors, as shown in Figure 10-6.

Each of these modules controlled several instrument loops, generally 1 to 4. They were connected together by a single high-speed data link, called a data high-

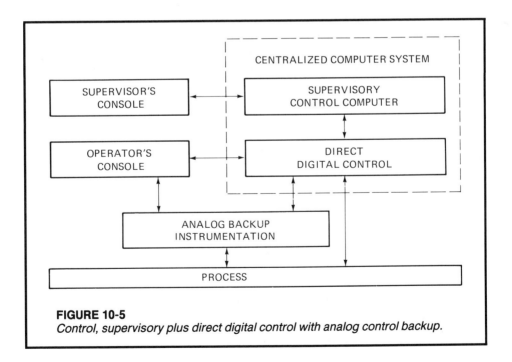

**FIGURE 10-5**
*Control, supervisory plus direct digital control with analog control backup.*

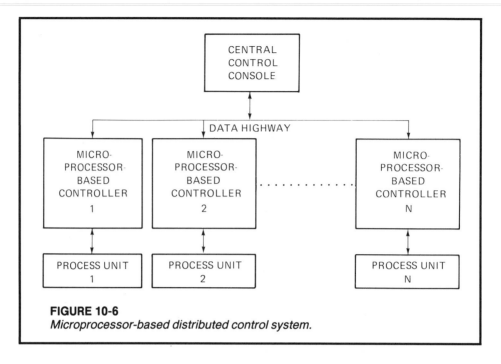

**FIGURE 10-6**
*Microprocessor-based distributed control system.*

way, permitting communications between each of the microprocessor-based modules and the central operator console. This allowed the operator to monitor the operation of each local process.

Another computer-based control system started in 1969 was called a programmable controller (PC). The PC was designed to replace relay-based logic systems and it will be fully discussed in the next chapter. The interesting thing to note is that both the PC and the distributed control system are computer-based control systems, but the word "computer" was not generally listed in the sales information by the vendors.

## Basics of Computers for Process Control    The digital computer used for process control has five basic elements:

1. Memory, which is used as storage for data used in computations and for instructions whose execution determines the behavior of the computer system.

2. Internal control, which interprets the instructions and directs the system to make logic decisions and to perform arithmetic functions.

3. Arithmetic unit, which performs operations such as add, subtract, multiply, divide, and compare.

4. Input registers, which provide a path into memory for the program or the data (constants, parameters, new measurements) upon which the system operates.

5. Output registers, which provide a path out of memory for direct contact or information to the outside world.

A block diagram of a basic computer is shown in Figure 10-7.

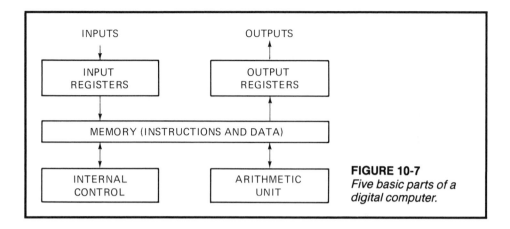

**FIGURE 10-7**
*Five basic parts of a digital computer.*

The additional equipment needed to obtain a functional process computer system are shown in Figure 10-8.

The elements that distinguish the process control computer (particularly for the lower levels) from computers in general are the following:

1. External interrupts
2. Real-time clock

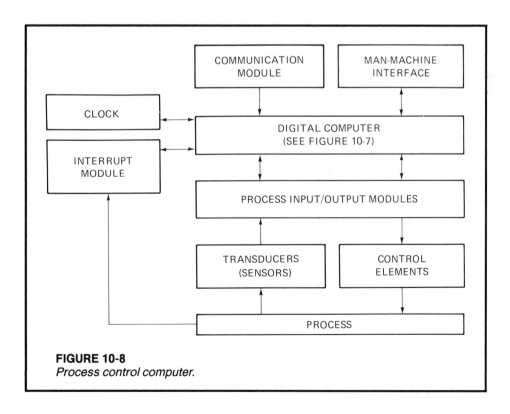

**FIGURE 10-8**
*Process control computer.*

3. Man-machine interface

4. Process input-output

5. Intrasystem communication

In addition to the above, process control computer systems generally have one or more of the several features designed to promote overall reliability. These additional features are as follows:

1. Memory or storage protection.

2. Parity or error detection on transfer of data between machine elements.

3. Dual redundancy or other fail-safe practices.

## Microcomputer Basics
A microcomputer can be defined as a collection of digital circuit elements connected together to form an information processing unit. The three essential elements of a microcomputer are shown in Figure 10-9. The three elements are (1) a program memory that stores the program the system will execute, (2) a data memory to store the numbers being manipulated, and (3) a microprocessor that operates on the data in the sequence determined by the program. For example, if the system is required to find the sum of a set of numbers, then the numbers will be stored in the data memory, the summing program is stored in the program memory, and the actual calculations will be done by the microprocessor.

The microprocessor or central processing unit (CPU) is the focal point of the system, but it must have facilities for storing the program and there must be some sort of data storage. The program is stored in memory as a set of binary numbers (0 or 1) that are "coded" to represent the various steps the microprocessor must execute. The microprocessor contains digital circuits that can decode those program instructions and implement the prescribed program steps.

Inside the microprocessor are several digital circuits called "registers," which are used to store binary numbers of particular significance. The most important registers are:

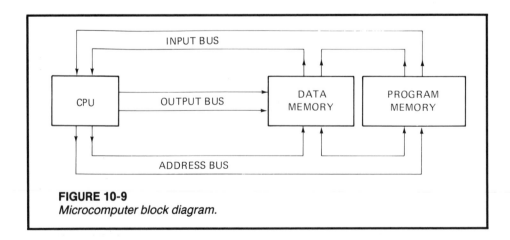

**FIGURE 10-9**
*Microcomputer block diagram.*

1.  The accumulator (ACC). It is the central point for all data manipulation (i.e., add, subtract, shift, etc.).

2.  The index resister. It is used to store and create data addresses that are important in a software program.

3.  The instruction resister. In order to have the microprocessor system execute a particular program, the program memory sends out a series of commands or "instructions" to the CPU. As each instruction is received by the CPU, it is stored in the instruction register. The CPU then carries out the operation required before receiving the next instruction.

4.  The program counter (P.C.): It is used to keep track of the CPU's progress through the program.

An important feature of a microcomputer is the way the three basic system elements (CPU, program memory, and data memory) communicate with each other by means of buses. A bus is defined as a set of physical connections along which parallel binary information can be transmitted. Only one word of parallel information can exist on a bus at any given time. For example, in Figure 10-10, it would not be permissible for the CPU to simultaneously send an address to both the program and data memory via the address bus.

Usually the CPU assumes control of the various buses by means of special signals sent out on control lines to the data and program memories. Sometimes these control signals are grouped together under the heading "control bus," but for clarity, the control paths are not shown in Figure 10-10.

In executing a program, the microprocessors use the data buses to exchange information in a well-defined manner. The complete sequence of information ex-

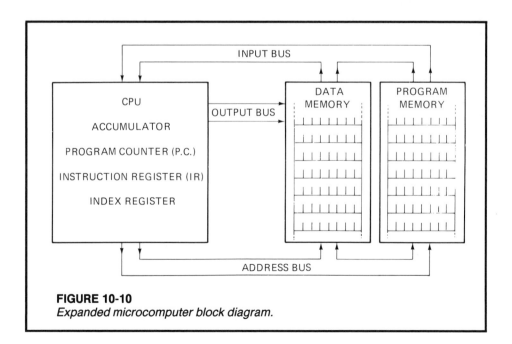

**FIGURE 10-10**
*Expanded microcomputer block diagram.*

change that carries out one program step is known as an "instruction cycle". A basic instruction cycle consists of the following:

1. Fetch the next instruction (i.e., program step) from the program memory to the instruction register.
2. Increment the program counter.
3. Execute the instruction.

The instruction cycle can be illustrated using the following simple program:

Step 1: Set the accumulator to zero.

Step 2: Increment the accumulator.

Step 3: Shift accumulator one bit to left.

At the start of any program, the program counter is set to zero by the CPU. In the first step of the program, the contents of the program counter are sent out on the address bus, as shown in Figure 10-11a. The program memory sends out the contents of the address accessed, which contains the instruction "Set the accumulator the zero," onto the input bus. The CPU receives the instruction and loads it into the instruction register. The contents of the program counter are then incremented, as shown in Figure 10-11b. Then the instruction is executed, which in this case sets the accumulator to zero, as shown in Figure 10-11c. This completes Step 1 of the program and, therefore, constitutes the first instruction cycle. The next two steps of the program are carried out in the same manner. The instruction cycle illustrated is sufficient for the operation of a simple microprocessor. However, since the input bus is normally only 8 bits wide in a standard microprocessor (some microprocessors are also 16-bit machines) all instructions would have to be encoded into 8 bits. This allows for only 256 different instructions (i.e., $2^8 = 256$). This proves to be inadequate for most applications, so, to overcome this problem, the concept of a multiple byte instruction is used. In a multiple byte instruction, the complete instruction is enclosed into a multiple of the byte size of the microprocessor. For an 8-bit (byte) machine, multiple byte instructions would be encoded into 16, 24, 32 bits, etc. The instruction is then split into a group of bytes and written in the program as a series of program steps.

For example, consider a simple three-step program:

Step 1 - Increment the accumulator.
Step 2 - Store the contents of the accumulator in data memory at address 10101010 10101010
Step 3 - Increment the accumulator.

In a typical CPU, the first two instructions might be encoded as follows:

Increment accumulator 01001100.

Store contents of accumulator in data memory at address 10101010: 10101010

In the program memory, the three program steps would appear as:

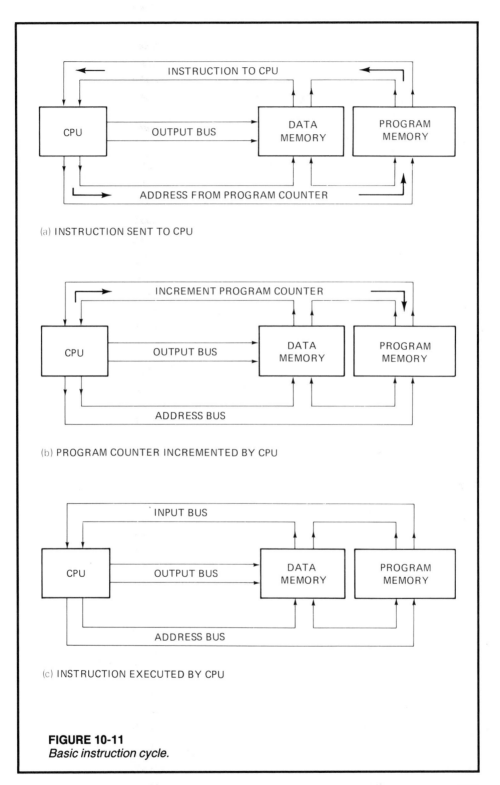

(a) INSTRUCTION SENT TO CPU

(b) PROGRAM COUNTER INCREMENTED BY CPU

(c) INSTRUCTION EXECUTED BY CPU

**FIGURE 10-11**
*Basic instruction cycle.*

Step 1: Address 0 contents (01001100) = Increment accumulator instruction

Step 2: Address 1 contents (01110111) = Store instruction
Address 2 contents (10101010) = Upper address
Address 3 contents (10101010) = Lower address

Step 3: Address 4 contents (01001100) = Increment accumulator instruction

Note that the "store" instruction has been split into three 8-bit bytes and the program requires 5 memory locations.

Even with simple programs, it is difficult to hand-write programs. Because the description of each instruction is rather long and the writing of the actual binary numbers for each instruction or memory location is tedious and prone to error, it is convenient to adopt shorthand schemes to assist in presenting a program in a more precise and concise manner. For example, consider the instruction:

"Add contents of memory location 1000:1000:1000:0010 to the accumulator."

This can be shortened to:

ADA [8882]

ADA is a mnemonic for "add to accumulator." The square brackets signify "the contents of the enclosed address," and 8882 is the address written in hexadecimal format (see Table 10-1).

Each microprocessor has its own unique set of program instructions and its own set of memories. Unfortunately, there is no standard set, but the manufacturers do provide detailed lists of their own mnemonics.

Most manufacturers have standardized on using the hexadecimal method of writing binary numbers. In this method, the binary number is split into blocks of 4 bits and then each block is written down as its equivalent decimal number. For the binary numbers in the range 1010 (ten) to 1111 (fifteen), the first six letters of the

**TABLE 10-1**
**Binary to Hexadecimal Conversion Table**

| Binary | Hex | Binary | Hex |
|--------|-----|--------|-----|
| 0000 | 0 | 1000 | 8 |
| 0001 | 1 | 1001 | 9 |
| 0010 | 2 | 1010 | A |
| 0011 | 3 | 1011 | B |
| 0100 | 4 | 1100 | C |
| 0101 | 5 | 1101 | D |
| 0110 | 6 | 1110 | E |
| 0111 | 7 | 1111 | F |

alphabet are used. The complete conversion table is shown in Table 10-1. There are also pocket calculators on the market that convert from binary to hexadecimal and hexadecimal to binary to aid in programming microprocessors. It should be clearly understood that all instructions and data are stored in the microcomputer as binary numbers. Also note that there are two shorthand methods for writing an instruction. The first is a mnemonic giving the function of the instruction (e.g., ADA), and the second method is using the hexadecimal code for the binary form of the instruction.

For example, ADA [8882] has the binary code

| 1011:1001 | operating code |
| 1000:1000 | address |
| 1000:0010 | address |

which can also be written as

B9

88

82

in hexadecimal code.

Programs written either in pure binary code or in hexadecimal code are generally referred to as being written in "machine code". Programs written using mnemonics and hexadecimal addresses are called "assembly language programs".

**Designing with Microprocessors**   Microprocessors have been used in a wide range of applications, such as control systems, programmable controllers, intelligent instruments, automotive controls and indicators, personal and home computers, and home appliances. This chapter is concerned only with the design of process industry control systems using microprocessors.

A typical microprocessor-based control system is shown in Figure 10-12. The electronic circuits inside the microcomputer sense the process through its inputs and control the process from its outputs. The inputs come from external instruments that measure process variables such as temperature, pressure, flow, equipment status, etc. Output loads are typically control valves, motors, relays, displays, etc. Normally, a CRT display unit and an operator keyboard are connected to the microprocessor unit through the appropriate interface circuitry.

The way the microcomputer-based control system functions when power is turned on is determined by the circuits in it and the control program in the microprocessor. Therefore, the design of a microprocessor system involves both hardware and program design. Since the requirements for designing and documenting the program are similar to those for the hardware, it is useful to review a standard hardware design and documentation method.

**Hardware Design Procedure**   Figure 10-13 shows the five-step method for designing a microcomputer system. These five steps are the engineering version of the standard four steps to problem solving, shown on the right side of Figure 10-13.

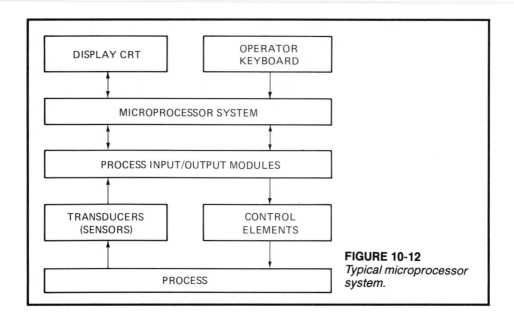

**FIGURE 10-12**
*Typical microprocessor system.*

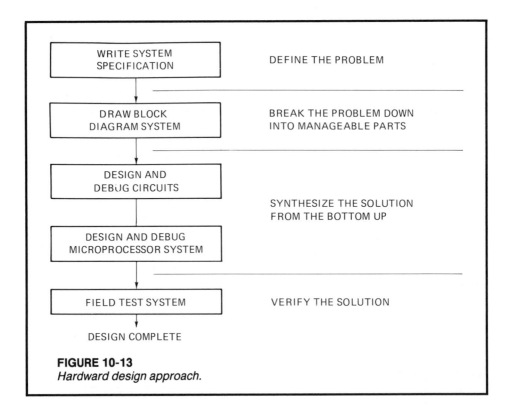

**FIGURE 10-13**
*Hardward design approach.*

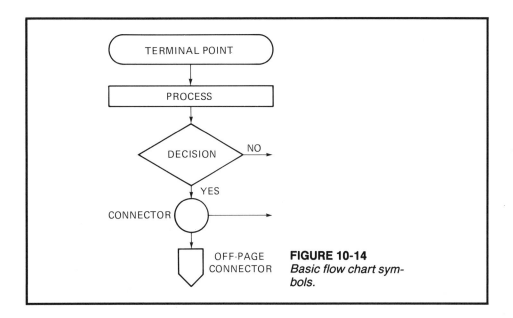

**FIGURE 10-14**
*Basic flow chart symbols.*

The system specification is used to clearly define the design problem. The block diagram method breaks down the design problem into bite-sized chunks. In the synthesize cycle, first the circuits are designed and debugged, then the circuits are used to design subsystems, and, finally the microprocessor system is designed and debugged. The field trials are then used to verify the design solution in the real world. The important characteristic of this design process is that it is modular.

**Software Design Procedure**   Software design is also a modular process. The design starts by breaking the problem down into understandable modules through the use of flow charts, which are simply a tool for describing a sequence of events or processes. The symbols used in flow charts are shown in Figure 10-14. The two most important symbols are a block for a single process and a diamond for a decision. The number of flow chart pages, as with block diagrams, is strictly a function of the complexity of the program.

Once the flow chart has defined a module, a specification should be written for that program module. Then the design process shown in Figure 10-15 can start. This figure shows a step-by-step design procedure, which is the dual of the one shown for hardware in Figure 10-13. Since the program documents will be used by the same people as the hardware documents, they should as far as possible resemble their hardware equivalents.

**Microprocessor Design Application**   Let's assume a microprocessor system is required to replace the conventional electro-mechanical logic (bimetallic thermostat, relays, switches, etc.) associated with the control of the start-up/shutdown of a heating system and with the regulation of the temperature within a building. The controller is also to act as a digital clock and provide a display in hours and minutes. The heating system is switched on or off via a power contactor

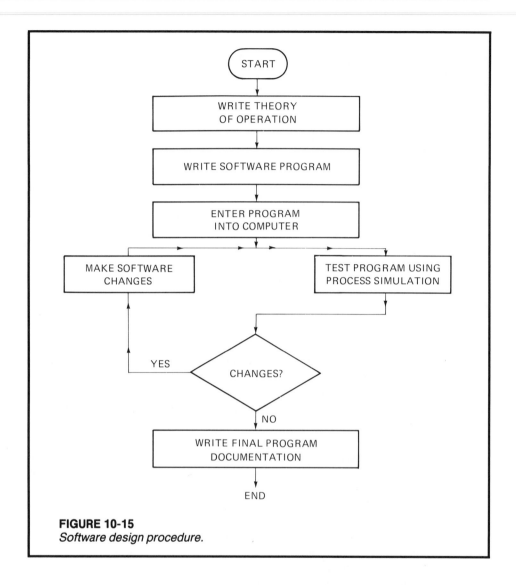

**FIGURE 10-15**
*Software design procedure.*

with a low voltage coil; the temperature inside the building is monitored using a single-point temperature measurement ($\theta$). The startup time ($t_s$), the shutdown time ($t_f$) and the desired setting for the inside temperature ($\theta_D$) are to be selected by the user after the controller has been installed. A typical inside temperature profile is shown in Figure 10-16. Simple ON/OFF control is acceptable for regulation of the inside temperature when the building is occupied. Outside the occupancy period, the heating system is to be switched off.

Since 8-bit resolution provides sufficient accuracy for this control application, an 8-bit microprocessor system is the most appropriate. A block diagram of the control system is shown in Figure 10-17. Since the control program is fairly simple, a single read-only memory (ROM) integrated circuit chip can hold the en-

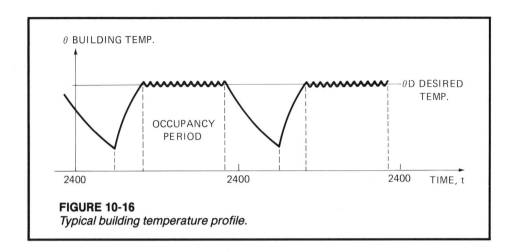

**FIGURE 10-16**
*Typical building temperature profile.*

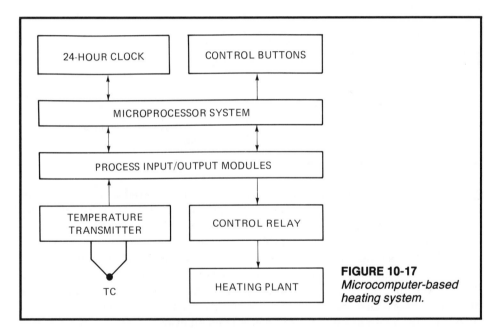

**FIGURE 10-17**
*Microcomputer-based heating system.*

tire program and an another random access memory (RAM) chip provides sufficient data storage for this application.

A four-digit seven-segment display indicates the current time based on a 24-hour clock implemented in software. The clock display is also used in association with two push button controls to allow the user to enter the desired start and stop times. Under program control one button causes the displayed time to be held or to be incremented at high speed. The other button enters the currently displayed value of time into a particular location in the data memory.

A simplified flow chart for the program is shown in Figure 10-18. When power is first applied to the system, program execution starts. The working regis-

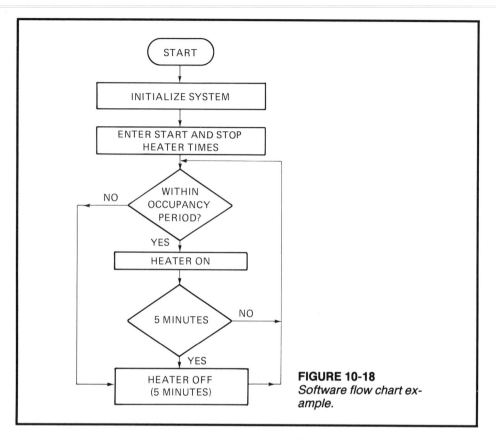

**FIGURE 10-18**
*Software flow chart example.*

ters and counters are initialized and the user enters the desired start-up and shut-down times using the control buttons. All input-output data transfers are made under program control via the I/O ports. During the occupancy period, control action is taken at 5-minute time intervals.

The first decision made by the control system is whether the time of day clock is within the occupancy period. If it is not, the building heater is turned off. If the clock is within the building occupancy period, the heater is turned on and the building heat is controlled to a set temperature for 5 minutes. Then, the heater is turned off for 5 minutes and the cycle is started all over.

## EXERCISES

10.1  List some of the disadvantages of the early centralized process control computers.

10.2  Discuss the function and purpose of each of the five basic elements of process control computers.

10.3  Describe the function(s) of the central processing unit in a microprocessor.

10.4  Give the names and list the functions of the main registers in a microprocessor.

10.5 Explain the steps of a typical instruction cycle in a microprocessor, using an example four-step program.

10.6 Convert the following binary numbers to hexadecimal format.
   (a) 01110101
   (b) 10111011
   (c) 00101111

10.7 Explain the difference between programs written in machine code and programs in assembly language.

10.8 Design a microprocessor-based home heating system that holds the temperature at 70°F between 6:00 AM and 12:00 PM and at 64°F the remaining time. Draw a block diagram of the system and a flow chart of the control program.

## BIBLIOGRAPHY

1. Williams, T.J., *The Use of Digital Computers in Process Control*, Instrument Society of America, 1984.

2. Burton, D.P., and Dexter, A.L., *Microprocessor Systems Handbook*, Analog Devices Inc., 1979.

3. *Microprocessor User's Guide*, Pro-Log Corporation, 1979.

4. Peatman, J.B., *Microcomputer-Based Design*, McGraw-Hill Inc., 1977.

5. Harrison, T.J., (ed.), *Minicomputers in Industrial Control, An Introduction*, Instrument Society of America, 1978.

# 11

# Programmable Controllers

**Introduction**    In the last chapter, we discussed the fundamental principles of microprocessors. In this chapter we will discuss a very important application of microprocessors and industrial computers: the design and use of programmable controllers (PCs) in process control.

PCs were originally designed to replace relay-based logic systems and solid-state hard-wired logic control panels. Their advantages over conventional logic systems are that they are easily programmed, highly reliable, flexible, small, relativity inexpensive, and able to communicate with other plant computers.

A PC examines the status of inputs and, in response, controls some processes through outputs. Combinations of input and output data are referred to as logic. Several logic combinations are usually required to carry out a control plan or program. This control plan is stored in memory using a programming device to input the program into the system. The control plan in memory is periodically scanned by the central processing unit (CPU), usually a microprocessor, in a predetermined order. The period required to evaluate the PC program is called the "scan time".

Regardless of size, cost or complexity, all PCs share the same basic components and functional characteristics. A PC will always consist of an input/output system, memory, a processor, a programming language and device, a power supply, and housings.

A typical PC system is shown in Figure 11-1 and consists of an I/O system, a power supply, a magnetic tape storage unit, a programming device, and a central processing unit.

The input/output system provides the physical connection between the process equipment and the central processing unit (CPU) as shown in Figure 11-1.

**Input/Output System**    The I/O system uses various interface circuits and/or modules to send and measure physical quantities of the process, such as motion, level, temperature, pressure, current, and voltage. Based on the status

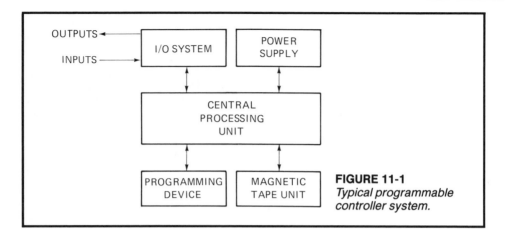

**FIGURE 11-1**
*Typical programmable controller system.*

sensed or values measured, the CPU controls various devices such as valves, motors, pumps, and alarms to exercise control over a machine or process.

**AC Input Modules**    A block diagram of a typical ac input module is shown in Figure 11-2. Input modules vary widely among PC manufacturers, but in general all ac input modules operate in a manner similar to that described in this diagram. The input circuit is composed of two primary parts: the power section and the logic section. The power and logic sections of the circuit are normally coupled with a circuit, that electrically isolates the input power section from the logic circuits. This electrical isolation is very important in a normally noisy industrial environment. The main problem with the early application of computers to process control was that the inputs and output were not designed for the harsh industrial environment.

The power section of an input module basically performs the function of converting the incoming voltage (115 V ac, 230 V ac, etc.) from an input device to a dc logic-level signal to be used by the processor during its program control scan. The bridge rectifier circuit converts the incoming ac signal to a dc level that is sent to a

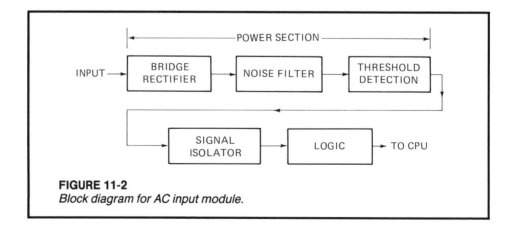

**FIGURE 11-2**
*Block diagram for AC input module.*

filter circuit, which protects against electrical noise on the input power line. This filter causes a signal delay that is typically 10-25 msec. The threshold circuit detects whether the incoming signal has reached the proper voltage level for the specified input rating. If the input signal exceeds and remains above the threshold voltage for a duration of at least the filter delay, the signal will be accepted as a valid input.

When a valid signal has been detected, it is passed through the isolation circuit, which completes the electrically isolated transition from ac to logic level. The dc signal from the isolator is used by the logic circuit and made available to the processor for its data bus. Electrical isolation is provided so that there is no electrical connection between the field device (power) and the controller (logic). This electrical separation helps prevent large voltage spikes from damaging the logic side of the interface (or the controller). The coupling between the power and logic sections is normally provided by an optical coupler or a pulse transformer.

Most input modules will have a power indicator to signify that the proper input voltage level is present (a switch is closed). A light-emitting diode (LED) indicator may also be available to indicate the status of the input. An ac input connection diagram is shown in Figure 11-3.

**Transistor-Transistor Logic (TTL) Input Modules**  TTL input modules allow the controller to accept signals from TTL-compatible devices, including solid-state controls and sensing instruments. TTL inputs are also used for interfacing with some 5 V dc-level control devices and several types of photoelectric sensors. The TTL interface has a configuration similar to the ac input modules; however, the input delay time caused by filtering is generally much shorter. TTL input modules normally require an external +5 V dc power supply with certain current specifications. Figure 11-4 shows a typical TTL input connection diagram.

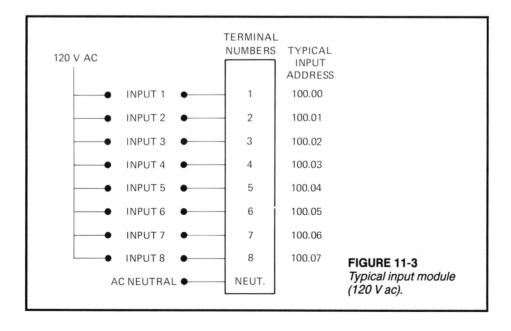

**FIGURE 11-3**
*Typical input module (120 V ac).*

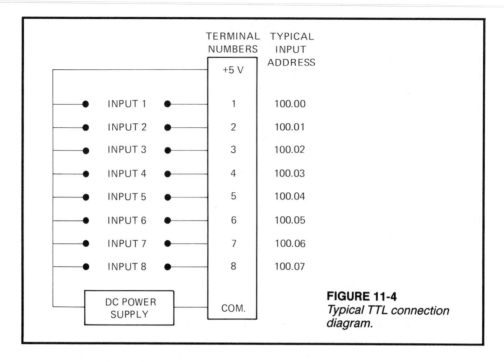

FIGURE 11-4
*Typical TTL connection diagram.*

**AC Output Modules**  Figure 11-5 shows a block diagram of the internal circuitry of a typical ac output module. AC output modules vary widely among PC manufacturers but the block diagram describes the basic operation of ac outputs. The circuit consists primarily of the logic and power sections, coupled by an isolation circuit. The output interface can be thought of as a simple switch through which power can be provided to control the output device.

During normal operation, the processor sends to the logic circuit the output status determined by the logic program. If the output is energized, the signal from the processor is fed to the logic section and passed through the isolation circuit, which will switch the power to the field device.

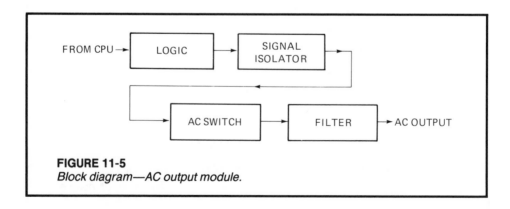

FIGURE 11-5
*Block diagram—AC output module.*

The switching section generally uses a triac or a silicon controller rectifier (SCR) to switch the power. The ac switch is normally protected by an RC snubber and often a metal oxide varistor (MOV), which is used to limit the peak voltage to some value below the maximum rating and also to prevent electrical noise from affecting the module operation. A fuse may be provided in the output circuit to prevent excessive current from damaging the ac switch. If the fuse is not provided in the circuit, it should be user-supplied.

As with input modules, the output module may provide light-emitting diode (LED) indicators to show the operating logic. If the circuit contains a fuse, a fuse status indicator may also be incorporated. An ac output module connection diagram is illustrated in Figure 11-6. Note that the switching voltage is field-supplied to the module.

Also notice that the PC output address starts with a zero (0). This is very common in programmable controllers, and it is used because it is easier for the system programmer to remember that all output addresses begin with a zero.

**DC Output Modules**   The dc output module is used to switch dc loads. Functional operation of the dc output is similar to the ac output, but the power circuit generally employs a power transistor to switch the load. Like triacs, transistors are also susceptible to excessive applied voltages and large surge currents, which could result in overheating and short circuits. To prevent this condition from occurring, the power transistor will normally be protected. Figure 11-7 shows a typical dc output module connection diagram.

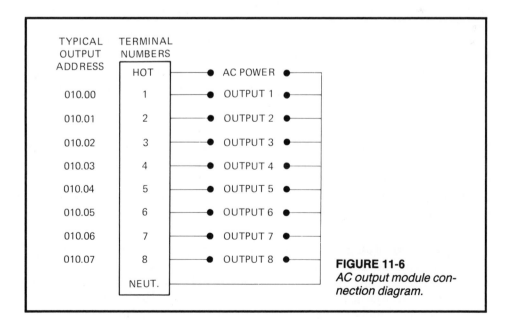

**FIGURE 11-6**
*AC output module connection diagram.*

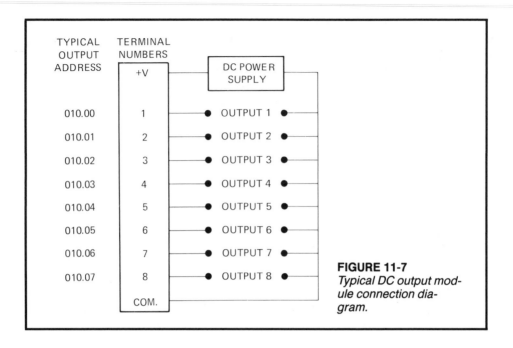

**FIGURE 11-7**
*Typical DC output module connection diagram.*

**Dry Contact Output Modules**   The contact output module allows output devices to be turned ON or OFF by a Normally Open (NO) or Normally Closed (NC) set of relay contacts. The advantage of relay or dry contact outputs is that there is electrical isolation between the power output signal and the logic signal. These modules will also generally have filtering, suppression, and fuses for circuit protection.

The contact output can be used to switch either ac or dc loads but are normally used in applications such as multiplexing analog signals and switching small currents at low voltage. High power contact outputs are also available for applications that require switching of high currents. The device connection for this output module is similar to the ac output module.

**TTL Output Module**   The TTL output module allows the controller to drive output devices that are TTL compatible, such as seven-segment LED displays, integrated circuits, and various 5 V dc logic devices. These modules generally require an external +5 V dc power supply with specific current requirements. A typical wiring diagram for a TTL output module is shown in Figure 11-8.

**Analog Input Modules**   The analog input interface contains the circuitry necessary to accept analog voltage or current signals from field devices. The voltage or current inputs are converted from an analog to a digital value by an analog-to-digital converter (ADC). The conversion value, which is proportional to the analog signal, is passed through to the controller's data bus and stored in a memory location for later use.

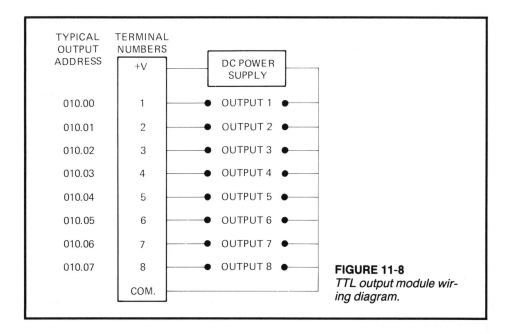

**FIGURE 11-8**
*TTL output module wiring diagram.*

Typically, analog input interfaces have a very high input impedance, which allows them to interface to low power (typically 4 to 20 mA output) field devices. The input line from the analog device generally uses twisted-pair conductors. The twisted-pair cable provides a lower noise input signal. The input stage of the interface provides filtering and isolation circuits to protect the module from additional field noise.

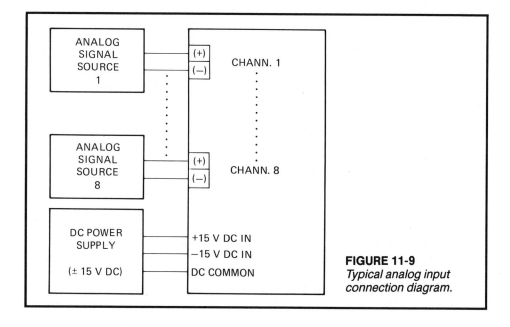

**FIGURE 11-9**
*Typical analog input connection diagram.*

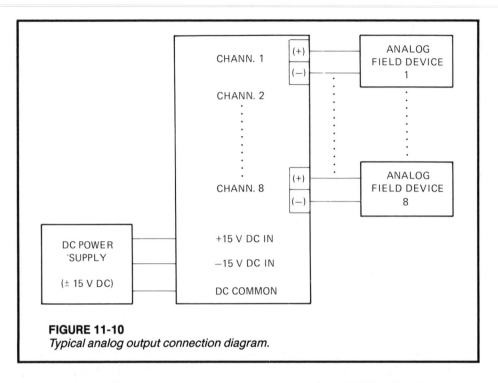

**FIGURE 11-10**
*Typical analog output connection diagram.*

The analog value (after conversion) is expressed as a BCD value that ranges from 000 to 999, where the low and high counts represent the low and full scale input signals. A typical analog input connection is illustrated in Figure 11-9.

**Analog Output Modules**   The analog output module receives from the CPU numerical data, which is translated into a proportional voltage or current to control an analog field device. The digital data is passed through a digital-to-analog converter (DAC) and the output is in analog form. Isolation between the output circuit and the logic circuit is generally provided through optical couplers. These output modules normally require an external power supply with certain current and voltage requirements. Figure 11-10 illustrates a typical device connection for an analog output module.

**Binary Coded Decimal (BCD) Input Modules**   The binary coded digital (BCD) input module provides parallel communication between the processor and input devices, such as thumbwheel switches. This type of module is generally used to input parameters into specific data locations in memory to be used by the control program. Typical parameters are timer and counter presets and process control set point values.

These modules generally accept voltages in the range of 5 V dc (TTL) to 24 V dc and are grouped in a module containing 16 or 32 inputs, which correspond to one or two I/O registers. Data manipulation instructions, such as a GET instruction, are used to access the data from the register input interface. Figure 11-11 illustrates a typical device connection for a BCD input module. In this module, each bit (1 or 0) from the thumbwheel controls one bit location in a word location in the PC.

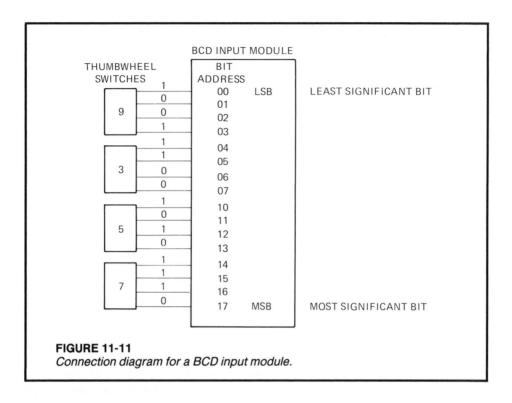

**FIGURE 11-11**
*Connection diagram for a BCD input module.*

**BCD Output Modules**   This numerical module provides parallel communication between the processor and an output device, such as a seven-segment LED display or a BCD alphanumeric display. The BCD output module can also provide voltage to TTL logic loads that have low current requirements. The register output module generally provides voltages that range from 5 V dc (TTL) to 30 V dc and have 16 or 32 output lines (one or two I/O registers).

When information is sent from the processor through a data transfer or I/O register instruction, the data is latched in the module and made available at the output circuit. Figure 11-12 shows a typical register output module connection.

# Special PC I/O Modules
In the previous sections, we discussed discrete, analog, and digital I/O modules that will normally cover 90% of the I/O applications encountered in PC systems. However, to process certain types of signals or data efficiently, the PC will require special modules. These special interfaces include those that condition input signals, such as thermocouple modules, or other signals that cannot be interfaced using standard I/O modules. Special I/O modules may also use an on-board microprocessor to add intelligence to the interface. These intelligent modules can perform complete processing functions, independent of the CPU and the control program scan. In this section, we will discuss the most commonly available special modules, such as thermocouple input, ASCII I/O, stepper motor output, and PID modules.

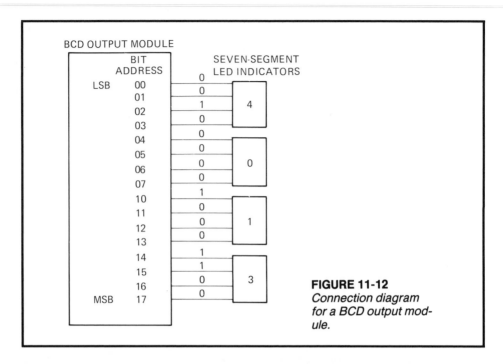

FIGURE 11-12
Connection diagram
for a BCD output mod-
ule.

**Thermocouple Input Module**    A thermocouple (TC) input module is designed to accept inputs directly from a TC; it also provides cold junction compensation to correct for changes in cold junction temperatures. The operation of this type of module is similar to the standard analog input with the exception that very low level signals are accepted from the TC (approximately 43 mV at maximum temperature for a J-type TC). (Refer to Chapter 6 for a detailed discussion of thermocou-

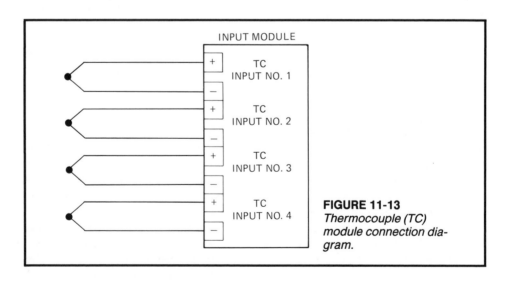

FIGURE 11-13
Thermocouple (TC)
module connection dia-
gram.

ples.) These signals are filtered, amplified, and digitized through an A/D converter and then sent to the CPU on command from a program instruction. The data is used by the control program to perform temperature control and/or indication. Figure 11-13 illustrates a typical thermocouple input connection diagram.

**ASCII Input/Output Module**   The ASCII input/output module is used to send and receive alphanumeric data between peripheral equipment and the controller. Typical peripheral devices with ASCII I/O include printers, video monitors, digital display instruments, and so on. This special I/O module, depending on the manufacturer, is available with communications interface circuitry that includes on-board memory and a dedicated microprocessor. The information exchange interface generally takes place via an RS-232C, RS-422, or a 20-mA current loop communications link.

The ASCII module will generally have its own RAM memory, which can store blocks of data that are to be transmitted. When the input data from the peripheral is received at the module, it is transferred to the PC memory through a data transfer instruction at the PC I/O data bus speed. All the initial communication parameters, such as parity (even or odd) or non-parity, number of stop bits, and communication rate, are hardware selectable or selectable through software.

**Stepping Motor Output Module**   The stepping motor module generates a pulse train that is compatible with stepping motor translators. The pulses sent to the translator will represent distance, speed, and direction commands to the motor.

The stepping motor interface accepts position commands from the control program. These commands are generally specified during program control, and, once the output interface is initialized by a start, it will output the pulses according to the PC program. Once the motion has started, the output module will generally not accept any commands from the CPU until the move is completed. Some modules may offer an override command that will reset the current position, which must be disabled to continue operation. The module also sends data regarding its status to the PC processor.

The step rate of pulses can range from 1 to 50 kHz with selectable step pulse widths. These modules generally require an external power supply. A typical stepping motor connection diagram is shown in Figure 11-14.

**Control Loop Module**   The control loop module is used in closed-loop control where the proportional-integral-derivative (PID) control algorithm is required. Some manufacturers call this interface the PID module, and it is typically applied to any process operation that requires continuous closed-loop control. Refer to Chapters 1 and 2 for a detailed discussion of PID control.

The control algorithm implemented by this module is represented by the following equation:

$$V_{out} = K_p e + K_i \int e \, dt + K_d \, \frac{de}{dt}$$

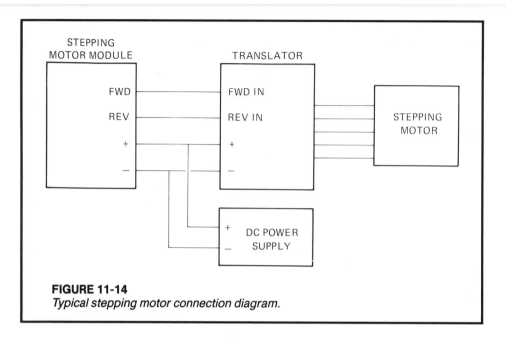

**FIGURE 11-14**
*Typical stepping motor connection diagram.*

where: $V_{out}$ = output control variable
e = PV – SP = error
$K_p$ = the proportional gain
$K_i$ = the integral gain
$K_d$ = the derivative gain

The module receives the process variable (PV), compares it to the set point (SP) selected by the operator, and computes the error difference. The operator or control engineer will determine the values of the control parameters ($K_p$, $K_d$ and $K_i$), based on the application.

The information sent to the PID module from the PC processor is primarily control parameters and set points. Depending on the PID module used, data can be sent to describe the update time, which is the period in which the output variable ($V_{out}$) is updated, and the error dead band, which is a quantity that is compared to the error signal. If the error is less than or equal to the signal error, no update takes place. Some modules provide square root extraction of the process variable, which can be used to obtain a linearized scaled output for use on flow control loops.

**Memory**   Memory is used to store the control program for the PC system, and it is usually located in the same housing as the CPU. The information stored in memory determines how the input and output data will be processed.

Memory elements store individual pieces of data called bits. A bit has two states—1 or 0, on or off, true or false, etc. Memory units are mounted on circuit boards and are specified in thousands or "K" increments where 1K is 1024 words (i.e., $2^{10}$ = 1024) of storage space in most cases. PC memory capacity may vary from less than one thousand bits to over 64,000 words (64K words), depending on the PC manufacturer. The complexity of the control plan will determine the amount of memory required.

The programs and data stored in memory are generally described using four terms, (1) Executive, (2) Scratch Pad, (3) Control Program, and (4) Data Table. The *Executive* is a permanently stored collection of programs that is the operating system for the PC. This operating system directs activities such as execution of the control program, communication with the peripheral devices, and other system housekeeping functions. The *Scratch Pad* is a temporary storage area used by the CPU to store a relatively small amount of data for interim control or calculations. Data that is needed quickly is stored in this area to increase the speed of data manipulation. The *Control Program* area provides storage for any programmed instructions entered by the user. The *Data Table* stores any data associated with the control program, such as timer/counter preset values, and any other stored constants or variables that are used by the main program or the CPU. It also retains the input/output status information.

The storage and retrieval requirement are not the same for the Executive, the Scratch Pad, the Control Program, and the Data Table; therefore, they are not always stored in the same types of memory. For example, the Executive requires a memory that permanently stores its contents and cannot be deliberately or accidentally altered by loss of electrical power or by the user. On the other hand, the user would need to alter the control program and/or the data table for any given application.

Although there are several different types of computer memory, they can always be classified as *volatile or nonvolatile.* Volatile memory will lose its programmed contents if all operating power is lost or removed. Volatile memory is easily altered and quite suitable for most programming applications, when supported by battery backup and/or a recorded copy of the program.

Nonvolatile memory will retain its data and program even if there is a complete loss of operating power. It does not require a backup system. Nonvolatile memory is generally not alterable, although some nonvolatile memory types can be changed. Volatile and nonvolatile memories used in PCs are explained in greater detail in the following sections.

**Memory Types**    This section will discuss the types of memory generally used in PC systems and their applications to the type of program and data stored. In selecting the type of memory to be used, a system designer is concerned with volatility and ease of programming. He is concerned with volatility because memory holds the process control program and, if this program is lost, production in a plant will be down. Ease in altering the memory is important since the memory is involved in any interaction that takes place between the user and the PC. This interaction begins with the initial system programming and debugging and continues with on-line changes such as changing timer and counter preset values.

### Read-Only Memory (ROM)
Read-only memory is designed to permanently store a fixed program, which normally can not or will not be changed. It gets its name from the fact that its contents

can be read but not written into or altered once the data or program has been stored. Because of their design, ROMs are generally immune to changes due to electrical noise or loss of power. The Executive or operating system program of PC is normally stored in ROM.

PCs rarely use ROM for the control applications program memory. However, in applications that require fixed data, ROM offers advantages where speed, cost, and reliability are factors. Generally, ROM-based PC programs are produced at the factory by the equipment manufacturer. Once the original set of instructions is programmed, it can never be altered by the user. The manufacturer will write and debug the program using a Read/Write-based controller or computer and then the final program is entered into ROM. ROM application memory is typically found only in very small, dedicated PCs.

### Random Access Memory (RAM)

Random access memory is designed so that data or information can be written into or read from any unique location. There are two types of RAM: volatile RAM, which does not retain its contents if power is lost, and nonvolatile RAM (see Core), which retains its contents if power is lost. Volatile RAM normally has a battery backup to sustain it during power loss. Programmable controllers, for the most part, use RAM with battery backup for application memory. RAM provides an excellent means for easily creating and altering a control program as well as allowing data entry. In comparison to some other memory types, RAM is relatively fast. The only important disadvantage of battery-supported RAM is the fact that it requires a battery that might fail at a critical time, but it is sufficient for most PC applications. If it is not feasible, a PC with a nonvolatile memory option can be used in combination with RAM (e.g., PROM, EPROM, or Core). This type of memory arrangement provides the advantages of both volatile and nonvolatile memory.

### Programmable Read-Only Memory (PROM)

The PROM is a special type of ROM that is rarely used in most PC applications. However, when it is used, it will most likely be a permanent storage backup to some type of RAM. Although PROM is programmable and, like other ROM, has the advantage of nonvolatility, it has the disadvantages of requiring special programming equipment and, once programmed, it cannot be erased or altered. Any program change would require a new set of PROM chips. PROM memory might be suitable for storing a program that has been thoroughly checked while stored in RAM and will not require further changes or on-line data entry.

### Erasable Programmable Read-Only Memory (EPROM)

The EPROM is a special type of PROM that can be reprogrammed after being completely erased using an ultraviolet (UV) light source. The integrated circuit chip for EPROM is built with a window on the top of the chip so the internal memory circuits can be exposed to the UV light. The EPROM can be considered a temporary storage device in that it stores a program until it is ready to be changed. EPROM provides an excellent storage medium for a control program where nonvolatility is required, but program changes are not required. Many manufacturers of equipment with built-in PCs use EPROM-type memories to provide permanent storage of the machine program after it has been developed, debugged, and is fully operational.

A control program composed of EPROM alone would be unsuitable if on-line changes and/or data entries are a requirement. However, many PCs offer EPROM control program memory as an optional backup to battery-supported RAM. EPROM, with its permanent storage capability combined with the easily altered RAM, makes a suitable memory system.

## Core Memory

Core memory is a nonvolatile memory that gets its name from the fact that it stores individual bits by magnetizing a small ferrite core in the 1 or 0 direction through a write-current pulse. Each core represents a bit and can hold a 1 or 0 even if power is lost. Core memory units are nonvolatile because power is not necessary to keep the core magnetized. The state of each core is also electrically alterable, which makes it a nonvolatile RAM.

Magnetic core was used in many of the first programmable controllers and is still used in a few PCs today. It provides excellent permanent storage and is easily changed. Some of the disadvantages of using core memory in PCs are its slow speed, relatively expensive cost, and larger physical space requirements.

**Memory Units (Bits, Bytes, Words)** PC memories can be visualized as a two-dimensional array of single storage cells, each of which can store a single bit of information in the form of 1 or 0. This single bit gets it name from BInary digiT. A bit is the smallest structural unit of memory and stores information in the form of 1s and 0s. Ones and zeros are not actually in each cell; each cell has a voltage present (indicating a one), or not present (indicating a zero). The bit is set or ON if the stored information is 1, and OFF if the stored information is 0.

In most cases it is necessary for the CPU to handle more than a single bit. For example, when transferring data to and from memory, storing numbers and, programming codes, a group of bits called a byte or word is required. A byte is defined as the smallest group of bits that can be handled by the CPU at one time. In PCs, byte size is normally 8 bits, but can be smaller or larger depending on the specific computer being used.

Word length is usually 1 byte or more in length. For example, a 16-bit word consists of 2 bytes. Typical word lengths in programmable controllers are 8, 16, and 32 bits. The basic structural memory units of a PC are shown in Figure 11-15.

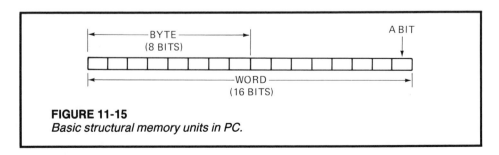

**FIGURE 11-15**
*Basic structural memory units in PC.*

**Memory Size**   The size of memory is an important factor in designing programmable controller-based control systems. Specifying the correct memory size can save hardware cost and avoid lost time later. Proper calculation of memory size means avoiding the possibility of purchasing a PC that does not have adequate capacity or that is not expandable.

Memory size is normally expandable to some maximum point in most controllers, but it is not expandable in some of the smaller PCs. (Smaller PCs are defined in this context as units that control 10 to 64 input/output devices.) Programmable controllers that handle 64 or more I/O devices are usually expandable in increments of 1K, 2K, 4K, etc., (K represents 1024 or $2^{10}$ word locations in memory). The maximum memory in the larger controllers is generally 64K.

The stated memory size of a PC is only a rough indication of the memory space available to the user, since some of the memory is used by the controllers for internal functions. Another problem is that generally two different word sizes, 8 bit and 16 bit, are used by PC manufacturers. Figure 11-16 shows a comparison of 2K of memory based on 8-bit and 16-bit words. It's clear that the 16-bit memory configuration has twice the storage capacity.

The main problem with determining memory size for an application is that the complexity of the control program is not determined until after the equipment is purchased. However, we generally know the number of I/O points in the system before the hardware is procured. Because memory size is estimated from this fact, a good rule is to multiply the number of I/O points by 10 words of memory. For example, if the system has 100 I/O points, the program will generally be equal to or less than 1000 words. We should keep in mind that program size is affected by the sophistication of the control program. If the application requires data handling or

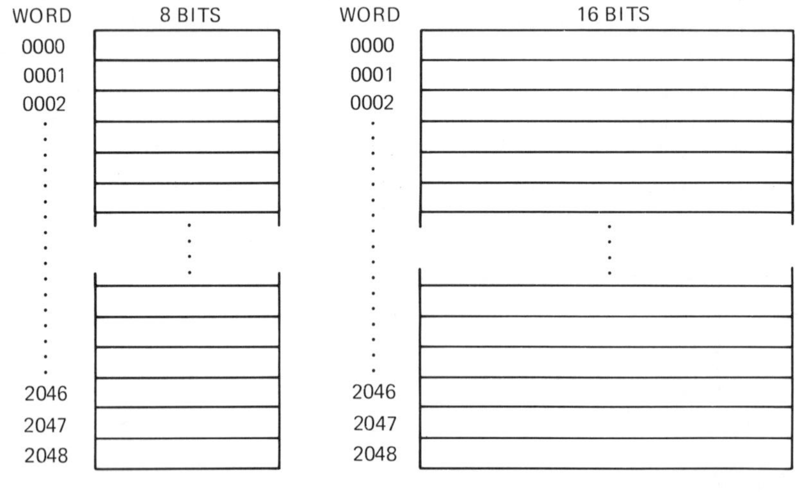

**FIGURE 11-16**
*Comparison of 2K of memory for 8- and 16-bit words.*

complex control algorithms such as PID control, then additional memory will be required.

After the system designer determines the minimum memory required for an application, he will normally add an additional 25 to 50% more for program changes, modification, or future expansion. To accurately size memory, we need to understand the overall organization of PC memory.

**PC Memory Organization**   The arrangement or organization of PC memory is known as a *memory map*. A memory map is used to show the location of both the system memory and the application memory; it is an aid to the PC programmer in writing the control program. A typical memory map is shown in Figure 11-17 that consists of the following units: executive, processor work area, the input/output table, data table, and the user program.

Normally the programmer does not have access to the executive or the process work area. These two areas are called the system memory. Care must be taken not to include this area as part of the available programming area when sizing the PC memory for an application. On the other hand, the data table and the user program areas are used by the programmer and are called the application memory. The PC memory, therefore, consists of three main parts: the system memory, the application memory, and the input/output table.

It is important to note again that some controller manufacturers include system memory in their total specified memory size. A controller with 64K of memory may have system memory of 32K and 2K of I/O image table, leaving only 30K for application memory. Fortunately, most PC vendors will exclude the system memory when they specify memory size, so that only the application memory size needs to be considered when designing a PC control system. Now for a closer look at application memory.

**Application Memory**   The application memory stores control program instructions and data that is used by the CPU to perform its control functions. A typical map of the application memory is shown in Figure 11-18. The application memory can be divided into two major areas: the *Data Table* and the *User Program*. All data is stored in the data table, while programming instructions are stored in the user program area.

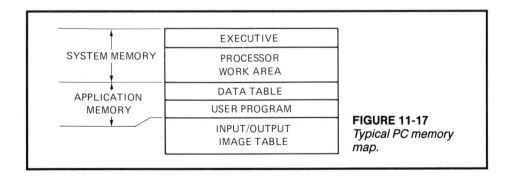

**FIGURE 11-17**
*Typical PC memory map.*

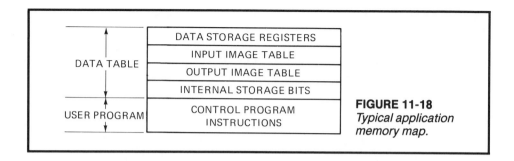

**FIGURE 11-18**
*Typical application memory map.*

The data table can be functionally divided into four areas:

1. Data storage registers
2. Input image table
3. Output image table
4. Internal storage bits

### Data Storage Registers

The information stored in the input/output table is ON/OFF status information, which is easily represented by 1 or 0. To denote any quantity having a value that cannot be represented by a single 1 or 0, groups of bits or memory words must be used. Memory words that store value-type information are also called storage registers. In general, there are three types of storage registers: input registers, holding registers, and output registers. The total number of registers varies depending on the controller memory size and how the data table is configured (ratio of data storage area to program storage area). Values stored in the storage registers are in binary or BCD format. Each register can generally be loaded, altered, or displayed by using the programming unit or a special data entry device offered by most manufacturers.

Input registers are used to store numerical data received, via input interfaces, from devices such as thumbwheel switches, shaft encoders, and other devices that provide BCD input. Analog signals also provide numerical data that must be stored in input registers. The current or voltage signal generated by various analog transmitters is converted by the analog interface. From these analog values, binary representations are obtained and stored in the designated input register. The value contained in the input register is determined by the input device and, therefore, is not alterable from within the controller or via any other form of data entry.

The holding registers are those required to store variable values that are program generated by instructions (e.g., math, timer, or counter) or constant values that are entered via the programming units or some other data entry method.

Output registers are used to provide storage for numerical or analog values that control various output devices. Typical devices that receive data from output registers are alphanumeric LED displays, recorder charts, analog meters, speed controllers, and control valves. Output registers are essentially holding registers that are designated "output" because of their particular nature (i.e., controlling outputs).

In addition to the I/O tables and storage register areas, some controllers allocate a portion of the data table for storing decimal, ASCII, and binary data. Typically, this table area is used for recipe data, report generation messages, or other data that can be stored or retrieved during program execution.

### Input Image Table

The input image table is an array of bits that stores the status of digital inputs from the process, which are connected to input modules. The number of bits in the table is equal to the maximum number of inputs. A controller with a maximum of 64 inputs would require an input table of 64 bits. Each connected input has a bit in the input table that corresponds exactly to the terminal to which the input is connected. If the input is ON, its corresponding bit in the table is ON (1). If the input is OFF, the corresponding bit is cleared or turned OFF (0).

The input table is continuously being changed to reflect the current status of the connected input devices. This status information is also being used by the control program. The input table is illustrated in Figure 11-19.

### Output Image Table

The output table is an array of bits that controls the status of digital output devices, which are connected to output interface circuits. The number of bits in the output table is equal to the maximum number of outputs. A controller with a maximum of 512 outputs would require an output table of 512 bits.

Each connected output has a bit in the output table that corresponds exactly to the terminal to which the output is connected. Note that the bits in the output table are controlled by the CPU as it interprets the control program and are updated accordingly during the I/O scan. If a bit is turned ON (1), then the connected output is switched ON. If a bit is cleared or turned OFF (0), the output is switched OFF. The output table is shown in Figure 11-19.

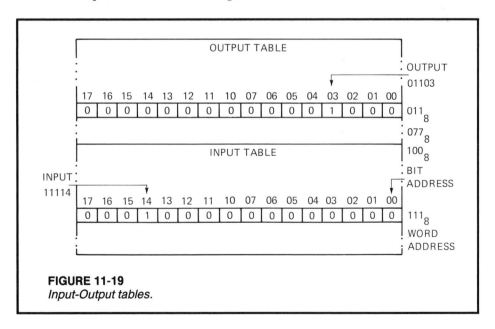

**FIGURE 11-19**
*Input-Output tables.*

### Internal Storage Bits

Most controllers assign an area for internal storage bits. These storage bits are also called internal outputs, internal coils, or internal control bits. The internal output operates just as any output that is controlled by programmed logic; however, the output is used strictly for internal logic programming and does not directly control an output to the process. Internal outputs are used for interlocking logic purposes in the control program.

Internal outputs include the "done" bits on counters and timers, as well as internal logic relays of various types. Each internal output bit, referenced by an address in the control program, has a storage bit of the same address. When the control logic is TRUE, the internal (output) storage bit turns ON.

The user program memory area of the application memory is used to store the process control logic program. All the controller instructions that control the machine or process are stored here. The addresses of the real and internal I/O bits are specified in this section of memory. When the PC is in the RUN mode, and the control program is executed, the CPU interprets these memory locations and controls the bits in the data table, which corresponds to a real or internal I/O bit. The interpretation of the control program is accomplished by the processor's execution of the executive program.

The maximum amount of user program memory available is normally a function of the controller memory size. In medium and large PCs, the user program size is normally flexible, through altering the data table size, so that it meets the minimum data storage requirements. In small PCs, however, the user program size is normally fixed.

## PC Programming Languages   The programming language allows the user to communicate with the PC via a programming device or panel. PC manufacturers use several different programming languages, but they all convey to the system, by means of instructions, a basic control plan.

The four most common types of languages encountered in programmable controllers are as follows:

1. Ladder diagrams
2. Boolean mnemonics
3. Function blocks
4. English statements

These languages can be grouped into two major categories. The first two, ladder and Boolean, form basic PC languages, while function blocks and English statements are considered high level languages. The basic PC languages consist of a set of instructions that will perform the most primitive types of control functions: relay replacement, timing, counting, sequencing, and logic. However, depending on the controller model, the instruction set may be extended or enhanced to perform other basic operations. The high level languages have been brought about by a need to execute more powerful instructions that go beyond the simple timing, counting, and ON/OFF control. High level languages are used for analog control, data manipulation, reporting, and other functions that are not possible with the basic instruction sets.

The language used in a PC actually dictates the range of applications in which the controller can be used. Depending on the size and capabilities of the controller, one or more languages may be used. Typical combinations of languages are:

1. Ladder diagrams only
2. Boolean only
3. Ladder diagrams and function blocks
4. Ladder diagrams and English statements
5. Boolean and function blocks
6. Boolean and English statements

## Ladder Diagram Programming
Since ladder logic programming is the most common type used in PC applications it will be covered in detail. But due to limited space in this chapter, the other languages will not be covered. To obtain information on other programming methods, the reader should consult the vendor literature or the sources listed in the bibliography at the end of this chapter.

The ladder language includes, as a basic set, the relay logic as well as timer and counter, arithmetic, data manipulation, and data transfer instructions.

Table 11-1 summarizes the five major types of operations and the instructions that are found in ladder logic programming. The main function of the ladder diagram program is to control outputs based on input conditions. This control is accomplished through the use of what is referred to as a ladder rung. Figure 11-20 shows the basic structure of a ladder rung. In general, a rung consists of a set of input conditions, represented by contact instructions, and an output instruction at the end of the rung, represented by the coil symbol.

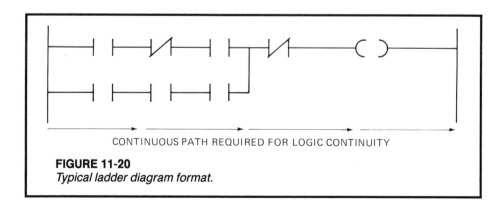

CONTINUOUS PATH REQUIRED FOR LOGIC CONTINUITY

**FIGURE 11-20**
*Typical ladder diagram format.*

Coils and contacts are the basic symbols of the ladder diagram instruction set. The contact symbols programmed in a given rung represent conditions to be evaluated in order to determine the control of the output; all outputs are represented by coil symbols.

**TABLE 11-1**
**Ladder Programming Symbols**

| Operation Type | Basic Symbols | Description |
|---|---|---|
| Relay logic | —| |— | Contacts (NO) |
| | —|/|— | Contacts (NC) |
| | —( )— | Output coil |
| | —( L )— | Latched output |
| | —( U )— | Unlatched output |
| Timer and counter | —( TON )— | Timer ON |
| | —( TOF )— | Timer OFF |
| | —( RTO )— | Retentive timer ON |
| | —( RTR )— | Retentive timer reset |
| | —( CTU )— | Up counter |
| | —( CTD )— | Down counter |
| | —( CTR )— | Counter reset |
| Arithmetic | —( + )— | Addition |
| | —( − )— | Subtraction |
| | —( X )——( X )— | Multiplication |
| | —( ÷ )——( ÷ )— | Division |
| Data manipulation | —| = |— | Equal to |
| | —| > |— | Greater than |
| | —| < |— | Less than |
| Data transfer | —|GET|— | Get data |
| | —( PUT )— | Store data |

When programmed, each contact and coil is referenced with an address number, which identifies what is being evaluated and what is being controlled. Recall that these address numbers reference the data table location of either an internal output or a connected input or output. A contact, regardless of whether it represents an input/output connection or an internal output, can be used throughout the program whenever that condition needs to be evaluated.

The format of the rung contacts is dependent on the desired control logic. Contacts may be placed in whatever series, parallel, or series/parallel configuration is required to control a given output. For an output to be activated or energized, at least one left-to-right path of contacts must be closed. A complete closed path is referred to as having logic continuity. When logic continuity exists in at least one path, it is said that the rung condition is TRUE. The rung condition is FALSE if no path has continuity.

In the early years, the standard ladder instruction set was limited to performing only relay equivalent functions, using the basic relay-type contact and coil symbols similar to those illustrated Figure 11-20. A need for greater flexibility, coupled with developments in technology, led to extended ladder diagram instruction sets that perform data manipulation, arithmetic, and data transfer. It is now commonplace to find controllers that include computer-like expressions similar to the diagram in Figure 11-21.

Although instructions and symbols may differ among controllers, the instructions described here are generic and apply to most controllers.

**Relay-Type Instructions** The relay-type instructions are the most basic of ladder logic instructions. They provide the same capabilities as hard-wired relay logic, but with greater flexibility. These instructions primarily provide the ability to examine the ON/OFF status of a specific bit addressed in memory and to control the state of an internal or external output. The following is a description of relay-type instructions that are most commonly available in any controller that has a ladder diagram instruction set.

**Normally Open Contact (NO)**
The normally open contact is used when the presence of the referenced signal is needed to turn an output ON. When evaluated, the referenced address is examined for an ON (1) condition. The referenced address may represent the status of an external input, or an internal program bit. If, when examined, the referenced address is ON, then the normally open contact will close and allow logic continuity (power flow). If it is OFF (0), then the normally open contact will assume its normal programmed state (open), thus breaking logic continuity.

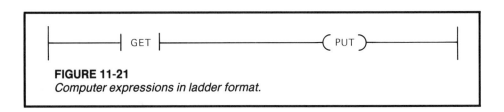

**FIGURE 11-21**
*Computer expressions in ladder format.*

### Normally Closed Contact (NC)

The normally closed contact is used when the absence of the referenced signal is needed to turn an output ON (1). When examined, the referenced address is checked for an OFF (0) condition. The referenced address may represent the status of an external input or an internal program bit. If, when examined, the referenced address is OFF, then the normally closed contact will remain closed, allowing logic continuity. If the referenced address is ON, then the normally closed contact will open and break logic continuity.

### Output Coil

The output coil instruction is programmed to control either an output connected to the controller or an internal control bit. If any rung path has logic continuity, the referenced output is turned ON. The output is turned OFF if logic continuity is lost. When the output is ON, a normally open contact of the same address will close, and a normally closed contact will open. If the output goes OFF, any normally open contact will then open, and normally closed contacts will close. An example of a rung using the previous instructions is shown in Figure 11-22. In this example, if either input 1100 or input 1200 is TRUE, the output 0300 will be TRUE.

### Latch Output

The latch output instruction is used if it is necessary for an output to remain energized, even though the status of the contacts that caused the output to energize may change. If any rung path has logic continuity, the output is turned ON and retained ON, even if logic continuity or system power is lost. The latched output will remain latched ON until it is unlatched by an unlatch output instruction of the same reference address. Although most controllers allow latching of internal or external outputs, some are restricted to latching internal outputs only.

### Unlatch Output

The unlatch output instruction is programmed to reset a latched output of the same reference address. If any rung path has logic continuity, the referenced address is turned OFF. The unlatch output is the only automatic means of resetting a latched output. Figure 11-23 illustrates the use of the latch and unlatch coils.

In this example, bit 111.15 must be TRUE to set the latch 200.00. If this bit (111.15) goes FALSE, the output coil will remain on until bit 100.00 is TRUE to un-

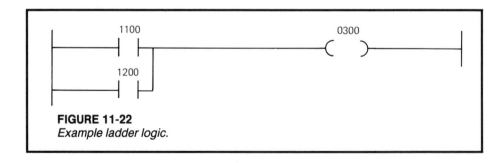

**FIGURE 11-22**
*Example ladder logic.*

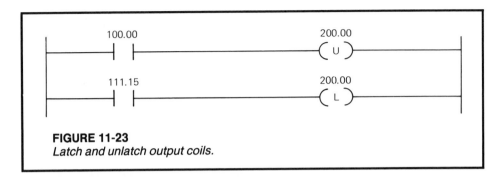

**FIGURE 11-23**
*Latch and unlatch output coils.*

latch the coil. In most PCs the unlatch output must be placed before the latch coil because the program is scanned from the top of the ladder to the bottom and the input image table is only updated at the end of a program scan.

**Timer and Counter Instructions**   Timers and counters are output instructions that provide the same functions as would hardware timers and counters. They are used to activate or de-activate a device after an expired interval or count. The timer and counter instructions are generally considered internal outputs. Like the relay-type instructions, timer and counter instructions are fundamental to the ladder diagram instruction set.

The operations of the timers and counters are quite similar in that they are both counters. A timer counts the number of times that a fixed interval of time (e.g., 0.1 sec, 1.0 sec) elapses. To time an interval of 3 seconds, a timer counts three 1-second intervals (time base). A counter simply counts the occurrence of an event. Both the timer and counter instructions require an accumulator register (word location) to store the elapsed count and a preset register to store a preset value. The preset value will determine the number of event occurrences or time-based intervals that are to be counted.

**Timer ON**   ————( TON )————
The timer ON output instruction is used to provide time-delayed action or to measure the duration of an event. If any rung path has logic continuity as shown in Figure 11-24, the timer begins counting time-based intervals and counts until the accumulated (ACC) time equals the preset (PR) value. When the accumulated time equals the preset time, the output is energized, and the timed-out contact associated with the output is closed. The timer-done contact can be used in the program as a normally open (NO) or normally closed (NC) contact to perform some logic operation. Most PCs have selectable time bases (TB) of 0.01, 0.1, or 1.0 second.

**Timer OFF**   ————( TOF )————
The timer OFF delay output instruction is programmed to provide time-delayed action. If logic continuity is lost, the timer begins counting time-based intervals until the accumulated time equals the programmed preset value. When the accumulated time equals the preset time, the output is de-energized, and the timed-out

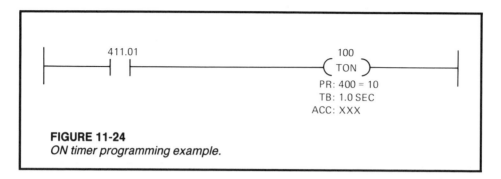

**FIGURE 11-24**
*ON timer programming example.*

contact associated with the output is opened. The timed contact can be used throughout the program as a NO or NC contact. If logic continuity is gained before the timer is timed out, the accumulator is reset to zero.

**Retentive Timer ON** —————( RTO )—————

The retentive timer output instruction is used if it is necessary for the timer accumulated value to be retained, even if logic continuity or power is lost. If the timer rung path has logic continuity, the timer begins counting time-based intervals until the accumulated time equals the preset value. The accumulator register retains the accumulated value, even if logic continuity is lost before the timer is timed out, or if power is lost. When the accumulated time equals the preset time, the output is energized, and the timed out contact associated with the output is turned ON. The timer contacts can be used throughout the program as a NO or NC contact. The retentive timer accumulator value must be reset by the retentive timer reset instruction.

**Retentive Timer Reset** —————( RTR )—————

The retentive timer reset output instruction is the only automatic means of resetting the accumulated value of a retentive timer. If any rung path has logic continuity, then the accumulated value of the referenced retentive timer is reset to zero.

**Up Counter** —————( CTU )—————

The up counter output instruction will increment by one each time the counted event occurs. A control application of a counter is to turn a device ON or OFF after reaching a certain count. An accounting application of a counter is to keep track of the number of filled cans that pass a certain point. The up counter increments its accumulated value each time the up-count event makes an OFF-to-ON transition. When the accumulated value reaches the preset (PR) value, the output is turned ON, and the counted-done contact associated with the referenced output is closed. Depending on the controller, after the counter reaches the preset value, the counter is either reset to zero or continues to increment for each OFF-to-ON transition. If the latter case is TRUE, a reset instruction is used to clear the accumulator.

**Down Counter** —————( CTD )—————

The down counter output instruction will count down by one each time a certain event occurs. Each time the down-count event occurs, the accumulated (ACC)

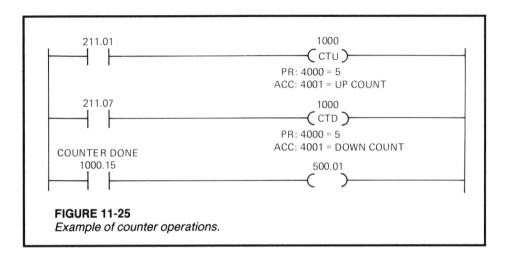

**FIGURE 11-25**
*Example of counter operations.*

value is decremented. In normal use, the down counter is used in conjunction with the up counter to form an up/down counter.

**Counter Reset**  ——————( CTR )——————

The counter reset output instruction is used to reset the CTU and CTD accumulated values. When programmed, the CTR coil is given the same reference address as the CTU and CTD coils. If the CTR rung condition is TRUE, the referenced address will be cleared. An example of counter operation is shown in Figure 11-25. In this example, the counter at location 1000 increments one count when bit 211.01 is ON, and decrements by one if bit 211.07 is energized. The done bit (1000.15 in this example) energizes after the count reaches 5, which turns on output 500.01 in the last rung.

**Arithmetric Operations**   The arithmetic operations include the four basic operations: addition, subtraction, multiplication, and division. These instructions use the contents of two registers to perform the desired function.

**Addition (ADD)**  ——————( + )——————

The ADD instruction performs the addition of two values stored in two different memory locations. How these values are accessed is dependent upon the PC. Some instruction sets use a GET (data transfer) instruction to access the two operand (registers) values, while others simply reference the two registers using contact symbols. The result is stored in the register referenced by the ADD coil. If the addition operation is enabled only when certain rung conditions are TRUE, then the input conditions should be programmed before the values are accessed in the addition rung. Overflow conditions are usually signaled by one of the bits of the addition result register.

**Subtraction (SUB)**  ——————( - )——————

The SUB instruction performs the subtraction operation of two registers. As in addition, if there is a condition to enable the subtraction, it should be programmed before the values are accessed in the rung. The subtraction result register will usually have an underflow bit to represent a negative result.

### Multiplication (MUL)  ———( x )——( x )———

The MUL instruction performs the multiplication operation, using two registers to hold the result of the operation between two operand registers. The two registers are referenced by two output coils. If there is a condition to enable the operation, it should be programmed before the two operands are accessed in the multiplication rung.

### Division, (DIV)  ———( ÷ )——( ÷ )———

The DIV instruction performs quotient calculation of two numbers. The result of the division is held in two result registers as referenced by the output coils. The first result register generally holds the integer, while the second result register holds the decimal fraction.

**Data Manipulation Operations**  In general, the manipulation of data using ladder diagram instructions involves simple register (word) operations to compare the contents of two registers. In the ladder language, there are three basic data manipulation instructions: equal to, greater than, and less than. Based on the result of a greater than, less than, or equal to comparison, an output can be turned ON or OFF, or some other operation can be performed.

### Equal To  ———| = |———

The equal instruction is used to compare the contents of two referenced registers for an equal condition when the rung conditions are TRUE. As in the arithmetic instructions, the values to be compared can be accessed directly or through a GET instruction, depending on the controller. If the operation is TRUE, the output coil is energized.

### Greater Than  ———( > )———

The greater than instruction operates like the less than operation, with the exception that the test is performed for a greater than condition. If the test condition is TRUE, the output coil is energized. Some controllers do not have this function, since a greater than function can be performed using the less than logic by reversing the orde  of the data and the less than function in the logic rung.

### Less Than  ———( < )———

Similar to the equal instruction, the less than instruction tests the contents of the value of one register to see if it is less than the value stored in a second register. If the test condition is TRUE, the output coil is energized.

**Data Transfer Operations**  Data transfer instructions, which involve the transfer of the contents from one register to another, can address any location in the memory data table, with the exception of areas restricted to user application. Prestored values can be automatically retrieved and placed in any new location. That location may be the preset register for a timer or counter or even an output register that controls an output display.

### Get Word  ———|GET|———

The GET instruction accesses the contents of the referenced address and makes it available for other operations. Some controllers use this instruction to access registers to perform math operations or comparisons.

**Put Word** ————————( PUT )————————

The PUT instruction is used to store the result of other operations in the memory location (register) specified by the PUT coil. PUT is generally used with the GET instruction to perform a move register operation. Figure 11-26 shows an example ladder diagram using arithmetic, data manipulation, and data transfer instructions.

In this example, if input 111.04 is true, the data in memory location 1600 is compared to the data value in location 1601, and, if they are equal, output coil 100.07 is energized. When output bit 100.07 is energized, the data in memory locations 1700 and 1701 are added and stored in location 1702. Finally, if logic bit 111.16 is ON, the contents of 1702 are transferred to output word 500.

**PC Power Supply**    The power supply for a PC system may integrated with the CPU, memory, and I/Os into a single housing, or it might be a separate unit connected to the system through a cable. As a system expands to include more I/O modules or special function modules, most PCs require an additional or auxiliary power supply to meet the increased power demand. PC power supplies are usually designed to eliminate electrical noise present on the ac power and signal lines in industrial plants. They are also normally designed for the higher temperature and humidity present in most industrial environments.

**PC Modular Housing**    Modular housing construction is one of the most popular features of programmable controllers. Most systems are designed so that the I/O modules can be removed without turning off the ac power or removing the field wiring. Most major PC components are mounted on printed circuit boards that can be inserted into an I/O housing or a card rack. The I/O housing can be mounted in a control panel or mounted on a sub-panel in a enclosure. Most housings are designed to protect the PC components from dirt, dust, electrical noise, and mechanical vibration.

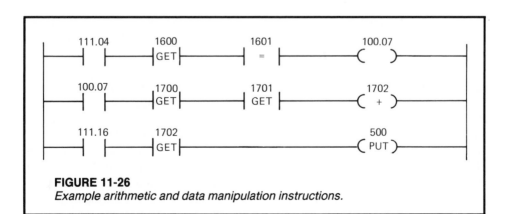

**FIGURE 11-26**
*Example arithmetic and data manipulation instructions.*

## PC System Design

As a general type of control system, the PC offers a wide variety of system configurations and capabilities. These range from a single machine relay replacement to an entire process control and monitoring system. After the decision has been made to use a PC in an application, the control systems engineer must do a complete system design. The four basic components of a system design are are: input/output, memory, programming, and peripheral equipment. Each of these areas will be discussed to give a step-by-step approach to PC design.

### I/O Requirements

Many different types of I/O may be needed for a given PC application. Limit switches, push buttons, selector switches, motor controls, solenoids, and pilot lights may require either ac or dc modules of different voltage levels. Solid-state displays and some electronic instrumentation may require +5 V dc logic interface modules. Process instrumentation for measurement of level, flow, temperature, or pressure may require analog-to-digital (A/D) conversion interfaces. Incremental encoders and stepping motors might need pulse-type input/output modules.

The interface to these I/O devices can be done with external "black boxes" to condition the signals, which would increase overall equipment cost for a system. Therefore, a PC should be selected with the correct input/output modules to match the process equipment.

The number of field devices that can be interfaced to a PC system is an important consideration in sizing the I/O. Each programmable controller has a maximum number of input and output devices that can be monitored or controlled. Most PC systems have I/O capacities ranging from 16 to 4096. These capacities can be divided into three categories: small, medium and large. A small PC system ranges from 16 to 256 I/O, a medium PC system encompasses 256 to 1024 I/O, and a large PC system has 1024 to 4096 I/O. To determine the PC system size required, simply add up the number of field and control panel devices and compare the total to the above classifications. The system designer must also define the type and number of I/O, because some PC systems are constrained as to the mixture that can be interfaced to a given I/O system.

Input and output totals can then be used to determine the number and type of I/O modules required. Each module can interface a certain number of I/O, such as 2, 4, 8, or 16. Divide the number of inputs or outputs by the number of I/O points per module and round up to the nearest whole number. This calculation must be performed for each type of I/O module, i.e., 120 V ac, 24 V dc, pulse, analog, etc.

### Memory Sizing

The amount of memory required for an application is primarily a function of control program complexity and the number of I/O points in the system. The most precise method of determining memory size is to write out the control program and count the number of instructions used in the program. Then multiply this count by the number of words used per instruction. (This number can be obtained from the PC programming manual. Also consult the programming manual on the amount of memory used by executive programs and the processor scratch pad.) The problem with this method is that, in a large system, the system programming sometimes takes months to complete and the system must be designed and purchased in advance. (A short cut method was given earlier that consists of multiplying the number of I/O points by 10 to obtain the memory required.)

An example of sizing memory using this simpler method is given in Example 11-1.

**EXAMPLE 11-1**

**Problem:** Calculate the memory size required for the process plant shown in Figure 11-27.

**Solution:** To calculate the memory size, we first need to calculate the number of I/O points in the system in the figure.

Remote Area 1: I/O points = 70 + 35 + 6 = 111

Remote Area 2: I/O points = 95 + 50 + 10 = 155

Main Process I/O points = 300 + 156 + 32 + 5 = 493

Total System I/O points = 111 + 155 + 493 = 759

Therefore, memory size = $10 \times 759 = 7590 \cong 8K$

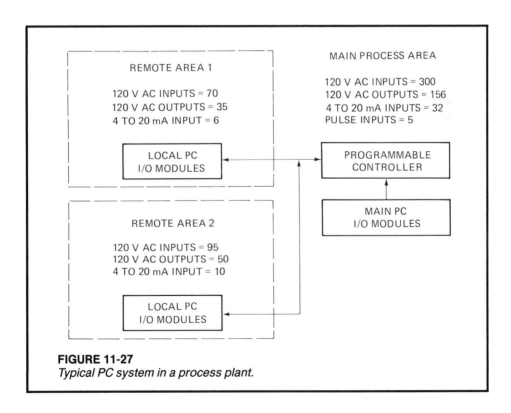

**FIGURE 11-27**
*Typical PC system in a process plant.*

**Programming Language Required**  As mentioned earlier, the four basic types of programming languages available in programmable controller systems are ladder diagrams, Boolean mnemonics, function blocks, and English statements. The type selected depends on the complexity of the control system and the background of the control system programmer and operators. Most PCs offer the basic relay ladder logic instructions plus a combination of the other types of languages. The most common type of language selected is a combination of ladder logic and function blocks, since this covers the basic ladder logic and some data transfer and manipulations.

**Peripheral Requirements**  The term "peripheral" refers to the equipment in the programmable controller system that is not directly involved in process control but increases the capabilities of the system. The most common peripheral is the PC programming device. This is generally available in three formats: a compact portable panel, a CRT (cathode ray tube) with a keyboard, or an industrial-type personal computer. The compact programmer normally has a small, limited function keypad and a seven-segment LED display and can handle only one logic rung at a time. It is normally used on small systems or for minor field changes to larger systems. The CRT-type programmer device is relatively portable and will normally display several rungs or logic functions at one time. The personal computer-based programmer has the greatest number of programming functions, but it is usually not portable and is normally used in a lab or office environment to perform the programming on PC systems.

Another common peripheral used in PC systems is a magnetic tape cassette unit. This unit is used to store the control program on magnetic tape so that in the event of a program loss, the backup program can be reloaded into the controller memory. If a personal computer is used in the PC system, the program can be saved on a floppy disk or a hard disk for future use. For hard-copy printouts of the control programs, a printer can be interfaced with the programming device to obtain a program listing. Some software programs can document the control program on special industrial computers or personal computers that interface to a programmable controller system.

It is important for a complete system design that the peripheral equipment be available to back up and document a control program because manual reprogramming and documentation can be expensive and time consuming.

Other common peripherals are PROM programmers, process I/O simulators, and communications modules. The PROM programmers are used to write and save control programs on PROM clips used in some controllers. The I/O process simulators are useful and time-saving devices for large and complex systems that can be fully tested before installation and start-up in the field. The communication peripherals are used to communicate between the programmable controllers and plant or personal computers and other controllers in a system.

## PC Application  
We are now ready to discuss a PC-based control system application. Consider the dehydration process shown in the simplifed process flow diagram of Figure 11-28.

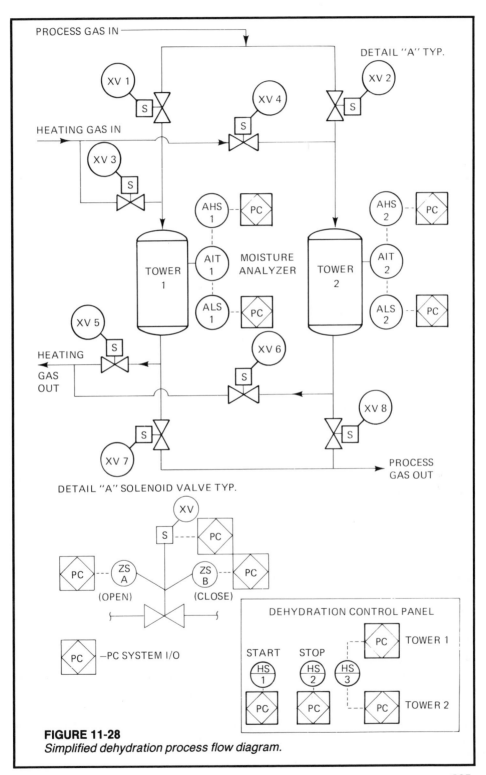

**FIGURE 11-28**
*Simplified dehydration process flow diagram.*

The design of a PC-based control system requires a process flow diagram or a P&ID, a process control description, sizing and selecting a PC, writing a system specification, system drawings and wiring diagrams, and final programming.

These design steps can be illustrated by using a PC to control the dehydration process of Figure 11-28. We already have the process flow diagram, which we can use to show the valve and/or equipment position for each step of the process. The next step is to write a preliminary process control description.

**Process Control Desciption**    The two process towers (towers 1 and 2) are used to remove moisture from natural gas. Generally one tower is *in service* (i.e., removing moisture from the process gas) and the other tower is being dried out or *regenerated*.

The steps of the process are as follows:

1. The operator selects the tower to be placed in service first by using handswitch 3 (HS-3) on the control panel shown in Figure 11-28.

2. Then the operator depresses the system start button (HS-1)

3. If we assume that tower 1 was placed in service first, process gas is fed to tower 1 by opening solenoid valves XV-1 and XV-7, and keeping valves XV-2, XV-3, XV-4, XV-5, XV-6, and XV-8 closed.

4. When the moisture content of tower 1 becomes high, as indicated by analyzer high switch (AHS-1), the PC control system places tower 1 in the regeneration mode by opening valves XV-3 and XV-5, and closing XV-1 and XV-7. At the same time, tower 2 is placed in service by opening valves XV-2 and XV-8. Note at this time that the heating cycle valves for tower 2, XV-4 and XV-6, are still closed.

5. When the moisture content of tower 2 is high and the moisture content of tower 1 is low, the control system will place tower 1 in service and tower 2 in regeneration by opening valves XV-1, XV-7, XV-4, XV-6, and closing valves XV-3, XV-5, XV-2, and XV-8.

After this preliminary control description is written and the process flow diagram is marked up showing valve and equipment status for the 5 process steps listed above, the designer is ready to size and select a PC system.

**Sizing and Selecting A PC System**    The number of inputs and outputs can be estimated from the dehydration flow diagram in Figure 11-28. There are eight (8) 120-V ac solenoid valves (eight 120-V ac outputs) and sixteen (16) limit switches (sixteen 120-V ac inputs) for the open and closed positions of the valves. There are also four moisture alarm switches and three control panel switches for seven (7) additional 120-V ac inputs. We arbitrarily selected 120 V ac for the input signal voltage to save on the types of modules and supply voltages used in the system. The handswitches HS1, HS2, and HS3 also have four ac indicator lights (i.e., *start, stop, tower* 1 and *tower* 2), so there are four more 120-V ac outputs from the PC. This results in twenty-three 120-V ac inputs and twelve 120-V ac outputs for a total I/O count of forty-six. Based on our size classifications for PC systems, this indicates a small system.

Let us assume that we select 8 point, 120-V ac I/O modules for use in our application PC system. The number of modules required can be calculated as follows:

120 V ac input modules
$(23 + 10\%) \div 8$ points/module $= 3.16 \cong 4$ modules

120-V ac output modules
$(12 + 10\%) \div 8$ points/module $= 1.65 \cong 2$ modules

**PC System Specification**   Writing a system specification is probably the most important step in the design of a PC system, because it contains information on both hardware and software. It also brings together all the information needed to purchase and program a system. The following is an outline of a typical PC system specification:

1.0 SCOPE
    1.1 General
    1.2 Hardware
    1.3 Software
    1.4 Drawings

2.0 PROCESS DESCRIPTION
    2.1 General
    2.2 Process Steps
    2.3 Process Logic

3.0 PC HARDWARE
    3.1 General
    3.2 Input/Output Modules
    3.3 Programming Capability
    3.4 Memory
    3.5 Peripheral Requirements

4.0 SOFTWARE
    4.1 General
    4.2 Documentation
    4.3 Simulation
    4.4 Alarms
    4.5 Report Generation
    4.6 Personnel Training

**System Drawing and I/O Wiring Diagrams**   A system drawing is used to give an overall view of the system hardware (I/O modules, processor, and peripheral equipment) and the system interface cabling. This drawing is also useful in identifying all the interface cables by model number.

A typical I/O wiring diagram is shown in Figure 11-29. This drawing shows the wiring of the system solenoid valves to an ac output module.

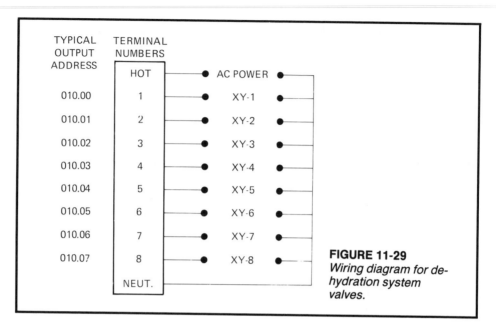

TYPICAL        TERMINAL
OUTPUT         NUMBERS
ADDRESS
                  HOT              AC POWER

010.00            1                  XY-1

010.01            2                  XY-2

010.02            3                  XY-3

010.03            4                  XY-4

010.04            5                  XY-5

010.05            6                  XY-6

010.06            7                  XY-7

010.07            8                  XY-8

                 NEUT.

**FIGURE 11-29**
*Wiring diagram for de-
hydration system
valves.*

It is recommended that the I/O program address number be put on the wiring diagrams for easier troubleshooting of the control program and the field wiring during installation and start-up. In our example application, a single ac line is used. However, in larger systems more than one ac line might be used, depending on loading requirements. The design engineer must also consider maintenance of the system, so that in our example application we might connect the wiring for tower 1 to one ac circuit and the wiring for the other tower to a second ac circuit. In this case, one tower could be taken out of service and the other tower could be kept on line during maintenance. Furthermore, the wiring for the control panel might be placed on a third ac power circuit.

**Application Programming**    The programming of a PC system can be done by the design engineer, process operations (plant) personnel, or the control system vendor. Programming by the system design engineer is the best choice, since it requires less documentation (flow charting, process description, etc.) and less time. The second best choice is to have the plant or operating personnel perform the system programming. More up-front documentation and time are required, but this method results in greater control system acceptance by plant personnel. Programming by a systems house is the poorest choice, since it requires more documentation and debugging time and more training time for plant personnel.

The selection of programming language type should usually be left to plant operations personnel, since they will have to maintain the software after the system is installed. However, in small systems like our example dehydration application, simple ladder programming is usually the best choice.

Ladder logic programming is the best choice in small systems because it is easily understood and relatively easy to troubleshoot and change. For example, let's consider programming the start/stop circuit for our application dehydration system. Let's assume that the start push button (HS1) is connected to input point 100.00 and that the stop push button (HS2) is input bit 100.01. The start/stop function can be programmed as shown in Figure 11-30.

The operation of this ladder logic circuit is relatively simple. When the start push button is depressed on the control panel, input bit 100.00 is TRUE and there is continuity in the ladder rung. This activates start coil 030.00, which seals the circuit ON once the push button is released. The start coil can be deactivated by depressing the stop push button.

Let's look at an example problem to study PC ladder programming in more detail.

## EXAMPLE 11-2

**Problem:** Add the required ladder rungs to the example start/stop program in Figure 11-30 to turn on the start and stop lights on the dehydration control panel. Assume that the start light is controlled by output bit 010.10 and that the stop light is energized by output bit 010.11.

**Solution:** The modified logic is given in Figure 11-31. We used START output bit 030.00 to energize the START LIGHT in rung 2 and the NOT START output bit to turn on the STOP LIGHT in rung 3.

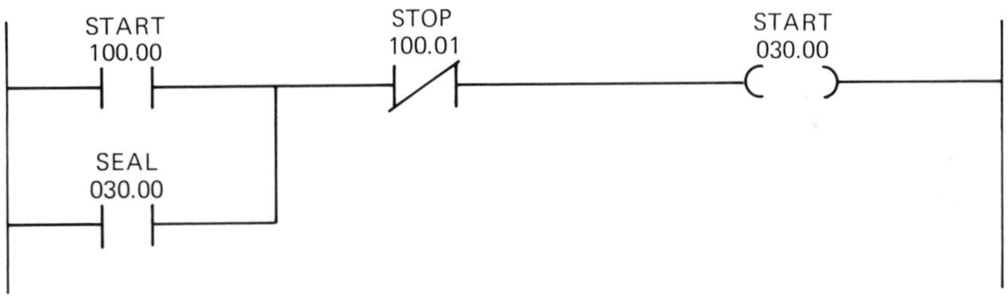

**FIGURE 11-30**
*Example start/stop ladder program.*

## EXERCISES

11.1  Refer to Figure 11.2 and explain the operation and purpose of each circuit in a typical ac input module.

11.2  List the advantages and disadvantages of the different memory types used in PC applications.

11.3  Explain the difference between volatile and nonvolatile PC memory.

11.4  Program an UP/DOWN counter that up counts to 10 and then down counts to zero.

11.5  Explain the function and purpose of each area of a typical PC memory map.

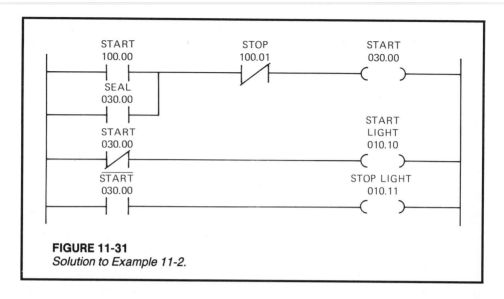

**FIGURE 11-31**
*Solution to Example 11-2.*

11.6  Write a ladder logic program to perform the following logic operation: If input A (bit 101.01) or input B (bit 101.07) and input C (bit 100.10) are TRUE (logic 1), then energize output D (bit 010.13).

11.7  Perform the I/O module sizing calculations for the PC system shown in Figure 11-27 using the following assumptions:
   (1) The 120-V ac input and output modules have 8-point capacity.
   (2) 4-20 mA input modules have 4-point capacity.
   (3) The pulse input modules have 2-point capacity.
   (4) The spare capacity required is 20%.

11.8  Complete the wiring diagrams for the dehydration process using input addresses starting at 100.00 and output addresses starting at 010.00. Assume 8-point ac I/O modules.

11.9  Write a PC ladder program to control the dehydration process, based on the P&ID and the process description.

## BIBLIOGRAPHY

1.  Jones, C.T., and Bryan, L.A., *Programmable Controllers, Concepts and Applications*, First Edition, International Programmable Controls, Inc., 1983.

2.  *Modicon 584; Programmable Controllers, Users' Manual*, Gould Modicon Division, January 1982.

3.  *PLC-2/30 Programmable Controller: Programming and Operations Manual*, Publication 1772-6.8.3, Allen-Bradley, 1984.

4.  Gilbert, R.A., and Llewellyn, J.A., *Programmable Controllers, Practices and Concepts*, Industrial Training Corporation (ITC), 1985.

# APPENDIX

# Standard Graphics Symbols for Process Control and Instrumentation

ANSI/ISA-S5.1-1984, Instrumentation Symbols and Identification, is generally used in the instrumentation and control field to document projects.

This standard provides sufficient information to allow a person with limited knowledge of process control to understand the means of measurement and control of a process when reviewing process documents and drawings. The information provided in this appendix is very limited and intended only to introduce the subject of graphics symbols. It is recommended that the standard be obtained from the Instrument Society of America.

One important function the standard performs is to provide a standard list of instrument line symbols to be used in documentation as shown in Table A-1.

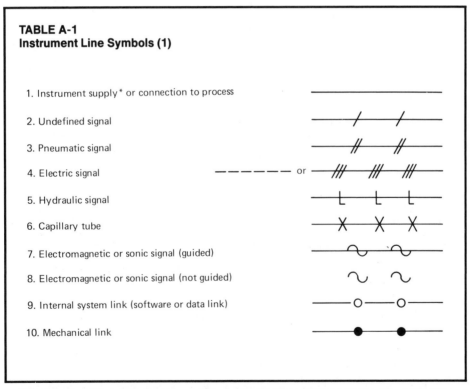

**TABLE A-1**
**Instrument Line Symbols (1)**

1. Instrument supply* or connection to process

2. Undefined signal

3. Pneumatic signal

4. Electric signal

5. Hydraulic signal

6. Capillary tube

7. Electromagnetic or sonic signal (guided)

8. Electromagnetic or sonic signal (not guided)

9. Internal system link (software or data link)

10. Mechanical link

*The following abbreviations can be used to denote the types of power supply: AS—Air Supply, IA—Instrument Air, PA—Plant Air, ES—Electric Supply, GS—Gas Supply, HS—Hydraulic Supply, NS—Nitrogen Supply, SS—Steam Supply, WS—Water Supply.

```
TABLE A-2
Typical Tag Number
─────────────────────────────────────────────

TIC 103    – Intrument Identification or Tag Number
T   103    – Loop Identification
    103    – Loop Number
TIC        – Functional Identification
T          – First Letter
IC         – Succeeding Letters
```

Another important function performed by the standard is to identify each instrument by an alphanumeric code or tag number as shown in Table A-2. Each instrument is represented on an instrument diagram by a symbol, and the symbol is accompanied by a instrument tag number.

The functional identification of an instrument consists of letters from Table A-3 and includes one first letter designating the measured or initiating variable and one or more succeeding letters denoting the functions performed.

Instrument tag numbering is according to the function performed and not according to the construction. For example, a differential pressure element measuring flow is identified by FE and not by DPE.

The following notes for Table A-3 were taken directly from ANSI-ISA-S5.1-1984, paragraph 5.1; used with permission.

## Notes to Table A-3

(1) A "user's choice" letter is intended to cover unlisted meanings that will be used repetitively in a particular project. If used, the letter may have one meaning as a first-letter and another meaning as a succeeding-letter. The meanings need to be defined only once in a legend, or other place, for that project. For example, the letter N may be defined as "modulus of elasticity" as a first-letter and "oscilloscope" as a succeeding-letter.

(2) The unclassified letter X is intended to cover unlisted meanings that will be used only once or used to a limited extent. If used, the letter may have any number of meanings as a first-letter and any number of meanings as a succeeding-letter. Except for its use with distinctive symbols, it is expected that the meaning will be defined outside a tagging bubble on a flow diagram. For example, XR-2 may be a stress recorder and XX-4 may be a stress oscilloscope.

(3) The grammatical form of the succeeding-letter meaning may be modified as required. For example, "indicate" may be applied as "indicator" or "indicating," "transmit" as "transmitter" or "transmitting," etc.

(4) Any first-letter, if used in combination with modifying letters D (differential), F (ratio), M (momentary), K (time rate of change), Q (integrate or totalize), or any combination of these is intended to represent a new and separate measured variable, and the combination is treated as a first-letter entity. Thus, instruments TDI and TI indicate two different variables, namely, differential-temperature and temperature. Modifying letters are used when applicable.

(5) First-letter A (analysis) covers all analyses not described by a "user's choice" letter. It is expected that the type of analysis will be defined outside a tagging bubble.

## TABLE A-3
## Instrument Identification Letters (1)

| | FIRST-LETTER (4) | | SUCCEEDING-LETTERS (3) | | |
|---|---|---|---|---|---|
| | **MEASURED OR INITIATING VARIABLE** | **MODIFIER** | **READOUT OR PASSIVE FUNCTION** | **OUTPUT FUNCTION** | **MODIFIER** |
| A | Analysis(5,19) | | Alarm | | |
| B | Burner, Combustion | | User's Choice(1) | User's Choice(1) | User's Choice(1) |
| C | User's Choice(1) | | | Control(13) | |
| D | User's Choice(1) | Differential(4) | | | |
| E | Voltage | | Sensor (Primary Element) | | |
| F | Flow Rate | Ratio (Fraction)(4) | | | |
| G | User's Choice(1) | | Glass, Viewing Device(9) | | |
| H | Hand | | | | High(7,15,16) |
| I | Current (Electrical) | | Indicate(10) | | |
| J | Power | Scan(7) | | | |
| K | Time, Time Schedule | Time Rate of Change(4,21) | | Control Station (22) | |
| L | Level | | Light(11) | | Low(7,15,16) |
| M | User's Choice(1) | Momentary(4) | | | Middle, Intermediate(7,15) |
| N | User's Choice(1) | | User's Choice(1) | User's Choice(1) | User's Choice(1) |
| O | User's Choice(1) | | Orifice, Restriction | | |
| P | Pressure, Vacuum | | Point (Test) Connection | | |
| Q | Quantity | Integrate, Totalize(4) | | | |
| R | Radiation | | Record(17) | | |
| S | Speed, Frequency | Safety(8) | | Switch(13) | |
| T | Temperature | | | Transmit(18) | |
| U | Multivariable(6) | | Multifunction(12) | Multifunction(12) | Multifunction(12) |
| V | Vibration, Mechanical Analysis(19) | | | Valve, Damper, Louver(13) | |
| W | Weight, Force | | Well | | |
| X | Unclassified(2) | X Axis | Unclassified(2) | Unclassified(2) | Unclassified(2) |
| Y | Event, State or Presence(20) | Y Axis | | Relay, Compute, Convert(13,14,18) | |
| Z | Position, Dimension | Z Axis | | Driver, Actuator, Unclassified Final Control Element | |

(6) Use of first-letter *U* for "multivariable" in lieu of a combination of first-letters is optional. It is recommended that nonspecific variable designators such as *U* be used sparingly.

(7) The use of modifying terms "high," "low," "middle," or "intermediate," and "scan" is optional.

(8) The term "safety" applies to emergency protective primary elements and emergency protective final control elements only. Thus, a self-actuated valve that prevents operation of a fluid system at a higher-than-desired pressure by bleeding fluid from the system is a back-pressure-type *PCV*, even if the valve is not intended to be used normally. However, this valve is designed as a *PSV* if it is intended to protect against emergency conditions, i.e., conditions that are hazardous to personnel and/or equipment and that are not expected to arise normally.

The designation PSV applies to all valves intended to protect against emergency pressure conditions regardless of whether the valve construction and mode of operation place them in the category of the safety valve, relief valve, or safety relief valve. A rupture disc is designated PSE.

(9) The passive function G applies to instruments or devices that provide an uncalibrated view, such as sight glasses and television monitors.

(10) "Indicate" normally applies to the readout - analog or digital - of an actual measurement. In the case of a manual loader, it may be used for the dial or setting indication, i.e., for the value of the initiating variable.

(11) A pilot light that is part of an instrument loop should be designated by a first-letter followed by the succeeding-letter *L*. For example, a pilot light that indicates an expired time period should be tagged *KQL*. If it is desired to tag a pilot light that is not part of an instrument loop, the light is designated in the same way. For example, a running light for an electric motor may be tagged *EL*, assuming voltage to be the appropriate measured variable, or *YL*, assuming the operating status is being monitored. The unclassified variable *X* should be used only for applications which are limited in extent. The designation *XL* should not be used for motor running lights, as these are commonly numerous. It is permissible to use the user's choice letters *M*, *N*, or *O* for a motor running light when the meaning is previously defined. If *M* is used, it must be clear that the letter does not stand for the word "motor," but for a monitored state.

(12) Use of a succeeding-letter *U* for "malfunction" instead of a combination of other functional letters is optional. This nonspecific function designator should be used sparingly.

(13) A device that connects, disconnects, or transfers one or more circuits may be either a switch, a relay, an ON-OFF controller, or a control valve, depending on the application.

If the device manipulates a fluid process stream and is not a hand-actuated ON-OFF block valve, it is designated as a control valve. It is incorrect to use the succeeding letters *CV* for anything other than a self-actuated control valve. For all applications other than fluid process streams, the device is designated as follows:

> A switch, if it is actuated by hand.
>
> A switch or an ON-OFF controller, if it is automatic and is the first such device in a loop. The term "switch" is generally used if the device is used for alarm, pilot light, selection, interlock, or safety.
>
> The term "controller" is generally used if the device is used for normal operating control.
>
> A relay, if it is automatic and is not the first such device in a loop, i.e., it is actuated by a switch or an ON-OFF controller.

(14) It is expected that the functions associated with the use of succeeding-letter *Y* will be defined outside a bubble on a diagram when further definition is considered necessary. This definition need not be made when the function is self-evident, as for a solenoid valve in a fluid signal line.

(15) The modifying terms "high," and "low," and "middle" or "intermediate" correspond to values of the measured variable, not to values of the signal, unless otherwise noted. For example, a high-level alarm derived from a reverse-acting level transmitter signal should be an *LAH*, even though the alarm is actuated when the signal falls to a low value. The terms may be used in combinations as appropriate.

(16) The terms "high" and "low," when applied to positions of valves and other open-close devices, are defined as follows: "high" denotes that the valve is in or approaching the fully open position, and "low" denotes that it is in or approaching the fully closed position.

(17) The word "record" applies to any form of permanent storage of information that permits retrieval by any means.

(18) For use of the term "transmitter" versus "converter," see the definitions in Section 3.

(19) First-letter *V*, "vibration or mechanical analysis," is intended to perform the duties in machinery monitoring that the letter *A* performs in more general analyses. Except for vibration, it is expected that the variable of interest will be defined outside the tagging bubble.

(20) First-letter *Y* is intended for use when control or monitoring responses are event-driven as opposed to time- or time schedule-driven. The letter *Y*, in this position, can also signify presence or state.

(21) Modifying-letter *K*, in combination with a first-letter such as *L*, *T*, or *W*, signifies a time rate of change of the measured or initiating variable. The variable *WKIC*, for instance, may represent a rate-of-weight-loss controller.

(22) Succeeding-letter *K* is a user's option for designating a control station, while the succeeding-letter *C* is used for describing automatic or manual controllers.

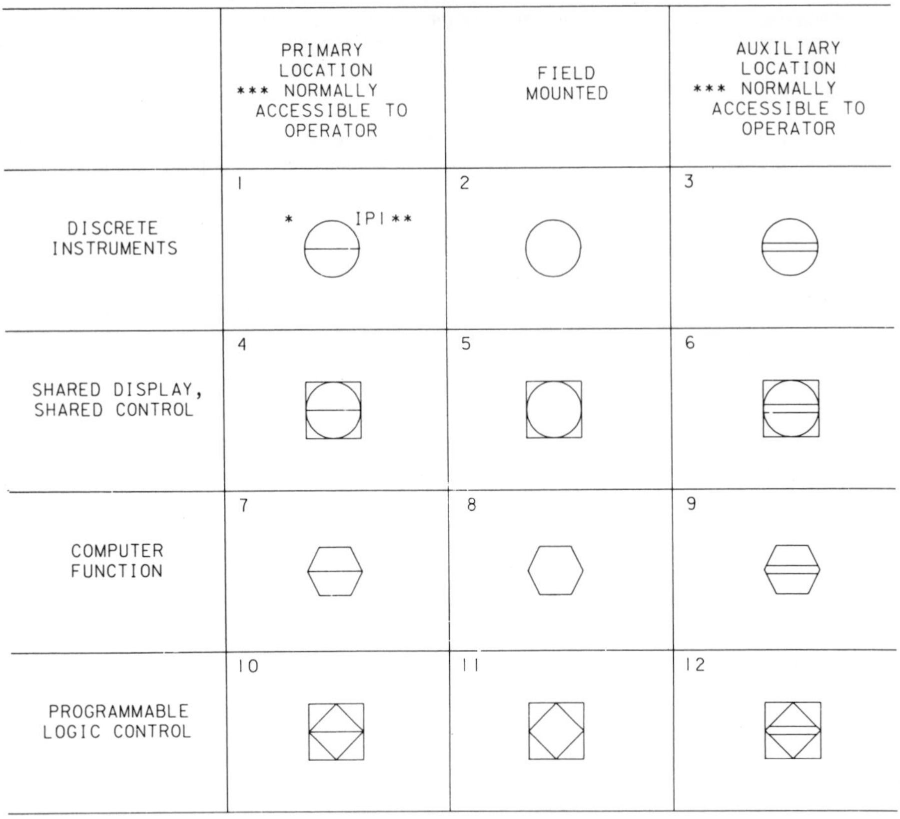

| | PRIMARY LOCATION *** NORMALLY ACCESSIBLE TO OPERATOR | FIELD MOUNTED | AUXILIARY LOCATION *** NORMALLY ACCESSIBLE TO OPERATOR |
|---|---|---|---|
| DISCRETE INSTRUMENTS | 1    * IPI ** | 2 | 3 |
| SHARED DISPLAY, SHARED CONTROL | 4 | 5 | 6 |
| COMPUTER FUNCTION | 7 | 8 | 9 |
| PROGRAMMABLE LOGIC CONTROL | 10 | 11 | 12 |

\* Symbol size may vary according to the user's needs and the type of document. A suggested square and circle size for large diagrams is shown above. Consistency is recommended.

\*\* Abbreviations of the user's choice such as IPI (Instrument Panel #1), IC2 (Instrument Console #2), CC3 (Computer Console #3), etc., may be used when it is necessary to specify instrument or function location.

\*\*\* Normally inaccessible or behind-the-panel devices or functions may be depicted by using the same symbols but with dashed horizontal bars, i.e.

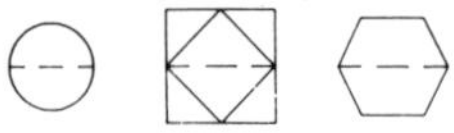

**FIGURE A-1**
*General instrument or function symbols. (Courtesy of Instrument Society of America)*

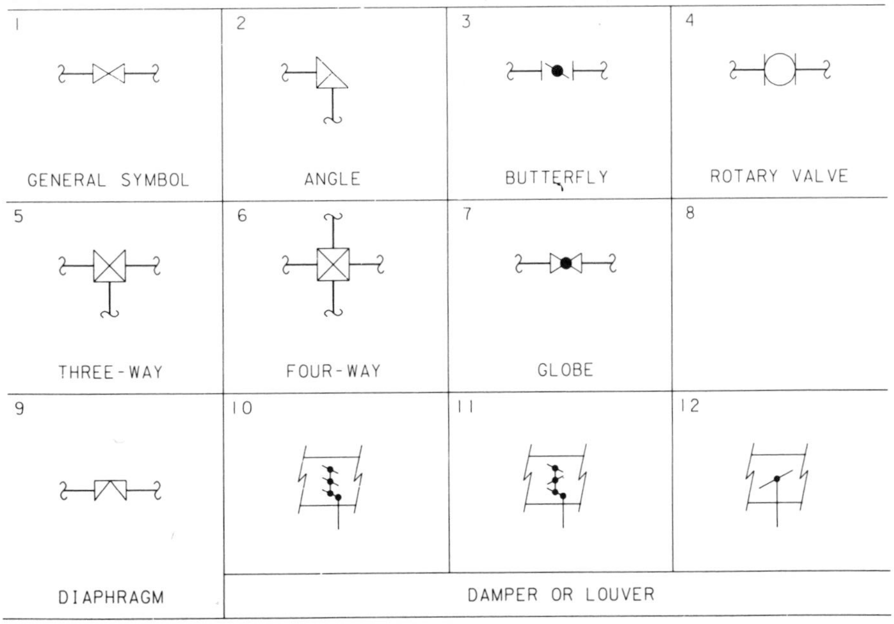

| 1 | 2 | 3 | 4 |
|---|---|---|---|
| GENERAL SYMBOL | ANGLE | BUTTERFLY | ROTARY VALVE |
| 5 | 6 | 7 | 8 |
| THREE-WAY | FOUR-WAY | GLOBE | |
| 9 | 10 | 11 | 12 |
| DIAPHRAGM | DAMPER OR LOUVER | | |

Further information may be added adjacent to the body symbol either by note or code number.

**FIGURE A-2**
*Control valve body symbols, damper symbols. (Courtesy of Instrument Society of America)*

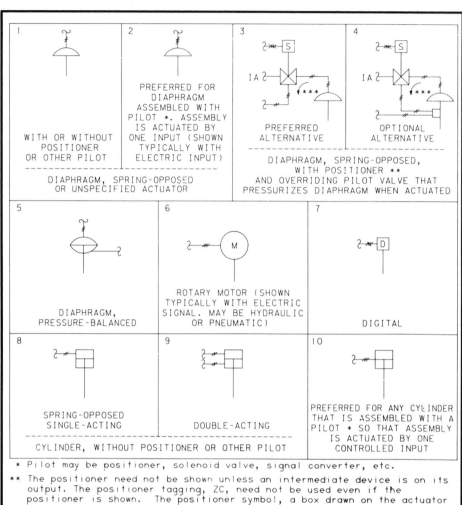

**1**    WITH OR WITHOUT
        POSITIONER
        OR OTHER PILOT

**2**    PREFERRED FOR
        DIAPHRAGM
        ASSEMBLED WITH
        PILOT *. ASSEMBLY
        IS ACTUATED BY
        ONE INPUT (SHOWN
        TYPICALLY WITH
        ELECTRIC INPUT)

DIAPHRAGM, SPRING-OPPOSED
OR UNSPECIFIED ACTUATOR

**3**    PREFERRED
        ALTERNATIVE

**4**    OPTIONAL
        ALTERNATIVE

DIAPHRAGM, SPRING-OPPOSED,
WITH POSITIONER **
AND OVERRIDING PILOT VALVE THAT
PRESSURIZES DIAPHRAGM WHEN ACTUATED

**5**    DIAPHRAGM,
        PRESSURE-BALANCED

**6**    ROTARY MOTOR (SHOWN
        TYPICALLY WITH ELECTRIC
        SIGNAL. MAY BE HYDRAULIC
        OR PNEUMATIC)

**7**    DIGITAL

**8**    SPRING-OPPOSED
        SINGLE-ACTING

**9**    DOUBLE-ACTING

CYLINDER, WITHOUT POSITIONER OR OTHER PILOT

**10**   PREFERRED FOR ANY CYLINDER
        THAT IS ASSEMBLED WITH A
        PILOT * SO THAT ASSEMBLY
        IS ACTUATED BY ONE
        CONTROLLED INPUT

* Pilot may be positioner, solenoid valve, signal converter, etc.

** The positioner need not be shown unless an intermediate device is on its
   output. The positioner tagging, ZC, need not be used even if the
   positioner is shown. The positioner symbol, a box drawn on the actuator
   shaft, is the same for all types of actuators. When the symbol is used,
   the type of instrument signal, i.e., pneumatic, electric, etc., is drawn
   as appropriate. If the positioner symbol is used and there is no
   intermediate device on its output, then the positioner output signal need
   not be shown.

*** The arrow represents the path from a common to a fail open port. It does
    not correspond necessarily to the direction of fluid flow.

**FIGURE A-3**
*Actuator function symbols. (Courtesy of Instrument Society of America)*

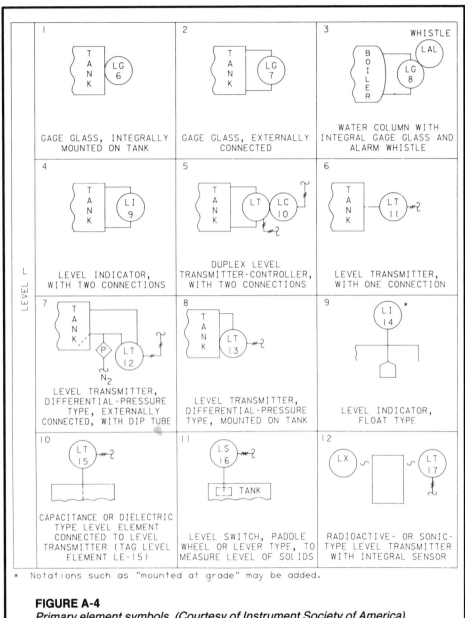

**FIGURE A-4**
*Primary element symbols. (Courtesy of Instrument Society of America)*

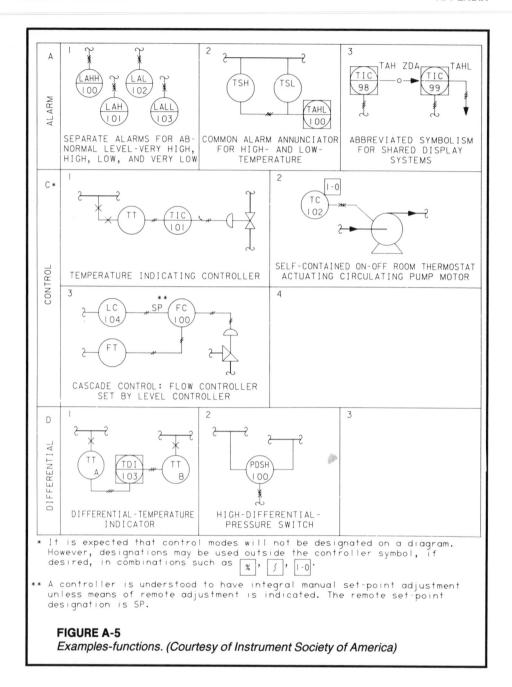

**FIGURE A-5**
*Examples-functions. (Courtesy of Instrument Society of America)*

## REFERENCE

1. ANSI/ISA-S5.1-1984, *Instrumentation Symbols and Identification,* Instrument Society of America, Research Triangle Park, NC, 1984.

# Index